Politics and Policy-Making in Israel's Eduation System

T0324367

Dedicated to
My Beloved Wife and Children

Politics and Policy-Making in Israel's Eduation System

Haim Gaziel

sussex
ACADEMIC
PRESS
Brighton • Portland • Toronto

2 4 6 8 10 9 7 5 3

First published 1996, reprinted 2012, in Great Britain by
SUSSEX ACADEMIC PRESS
PO Box 139   Eastbourne BN24 9BP

and in the United States of America by
SUSSEX ACADEMIC PRESS
920 NE 58th Ave Suite 300
Portland, Oregon 97213-3786

and in Canada by
SUSSEX ACADEMIC PRESS (CANADA)
8000 Bathurst Street, Unit 1, PO Box 30010, Vaughan, Ontario L4J 0C6

British Library Cataloguing in Publication Data
A CIP catalogue record for this book is available from the British Library.

Library of Congress Cataloging-in-Publication Data has been applied for.

Typeset by Sussex Academic Press, Brighton & Eastbourne.
Printed TJ International, Padstow, Cornwall.
This book is printed on acid-free paper.

Contents

Preface and Acknowledgments

This book is a contribution to what Ozga[1] calls "policy sociology," which is rooted in the social science tradition, is historically informed and draws on qualitative and illuminative techniques. The aim is to outline and apply the policy approach[2] to the study of education policy in Israel, and to provide an understanding of the changes in the Israeli policy in education from the 1970s (the period of the "great reform" toward social integration – the "equity era") to the 1990s (the era of excellence, quality, and efficiency). The task of social policy analysis is to evaluate the distributional impact of existing policies and proposals, and the rationales underlying them.[3]

The literature[4] provides two lines of inquiry for studying educational policies at the state level. The first line results from applying the traditional methods and concepts of political science to educational systems. It seeks to explain school policy by looking at the *distribution of power among stakeholders* in the system and following interactions among these power-wielding groups in order to reveal the process of decision-making. The research rooted in this tradition tries to establish when and how decisions are made, and it looks for explanations either in the institutional structures or in the personal actions of policy-makers.

The second line of research is less concerned with the role of political power in shaping decision-making processes. Rather, it concentrates on the *content and domain of actions of policy-makers on educational policies.* This line of research looks for the consequences of state action by measuring the changes during a certain time period. Mitchell and Encarnation[5] found that policy-makers are mostly interested in the following domains of action: school finances, student testing and assessment, curriculum, school governance and personnel training. For the purposes of this book, both strands of research have been employed.

vii

Statements and publications of the Ministry of Education and Culture and the Knesset Education Committee are used to examine trends of change and continuity in educational policy in Israel, and to explore the implications for the future. Information is gathered from the following sources: policy statements by Ministers of Education and Culture in the Knesset and public forums, discussions in the Knesset plenum and committees, reports and circulars of the Ministry of Education administration, education budget records, publications of the Central Bureau of Statistics, and a review of studies on related subjects.

I would like to take this opportunity to thank: ISES, the Institute for the Study of Educational Systems, founded by the Jerusalem Center for Public Affairs and the Foundations of the Milken Families, which financed the original study; Professor Daniel J. Elazar, President of the Jerusalem Center for Public Affairs and a member of the ISES Board; Zvi R. Marom, Director-General of the Jerusalem Center for Public Affairs and a member of the ISES Board, for his long-term support; Chaya Herskovic, coordinator of research programs at ISES, for providing me with administrative services; Dr Shmuel Himelstein for editorial assistance; and, finally, the anonymous readers for their useful comments.

The author is grateful to the Schnitzer Foundation for Research on Israeli Economy and Society, Bar-Ilan University and to the Research Authority of Bar-Ilan University for supporting the publication of this book.

*Politics and Policy-Making
in Israel's Education
System*

1

Linking Politics to Education

The belief that one can dispense with specific viewpoints and simply observe in a wholly impartial way the real nature of Israel's politics in education is widely held, and therefore deserves careful consideration, but this book takes a contrary view: because the study of politics is bound to involve political judgments, the *way* it is studied is of great importance.

The policy approach adopted is centered on government. This approach recognizes that in industrial states, "government" in its broad sense (parliament, ministries and local authorities) is an important fact of social, economic and political life. In Israel more than 90 percent of the teachers receive their main source of income from the government, in wages or in cash benefits such as unemployment pay and old-age pensions. The emphasis on government allows one to define politics "as government related." Actions can be called "political" if they involve government or are concerned with government.

For example, the members of parents' organizations would act politically if they attempted to influence members of the parliament (Knesset) or the Minister of Education to accept their demands. The scope of government is defined primarily in institutional terms: central government (including parliament) and the local authorities.[1] However, any attempt to define what is not "government" is fraught with difficulties and is a matter of judgment. There are always agencies and functions which are difficult to classify. Although the government is central in setting policy, it is a part of the wider society, subject to influences from outside its own boundaries, such as the economy and other parts of the social system. Thus neither the government nor the political system is autonomous, and indeed to some extent they are shaped by non-political forces.

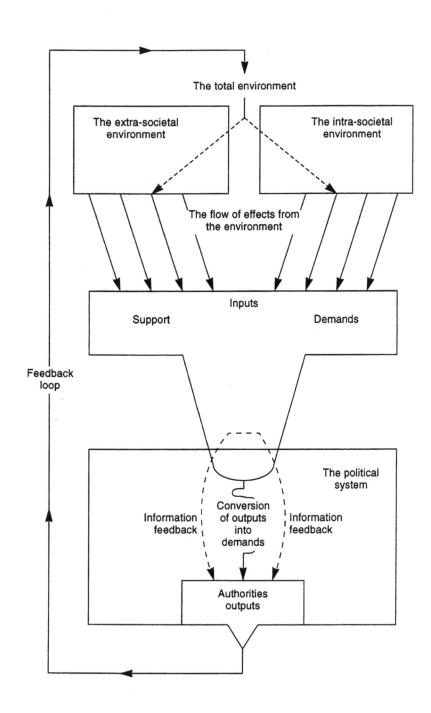

The Policy Approach: Features and Assumptions

The policy approach is concerned with examining what government chooses to do or to neglect, and with what consequences for its citizens. It is also concerned with what government should do.[2] The most important activity of any government is to formulate policies in diverse domains, including education. In order to formulate policy, governments engage in a series of actions. By studying these actions, an understanding can be gained of the activities of the government and their broader effects on society. Policy is the product of government and it includes rules, regulations and pronouncements. It also includes the amount of money allocated to different services and their impact upon the equity in a society.[3] The educational policy-making activities of government are best seen as a process. The process is cyclic, and is modified by its results or effects.

Following the Easton model,[4] government collects inputs: finances and political support. These inputs ("resources") are then processed into products or policies, which are applied to the citizens and consumed by them. Citizens also articulate demands for future policy provisions and provide support or opposition to policy proposals.

The figure on the opposite page indicates some of the main features of the policy approach. The emphasis is on policy as a means for studying government activities and the use of the notion of process as a way of visualizing the key operations of government.

The policy approach employs the following assumptions:

1. Government is central to the study of politics and policy-making. It helps to shape the broad political, social and economic context within which it operates. Its policies are not necessarily in congruence with public interests.
2. Although several phases of the policy-making process may be distinguished, it is still continual and involves the constantly varying interplay of many individual policy-makers (political leaders, the ruling elite and interest groups such as unions).
3. The policy process is cyclic; it is modified by its results.

Educational Policy-Making: Processes and Structures[5]

Various models are borrowed from political science and tradition-ally applied to education.[6] Public policy literature contains many models which are used to explain each government's policy-making structure. For the purpose of this book, however, those that meet the following criteria are presented:[7] (a) They have been found in research to have deductive power and theoretical coherence and that the module is based on facts,[8] (b) that they be simple to apply and of practical use.[9]

Various models of the policy cycle may perform differently, based on the evaluation criteria employed. Model evaluation then becomes the task of listing the pros and cons of different approaches. Equally true yet different models may perform differently in dif-ferent situations. The functions of the public policy models are to explain, understand, interpret and organize data concerning the making of decisions by public bodies such as government.

When presenting the policy-making models a distinction is made between the *structure* of policy-making responding to the question of which are the key bodies (parliament, government, political parties, the unions, a ruling elite, other public interests) in shaping the policy, and the *process* responding to the "how" question, that is how the main actors in the policy-making process make decisions (by rational processes, incrementalism or the motives of the public actors).

"Main Actor" views in the literature are either descriptive or nor-mative with regard to the structure of the policy-making process.[10] For the purpose of the present book only the descriptive aspects of those views will be of concern.

According to the *conventional view*, the key elements in policy-making are the elected institutions (representative and responsible). Power is in the hands of the citizens but is mediated through the members of the representative assembly, who have the dual role of being accountable to the public and of controlling the executive, such as the local council committee system or the parliamentary scrutiny of the work of government agencies and the responsi-bility of individual ministers to parliament for the work of their departments. In almost every country the parliament plays a role in formulating policy. The question is whether it has a major role or a marginal role in making policies. Opinions are at odds on this point.

In Israel, some researchers[11] argue that the parliament – the Knesset – plays an important role in deciding about the budgets designated for ministries. Others contend[12] that the parliamentary members are no more than a rubber stamp of the budget already decided upon by the executive. This is a question that will be examined in detail in the following chapters.

The second view see the *political parties* as the key institution in shaping public policy, rather than elected members. It is political parties that mediate the public's opinion, which they then fuse into broad policy proposals; it is political parties that control the operations of the assembly. According to this view, party activists form the main body of policy-makers, and party leaders are the key personnel. Governments act in conformity with the policies and demands of the party in power. These policies are formulated within the party in line with the wishes of party activists and in keeping with that party's ideology and values.[13] From the descriptive point of view this view is valid when analyzing the Israeli education policy. (It is quite clear that when the Conservative Party in Britain is in power, its leaders, who also head the party, have an interest in realizing the party's values and ideology.[14])

The third view mentioned in the literature is the *bureaucratic power view*,[15] which focuses on government institutions, especially ministries and local government departments, as the key components in the policy-making system. These institutions are at the centers of the policy process; most if not all policies have to pass through them, and some policies are actually generated within them. Thus, the argument goes, these bodies either create policies or significantly shape them. Their substantial role in policy-making is a result of their position at the heart of government and their supremacy is exercised through their superior knowledge, control of information, continuity (politicians come and go) and the ability to work away from the glare of publicity that inevitably surrounds politicians. According to this view, government is seen as central to policy-making, with its personnel, especially officials, managing the policy process. They regulate policy demands by interpreting those demands and preparing responses for ministers to articulate. They also supervise, and to some extent control the flow and application of policy ideas and decisions. A review of studies in other countries reveals that bureaucrats have a considerable amount of power in shaping educational policies.[16]

Derived from the bureaucratic power view is the *technocratic view*. According to this view, power lies in the hands of those who possess technical skills and know-how: the specialists or professionals. It is these individuals who constitute the main policy-makers. It is they who are "most competent" and thus most able to make judgments about policy matters. The system lays emphasis on expertise rather than on seniority on the job, bureaucratic position or personal connections.[17]

Contrary to the views mentioned above, the technocratic view claims to be normative and in recent years it has gained more and more supporters among management specialists and even among some politicians who seek efficiency in the educational sector.[18]

While the previous views emphasize formal institutions (parliament, political parties, government bureaucrats or technocrats) as the main actors in the policy-making structure, the next view emphasizes *interest groups* as the key element in the policy-making system. Society is seen as being made up of interest groups such as unions, businessmen and parent associations. Some groups are organized while others are amorphous. Some researchers argue[19] that policy emerges as conforming to the demands of particular interest groups, which act against the real interests of the majority of the population. Politicians and officials exercise political power in congruence with these particular groups. The problem with this view is that it is less tangibile than the previous four views in that it is concerned with ideas, desires and demands that are difficult to prove, rather than with institutions like the parliament or government ministries.

Studies done in other countries on a comparative basis reveal that state education policy is typically shaped by a very small number of key actors.[20] State policies are very much affected by state cultures.[21] Professional interest groups play an important role in shaping policies.

All five views above are different ways to look at the operation of the education policy-making system. They are neither "right" nor "wrong." Each view focuses on different elements and questions. What is important when analyzing the policy system of a certain country is to look for the *weight* of each of these in the formulation of a certain education policy.

The politics of education theory is also interested in how decisions are made, as the following models will attempt to explain.

Public Policy-Making Processes

Rational Decision-Making[22]

A rational strategy for tackling policy issues involves proceeding through a sequence of stages which follow on logically from one another. A policy-maker, having identified a problem which requires a response, should:

1. Identify, and rank in order of importance, his objectives;
2. Identify all possible responses to the problem;
3. Go on next to consider all possible consequences resulting from the adoption of each response;
4. And finally, select the response which will most nearly achieve the desired objectives.

The assumption behind this model is that decision-makers have complete knowledge about the alternatives and the environment of each issue involved, in order to weigh the consequences of each alternative. Several researchers have already demonstrated that that assumption is false, because it is beyond human capacity.[23]

While rational decision-making rules are attractive theoretically, they are weak in explaining how public (education) policy-makers decide, because while in theory the choices are a function of the goals which have been set and the technology that is available, it is known that education policy goals are neither precise nor clear and often include potential contradictions,[24] On the other hand, the technology employed is clearly imperfect. If that is the state of the goals and the technology, then it is far from evident that the behavior devised by the rational decision model is the most appropriate.[25] Thus the rational decision model may be more attractive as a regulative notion than as a tool for understanding how policy-making actually takes place.

An alternative explanation to the rational model of how policies are made is suggested by Lindbloom in his incremental model.[26]

The Incremental Model

An increment is a small step away from an existing position. As an approach to policy-making, incremental theories share certain characteristics:

1. According to this view, policy-making is restricted, in that policy-makers do not wander from the status quo. They seek new policies or responses to problems which differ only marginally from existing policies, a good example of this being the marginal changes in public budgets.[27]
2. Means rather than objectives determine policies. If, for example, there is a shortage in the teacher supply, policy-makers would reject an interest group's demand for extending the school day.
3. Incremental strategies are remedial. They deal with issues or problems as they arise. Policy-makers do not go out in search of work and have no idealized future state by which to test whether or not a particular action toward which they are working is actually needed. The status quo is satisfactory until it cannot be maintained any longer due to dissatisfaction with it.[28]

Finally, incrementalism is fragmentary. Policy is made across space. By "across space" is meant that different actors and institutions are involved in the same policy area. Vocational education in Israel is a good example. Because of its division among several institutions (the Ministry of Education, Ministry of Labor, private organizations and local authorities), its efficiency is put in question.

For all of its simplicity, the incremental model may be too crude in regard to the complexity of the policy process. This model does not offer a useful clear distinction between the incremental and non-incremental. Its general validity is doubtful and its theoretical appeal is decreased by the obvious voluntaristic aspect of action, including collective action. It may well be true that educational policy-making cannot possibly consider all the alternatives and rank all the outcomes as incrementalism predicts, but it does not follow that decision-making is therefore bound to be limited in scope. Decision-making, faced by uncertainty and focusing only upon a few alternatives and values, does not ipso facto have to be marginal. Decision-making may be comprehensive in terms of the changes aimed at.

If major structural changes are at odds with incremental modeling, how do we explain the occurrence of these types of policy changes?

Like the rational model, the incremental model offers a useful explanation of some aspects of the behavior of the policy-makers, such as partisan mutual adjustment and common ground, which may explain the lengthy time-scale of policy-making, with its emphasis on coordination and negotiation.

The Public Choice Models

The assumption of the public choice model of policy determination is to reject any such traditional notion of policy as a search for public interest. Politicians are no different from private entrepreneurs, and their involvement in public policy is motivated by private concerns to the same extent as are the concerns of the profit maximizer.[29] What is the objective function that a politician maximizes, and what are the implications for the understanding of policy-making? According to the well-known Hotelling–Downs model of the politician, the politician's behavior is a function of the probability of re-election.[30] Although models regarding political behavior are simple and have deductive power, their chief weakness lies in their empirical bases; the evidence is mixed and it is difficult to arrange proper tests.[31]

Studies looking for how education policies are made reveal that in most cases the incremental model is the one closest to reality.[32] This is explained by the fact that policy-making is made manageable when only limited comparisons with the status quo are made. For most actors, focusing on the familiar is more comfortable than assessing the unknown.

Policy Content and Actions

In recent years, research on state systems has tended to shift away from process-oriented political studies to more content-oriented policy analysis. The main questions interesting researchers have been the following: What are the main issues on the government's education agenda? Is there any systematic taxonomy of state policy actions – a taxonomy providing a comprehensive overview of possible domains within which the state is acting?

According to Odden and Dougherty,[33] there are seven general patterns of state policy actions: workforce improvement, curricular guidance, program review, comprehensive improvement program, assistance programs, testing programs and parent involvement programs.[34]

Cobb and Elder argue that the emphasis put on an issue (or

domain of action) is different from state to state and even from time to time in the same state, and the emphasis depends mostly on the support that the issue has from the political parties and the powerful interest groups. For example, the extending of the school day in Israel became an important issue only when the powerful social lobby in Israel demanded the extension of the school day for social deprived students and for greater equality in the distribution of the education budget. Otherwise, the lobby threatened, it would bring down the government, and this tactic worked. The government gave in to its demand and appointed a committee to deliberate on the issue and to offer recommendations within half a year at the latest.

Government members may put more energy in a particular domain of action because it may promote their political interest. A good example is the significant increase of the educational budgets to the Arab sector in Israel by the former Minister of Education, Shulamit Aloni, as a form of recognition of their votes for her party during the 1992 parliament elections.[35] A particular domain of action may emerge because of an unanticipated event, such as changes in economic policy, ecological changes, population movement or technological changes. Changes in Israeli educational policies since the early 1970s can also be explained by the Cobb and Elder theory.

An alternative explanation has given by Wirt, Mitchell and Marshall.[36] Variation among states in the education policy domain of action is explained by them as due to the particular states' political cultures. At the core of meaning of a political culture are its common values, preferences for action, and beliefs. The state culture is reflected in its codes. These codes may be the educational laws, specific curriculum contents, instructions on school governance, parental involvement or particular program budgets. Wirt, Mitchell and Marshall, in their study analyzing educational policies of several states in the United States, found three dominant cultures explaining the variation among the policy domain of their actions.

The meritocratic culture (or the culture of professionalism) would be evidenced in code references to the quality and efficiency values.[37] This culture features an elite to set standards of service, to have the veto in personnel approval and to evaluate its own work. This model is found mostly in Illinois. The preferred domain of actions there was finance and school governance.

The democratic culture is evidenced by choice references, with non-professional control of schooling policy through board elections and referenda.[38] This model was found mainly in Wisconsin.

The egalitarian culture is evident in equity values that seek to redress the maldistribution of schooling resources,[39] found mostly in Wisconsin.

The cultural thesis may be used in testing changes in Israeli educational policy contents and actions.

Summary

To summarize, an educational policy may be tested by one or more line of inquiries. It may be tested by its structure; by who is involved in the policy-making process and what his weight is in formulating policies. It can be tested by its processes: how decisions are made. It can also be tested by its contents and domains of actions. In the following chapters, Israel's macro-educational policy is analyzed according to its structures (chapter 3), according to its perspectives (chapters 4 and 5), and according to its actions (chapters 6 and 7).

2

Shaping Education Policy

After World War II, the Western world underwent social upheavals that impacted on the direction of education policy. The postwar period was marked by substantial demographic growth, coupled with economic rehabilitation and prosperity.[1] As standards of living rose, so did the demand for education services, especially among the peripheral social strata, whose expectations grew even more than did those of the rest of the population. One can explain these changes as being based on the belief that education improves the quality of life,[2] as well as on research findings showing that education increases the income of both individuals and society.[3] Indeed, education is perceived as a worthwhile economic investment at both the individual and the societal levels. From the individual's point of view, education facilitates an increase in one's direct income and social status; from society's standpoint, it helps create high-quality human resources and furthers economic and industrial development in an era of high technology and competition. The increase in demand for education caused the education system to grow in terms of number of workers, number of buildings, quantity of scholastic equipment, and size of education budgets.

Just as the education system was in the midst of rapid development, economic activity in the Western world slowed (especially after the oil crisis of the early 1980s), and this led to cutbacks in all social-service budgets, including those for education.[4] The shrinking public budget pie became a focal point for struggles among all public sectors, including welfare, education, and health services. As different fields of education contested for their share of the overall education budgets, questions of priority arose, such as whether to invest in pre-school education as opposed to post-primary education, or whether to develop vocational education at the expense of academic education or vice versa.[5] Should the education system be led toward equality, or should elitism be preferred? These were by no means the only questions. These problems worsened as ideological schisms in society deepened and the budget pie shrank. Larry Cuban, of the Stanford University College of Education, argues that education system reforms, including restructuring (centralization versus decentralization), curriculum changes (academic versus vocational), and changes in teaching methods (frontal versus activational), are always based on ideological and value considerations.[6] Furthermore, when decision-makers in education seek to revise an existing policy or devise a new one, their behavior is based on ideology and rationality. The ideological basis for their behavior manifests itself in the shaping of the education goals meant to reflect a scale of values shared by the policy-makers and the dominant group or groups in society. The rational basis for their behavior, in contrast, is reflected in the consistent correlation between the goals of education and the resources earmarked for their attainment. Thus, for example, the cult of efficiency of early 1960s American society manifested itself most substantively in the education system – in its subject matter, teaching methods, and administrative and supervisory modalities. In a pluralistic society, education policy-makers proffer different sets of values, which, to a great extent, exist in a state of conflict. Change in such situations is usually the outcome of compromise among politicians who represent the conflicting interests and different scales of values.[7]

What, then, are the value dilemmas that education policy-makers face, and can they in fact be bridged?

Value Dilemmas in Education Systems

Efficiency (as an Economic Value) versus Equality
(as a Social Value)

Efficiency as a basic value in education policy means the adoption of the most productive policies possible, i.e., those of lowest cost and highest yield.[8] This definition is also valid with regard to school efficiency. It elicits the questions of what yield in education is comprised of – scholastic achievement? pupils' satisfaction with their school? the acquisition of new attitudes and values? Even if we focus on only one component of the yield in education, say, scholastic achievement, the question remains: Can one actually measure the school's net contribution to scholastic achievement, disregarding the contribution of the home and the mass media to the totality of the pupil's knowledge? If we find it hard to calculate the net utility of the school in pupil achievement, and to estimate all the costs and benefits of school, how is it possible to perform a cost-benefit analysis of teaching and study in the school? Furthermore, if we focus on cognitive achievement as the measure of educational utility, we are forced to disregard many other kinds of education-system benefits. These may be tangible and measurable outputs, such as the contribution of education to the pupil's future income, or intangibles such as education for ethics, patriotism, love of others, etc. It is equally hard to measure the contribution of the education system to the individual's ability to adjust to change – a vastly important skill in the present era.[9] If the yardstick of education policy is efficiency, curricula that fail to meet the criterion of high yield and low cost are unjustifiable. Should we accept this yardstick, we would urge the Ministry of Education and Culture to downscale or eliminate inputs invested in certain social groups, because investments in these groups are not economically viable.[10] If this is done, what becomes of the non-economic values that guide education policy?

In view of the difficulties that arise in measuring efficiency in education, and in view of the predictably adverse social effects of the application of efficiency as a preferred value in education policy, education decision-makers have been motivated to seek a *conceptual alternative to efficiency*. Such a concept should not only give expression to the economic aspects of education but also embrace other education goals. The concept of effectiveness, instead of efficiency, is consistent with this intent. On the macro level, the concept of effectiveness is not limited to money-saving ways of carrying out a given education policy, although it does include these. The concept also concerns itself with the social correctness and desirability of the policy in question. In other words, the concept of effectiveness in education is more comprehensive than mere efficiency, and better suited to use in education systems. On the micro level, the effectiveness-in-education concept relates not only to scholastic achievement in school but also to the qualitative components of school work: teacher and pupil satisfaction, morale, commitment to one's school, and faculty adjustment to changes and innovations in the school environment.[11]

The preference for effectiveness over efficiency as an educational goal has presented researchers with several questions. First, for whom should the system be effective? In other words, who should benefit from education resources? In a democratic society, all citizens are entitled to benefit from education resources,[12] but does this really happen? Studies in the United States,[13] Europe,[14] and Israel[15] indicate that some people benefit disproportionately. These findings have catapulted the subject of equality in education to the top of the public agenda. Indeed, most of the speakers at an OECD conference in Paris in 1970 asked how to ensure equality in education – this being a basic value in democratic society – without harming the quality of education.[16]

Equality in Education

Equality as an education system objective is not a unique discovery of the twentieth century. The belief that people are entitled to equal opportunity in education is anchored in the classical Liberal philosophy of the eighteenth century.[17] In this *weltanschauung*, all persons are entitled to equal rights, and all artificial impediments to the attainment of social status commensurate with individuals' natural traits should be eliminated. The basis for success should be determined by individuals' attributes, not their social background. Then as now it was widely believed that equality in education opportunities would almost automatically lead in the long term to greater equality in educational achievement and greater equality among social strata. Education is regarded as a key to social mobility for the disadvantaged, and for this reason many espouse equality in education as a way to vitiate the enmity of the poor toward the rich.[18]

The ascent of the value of equity in the Western world and, in its wake, the demand that the principle of equal opportunity in education be honored, have brought the following question to the fore: Where, in practical terms, does one implement this equality? Does one equalize the budgets of all local education authorities or districts?[19] Does one equalize the inputs that all schools within a local education authority receive, or does one equalize per-capita spending? Should equality pertain to inputs only, or to the results as well? Formal equality in total inputs means uniformity – in standards, equipment, curricula, and teaching personnel. The administrative meaning of such uniformity is centralization, and its pedagogic meaning is a decrease in the autonomy of schools and teachers.[20] Uniformity also means placing schools under close inspection, to ensure the fulfillment of the principles of equality and uniformity and to prevent schools breaching the limits set forth in Ministry of Education policy. The immediate budgetary significance of such a policy is budgeting for schools using a line-item method. The main characteristics of such a system are two: budgeting by item irrespective of the necessity of each item, and rigid control of all outlays. Within this type of rigid budget, only the central authority is given discretion in the apportionment of resources. To maintain the size of the budget from year to year, surpluses are frittered away in various activities, irrespective of their relevance or irrelevance to the organization's goals. This method of budgeting encourages inefficiency and waste.

Education observers have subjected the horizontal-equality method to withering criticism, with Swedish educationist Thorsten Husen calling it "Social Darwinism."[21] True, all children are given equal inputs, but success ultimately belongs to the "strong" students who know how to benefit from them; the "weak" students will fail more. Israeli educational philosopher Fritz Kleinberg therefore adds the following questions: Do equal efforts for all children affect all children equally? Will all children treated in this fashion be equal in knowledge, skills, approaches, and attitudes?[22] As a consequence of this criticism, voiced in various parts of the world, a turnabout took place in the meaning of "equality in education"; equality of inputs was replaced by "equality in results."

A famous study by sociologist James Coleman had much to do with this watershed.[23] One of Coleman's surprise findings was that, even when schools were given equal inputs, the outputs varied significantly, evidently because of sociological differences among students. Other American studies verified Coleman's findings.[24] Coleman reinforced the hypothesis that equal opportunity in education must be an efficient equality, one that manifests itself in those qualitative components that contribute to the learning process and assure greater equity in results. Coleman's findings and those of other scholars led to the conclusion that equal opportunity based on inputs only will not suffice; equal opportunity based on results should be present as well. The goal of formal equity should be replaced by real equity, and horizontal equity by vertical equity. Vertical education means compensating disadvantaged groups by offering complementary education activities, i.e., a deliberate focus of physical and human resources on the culturally and educationally disadvantaged. American researcher S. J. Carroll claims that the effectiveness of a budget earmarked for the disadvantaged is a function of the degree to which it focuses on the improvement of teaching and learning processes.[25]

Jencks *et al.* went one step further, concluding that even positive discrimination toward the disadvantaged will not improve their achievement.[26] These findings were corroborated by Lesterc.[27] These arguments stunned the educational community and the proponents of result-based equality. Had these findings been accepted verbatim, the policy of equality in education might have been dealt a staggering blow. Accordingly, the education community responded by criticizing both the research modalities used and the findings themselves.[28] The core of this criticism was the argument that accepting Coleman's conclusions would repudiate the ability of the school, and its educational and scholastic efforts, to help the disadvantaged. Adoption of Coleman's conclusions might create a social tinderbox.

These findings undoubtedly helped Western conservative circles to press their demand that financial resources be earmarked for the promotion of elitism and excellence in education. These circles preferred this method to an investment in socio-educational integration, which might lead society toward mediocrity and adversely affect the training of future leadership elites, a necessity of every society.[29]

Educational Equality versus Educational Elitism

The demands of socioeconomically well-off pressure groups came as a counterpoint to the liberal and egalitarian tendencies of the education system. These groups favored the training of those best suited to making the greatest possible contribution to the common weal. They also espoused the maintenance of the necessary balance in the supply of people with certain skills and propensities. The egalitarian culture preached equality in both education inputs and scholastic results as a central value; this was opposed by a culture of meritocracy, which stressed values such as elitism and excellence. The disciples of meritocracy argued that the realities of differential results should be allowed to manifest themselves. They also contended that uniformity and egalitarianism in education might subvert their rights as members of a democratic society. According to their reasoning, an education policy which aspired to equalize the "educational rights" of all students would increase the allocation of public resources for the disadvantaged. At a time of cutbacks in public budgets, this would amount to the funding of education services for the disadvantaged by the affluent, and they opposed this. The advocates of meritocracy also rejected positive discrimination toward the disadvantaged, arguing that the slice of the budget pie meant for education in a democratic society, which has multiple goals and serves many customers, should be apportioned equally among all social sectors and strata.[30]

The meritocrats did advocate a reform in school budgeting – with a transition from input-based to output-based budgeting.[31] The public treasury should fund schools in accordance with their quality, educational level, and the quality of their graduates. By this method, the state would increase its share of assistance only for schools that demonstrated higher efficiency and effectiveness; the automatic allocation of budget resources based only on inputs would be stopped. The changeover to output-based budgeting would undoubtedly lead to a restructuring of the education system – from centralized to decentralized. Schools would have to streamline in order to obtain a larger slice of the public budget. This streamlining would manifest itself in the planning of school administration, teaching, and a display of accountability to taxpayers. The meritocrats acknowledged the existence of a basic contradiction between their philosophy and the doctrine of educational equality. Hence an essential question arose: is it not possible to assure excellence in education even in an egalitarian society? Some would answer this question in the negative; for them, the best way to assure excellence in education is by moving from "coercion in education," which seeks to ensure equality, to "parental choice."[32] Others answer in the affirmative; they regard parental choice as the best way to obtain both excellence and equality in education.[33] But does "parental choice" truly promote equality and integration in education, or does it support social selectivity? The issue requires examination, and I consider it below.

Educational Choice as a Basis for Education Policy[34]

Another educational policy dilemma that has caused vacillation in democratic societies and which has implications for educational policy is the dichotomy between values of equality that have an element of coercion (e.g., compulsory attendance in integrated schools) and that of parents' and children's "right to choose" the kind of education that they desire. This dichotomy is best summed up by the phrase "educational coercion versus educational choice."

Even though the options among which one may choose are numerous, diverse, and sometimes mutually exclusive, the principle remains the same: parental choice means greater parental freedom to choose the school that they wish their children to attend and that meets their needs, without government intervention by way of compulsory enrollment districts. Several rationales underlie the concept of educational choice:

The philosophical rationale – Freedom of choice for individuals is a supreme value, deriving from the very existence of the individual.[35]

The psychological rationale – Every individual has needs and areas of interest that are particular to him/her. The education system is supposed to respond to these needs.

The economic rationale – The possibility of choice among many schools will force schools to compete for students and, consequently, to achieve efficiencies and offer attractive programs. This will eventually improve individuals' scholastic achievement, to the ultimate benefit of society as a whole – monopolism harms efficiency, while competitiveness promotes it. Furthermore, the elimination of districting restrictions will permit disadvantaged children to choose schools that may not be in their areas of residence.[36]

The social rationale – The social goal of education is to meet the expectations of families and their children; this can be accomplished only when parents are given a choice. Thus schools that fail to attract parent/child demand will simply close.

Researchers agree that these rationales are important.[37] However, the following counterclaim has been voiced: If the ideal of parental choice is fulfilled, any group of parents may devise its own curriculum, irrespective of the national interest of imparting a basic shared curriculum to all children in the culture. What will become of basic subject matter that all children within a given culture, even a free and democratic one, must know? This subject matter includes a shared language; mathematics and science; economics, investment, and savings; the meaning of the rule of law; equal rights and duties of every citizen; and conflict resolution by political means. What will happen if certain parent groups decide that the curriculum can omit these subjects?

In cases such as these, the education system may again stand at a crossroads between two conflicting trends: the individual's freedom of choice versus society's desire to provide all its constituents with a common base. Alternately stated, the clash is between society's right to reproduce its accepted values and norms by exposing pupils to them through a shared educational experience, versus the individual's right to choose the norms that he or she accepts.

Educational researcher Bruce Cooper of Fordham University (New York) argues that legitimizing parental choice means greater trust by society in the market mechanism than in the government mechanism as the agent of improvement in the educational system.[38] Educational choice admittedly substantiates the value of freedom in a democratic society, but it also legitimizes additional values such as efficiency and elitism. This efficiency will manifest itself in the closure of schools that children and their parents do not choose. Elitism will be reflected in schools' choice of the students they want, and these will usually be members of the affluent strata. Even if legislation bans discrimination in the selection of students on the basis of gender, race, ethnic origin, or even scholastic achievement, there is still a risk that the children of the poor will receive education of lesser quality than that offered to children of the rich, because the poor will have limited access to information about prestigious schools. Consequently, children of the rich will be the first to enroll in the schools; the disadvantaged, lacking suitable information and guidance, will attend inferior schools.

A contrary view is proffered by advocates of educational choice who favor equality: parental choice will actually promote equality and integration among social strata, provided that the schools are "special," i.e., differentiated by ideology or subject matter. Enrollment in special schools would be determined in a manner consonant with the interests and qualifications of the child, irrespective of his or her origin and parental income. The disadvantaged would be compensated by vouchers given them by the state, which they would use to purchase the education that they prefer. This method ostensibly eliminates the conflict between efficiency, excellence, and equality by invoking the parental choice principle. However, several questions still remain. Is society really able to set up efficient school inspection mechanisms that would allow educational equality and educational choice to coexist? Legislation might outlaw discrimination in school admission on the basis of gender, race, and ethnic origin, and might apprise the entire public of the scholastic opportunities available to it, but would such legislation truly cope with the risk that the schools would choose the pupils, and not vice versa?[39]

The tension between these conflicting trends in the education system have implications both on the way education resources are allocated and on the nature of the curriculum (see chapter 5). In any event, it is clear that parental choice increases the extent to which parents (especially middle-class parents) would have to share in the expense of their children's studies, and would reduce the budgetary burden that the public system bears. The result would be privatization by the back door.

Summary

Every democratic country that wishes to preserve or modify its education policy has to ask itself the following questions:

1. What is the value/ideological base that interest groups in the society prefer or agree upon?
2. How can one sustain an education policy that will meet most of the expectations of citizens in a pluralistic society, but which lacks an ideological consensus?
3. Equal opportunity in education is a value of paramount importance in a democratic society. However, if society wishes to survive in a competitive, frequently changing world, it must maintain the quality of its educational outputs; mediocrity cannot be accepted. This being the case, how can educational equality and quality be made to coexist?
4. Democratic society preaches freedom of choice. However, is there not a risk that educational choice will lead to social inequality? If the risk exists, how can society accept disparities in education among its different segments?
5. An education policy which regards equality as a value will have to claim a growing share of the public budget; one based on

the market mechanism will make growing financial demands on households.

6. An education policy that wishes to provide all citizens with a shared educational base must promote a certain degree of uniformity and centralization; the shapers of an education policy that seeks to meet the diverse needs of its citizens will have to encourage decentralization. However, is it truly possible to devise a policy when conflicting orientations exist?

These six questions indicate the problematic nature of policy-making in a democratic society. Those who shape education policy are at a crossroads; the question they face is how to maneuver among conflicting ideological trends and diverse interests.

Educational policy researcher Larry Cuban believes the choice of education policy is ultimately a sociopolitical one.[40] The central government will support a policy that expresses the views of interest groups that belong to the social mainstream. In reality, Cuban derives his outlook from the sociological theory known as functionalism, according to which the education system and the society in which it operates are interdependent.[41] The education system depends on society's legitimacy and resources, whereas society needs the education system to ensure its continuity (socialization) and to meet other existential needs, such as trained manpower for its economy.[42] Since the social system has an interest in keeping its constituents in equilibrium and preventing internal conflicts, the function of schools is to maintain the status quo.[43] Change in the education system would be the result of malfunction, dysfunction,[44] or endogenous pressures that bring new social needs to the fore. According to sociologist G.C. Homans, any change of this type is carried out in a controlled fashion in order to prevent shocks that may threaten the status quo and lead, *inter alia*, to a redistribution of rewards and resources.[45]

Group theory reinforces the structural/functional hypothesis. According to this theory, public policy is a product of the efforts to balance different interest groups, in order to prevent confrontation, produce a general solution when one is needed, or confine a confrontation to agreed-upon limits.[46] Accordingly, one cannot expect revolutions in policy.

By implication, as long as education policy keeps the ideologies and interests of the different groups in equilibrium, and as long as the education system functions in keeping with these expectations, no changes will take place. However, when the education system malfunctions and fails to meet its consumers' expectations, a profound, change-catalyzing crisis takes place. The intensity of the resulting change is a function of the degree to which it breaches the socio-ideological equilibrium.

Our hypothesis in this book is that the intensity of these dilemmas in the shaping of education policy will be greater in Israel for the following reasons:

1. Israel is a democratic, pluralistic state that espouses equality as a central value, as manifested both in its Declaration of Independence and in the State Education Law, 5713–1953.[47] Its leaders have declared on various occasions that they favor an egalitarian ideology that implies, *inter alia*, uniformity in curricula and teaching methods coupled with administrative centralization and control.

2. Israel is poor in physical resources, has a negative balance of payments, and depends on loans and grants from the United States and world Jewry.[48] Therefore, it cannot disregard the value of efficiency in its education policy.

3. Israel is a modern, progressive state which, in view of its scanty resources, cannot forfeit quality and a high technological level if it wishes to ensure its economic survival in a competitive world. For this reason, it must include excellence as one of the values in its policy base, develop accelerated programs for elites, and encourage the gifted.

4. Israel is a pluralistic state in which Jews and Arabs, non-religious and religious Jews, and those of European/American and Asian/African ethnic origin live alongside each other. Israeli sociologist Moshe Lissak has described Israel as having a "multischism society."[49] Consequently, education policy should give expression to these differences even as it maintains national unity. It was for good reason that the 1953 State Education Law recognized the religious sector's right to autonomy in the sense of separate institutions, teachers, principals, inspectors, and curricula. In other words, every parent is entitled to enroll his or her children in a State, State–Religious, or *haredi* (ultra-Orthodox) school. (The *haredim* have their own education systems.) Education decision-makers face the dilemma of the right of the religious to autonomy (and, to a certain extent, to separatism), on the one hand, and the

need to ensure the attainment of additional goals of state education that are no less important – equality among all education sectors and maintaining the principle of efficiency in resource allocation in education – on the other.

Israel has also recognized educational autonomy in the Arab sector.[50] The Arab population accounts for 17 percent of Israeli citizens – a minority in Israel but part of a substantial majority in the Middle East. Israeli Arabs regard themselves as part of the Arab world by virtue of their shared culture, language, and religion. For this reason, they wish to maintain their national and cultural identity and have no desire to assimilate into the Jewish majority in Israel. The educational expression of this aspiration is manifested in the existence of a separate education system with separate institutions, teachers, and curricula. The Arab-Israeli conflict has intensified Israeli Arab separatism. The education system faces a dilemma: how to assure educational autonomy for the Arabs of Israel while ensuring educational equality for all citizens of the state.

The question, then, is how can education policy-makers maneuver among the conflicting goals of education policy. Israeli sociologist S. N. Eisenstadt argues that Israeli society is composed of core and peripheral groups, dominant and marginal groups. When the core interest groups are entrenched in the Israeli social and political structure, they do not press for change but tend to safeguard their sphere of influence in a process that may be defined as "dynamic conservatism."[51] Eisenstadt's argument actually reinforces the structural-functional hypothesis in sociological theory and supports the central precept of group theory.

I argue that the shapers of education policy in Israel, operating in a pluralistic, multi-value society that cannot reach consensus on the aims of education, will maneuver among the various interest groups in keeping with the pendulum principle, itself a product of group theory. The pendulum stabilizes at a different point of equilibrium after each change (most such changes are incremental), but the equilibrium among the contrasting social trends is not breached. When exogenous environmental changes (social, economic, political) do not threaten the core interest groups, the changes in education policy are chiefly incremental, i.e., marginal. However, when the education system malfunctions, i.e., fails to perform the new functions warranted by rapid environmental changes, and when a significant breach of the social equilibrium is perceived, the system is engulfed in a crisis of confidence. As the values for which national consensus exists are threatened, the different interest groups press for change and force the education policy-makers to carry out a more comprehensive reform. To prevent violent clashes between interest groups, the policymakers struggle to stop the pendulum at a new point of equilibrium, at which a response is given to the changing environmental expectations and the new balance of social forces.[52]

The following chapters will demonstrate how the above scenario has influenced Israeli education policy.

3

History of Education Policy in Israel

The sources of educational policy in Israel after the establishment of the State hail back to the Yishuv era preceding its establishment.[1] The educational policy during the Yishuv era was developed outside the framework of a sovereign state, and was shaped by those political forces which were active in the Zionist movement. Inevitably, the values reflected in this policy were derived from the political and ideological views within the Zionist movement. These included, for example, the ideological struggles between religion and secularism, between socialism and capitalism, between equality and elitism, and between centralization and decentralization. These ideological struggles, which began during the Yishuv era, continued after the State was established and, in fact, have continued to the present.[2]

At the beginning of the Yishuv era (up to 1920), one cannot speak of a clearly formulated educational policy, because Jewish education in Palestine had neither a common language nor a common goal nor a common policy. The schools in the earliest era resembled – in structure, curriculum and educational method – the schools in Eastern Europe or in Western countries. The great majority were yeshivot, *hadarim* or Talmud Torah schools in the old traditional mold. At the end of the nineteenth century and the beginning of the twentieth century, a number of modern schools were established in Palestine by various Jewish philanthropic organizations. The aim was to establish such schools in Palestine as existed outside the country, the goal being to instill in their students the culture and language of the motherland of its founders. For example, the Alliance Israelite Universelle fostered French culture and the French language among the Jews, whereas the Ezra society promoted German culture and the German tongue. The Hebrew language schools received their impetus from the Hovevei Zion movement,[3] which founded the first Hebrew-language school and teacher's seminary in Jaffa. There were also schools under the control of local authorities, i.e., under the control of the governing bodies of different Jewish settlements (such as those founded in Tel Aviv). None of these, though, can be considered to have coalesced into an educational system.

In the period between 1920 and the establishment of the State in 1948, the British were in control of Palestine under a League of Nations mandate. It was during this era that a process began of the nationalization of the Hebrew educational system by the Zionist Organization, which strove to attain uniformity and a clearly delineated educational policy for the Jewish Yishuv in the country. For this purpose, it founded the "Education Committee" in 1914, a committee composed of nine members. Its members represented the Zionist Organization, the Teachers Union and the Yishuv as a whole. From 1927 there was also a representative of the Education Department of the British mandatory government. The Education Committee regarded as its primary mission the uniting of all educational institutions under a single language and under a single administration. In 1919 another body was established to coordinate matters and to implement them, this being named the Education Department. By 1920 the Zionist Organization already had under its supervision a total of 110 schools with 11,220 students.[4]

The British mandate gave the Hebrew education system autonomy and a very limited amount of budgetary support, covering about 1.5 percent of the budget of the Hebrew educational system, the same way it aided private schools of the Christian churches.[5] This policy of the mandatory government was accepted with a certain degree of understanding by the Zionist Executive, because at least it granted pedagogic autonomy to the Jewish schools – something that the Zionist Executive wanted very much to preserve. At the same time, the Executive expressed extreme opposition to the gross disparity between the allocations to Jewish education and those to Arabic education. The Arabic education system was public (as a continuation of the tradition dating back to Ottoman times in Palestine), so that it was totally funded by the mandatory government. The Briton Humphrey Bauman[6] claims that even if the mandatory government had wished to aid the Zionist Executive financially and had increased the budget to its schools, it is doubtful whether the Executive would have been willing to limit the autonomy which it enjoyed in return for an increase in the amount paid by the mandatory authorities to the Hebrew educational system. This claim is probably correct, for in 1927 the British mandatory government recognized the Hebrew educational system as a public school system and as a result increased its contribution to the system tenfold, but, in return, it demanded greater involvement in determining the policies of the Hebrew educational system.[7]

At that time the Zionist Executive was opposed to this. As a result, there was a return to the limited support of the mandatory authorities, amounting to 3.2 percent of the budget of the Hebrew educational system. This cut in British support to the Hebrew educational system was a major burden on the budget of the Zionist Organization. In spite of an increase in the number of students of about 60 percent between 1920 and 1927, not only did the educational budget not increase, but it actually decreased by 30 percent. (In 1919, the Zionist Executive bore 89 percent of the educational budget of the Hebrew educational system.) The result of these cuts was a decision by the Zionist Organization to concentrate on elementary schools and to terminate its aid to high schools and kindergartens.[8] As a result, the high schools were forced to raise their fees so that they were no longer dependent on external support, and they thus became more independent. Private high schools were opened, their professional quality declined, and their public school image dissipated.[9] While academic high schools flourished, vocational high schools almost ceased to exist due to a lack of students. The privatization of the high-school system resulted in having only students whose parents had the means attending high schools. The high school became an elitist institution.

The literature of the era would seem to indicate[10] that the reasons why the Zionist Organization decreased its expenditures on education were not only budgetary but also ideological. There were those in the Zionist Organization who regarded investment in education as being non-productive when compared to investment in other sectors, and it was they who sought to have the educational budget in Palestine decreased.

The poor financial situation brought about a proposal at the 13th Zionist Congress to have education moved from the Zionist Executive to the local authorities, which would have meant a decentralization of education and a transfer of the focus of power from the Zionist Organization and its Education Department to the local authorities and to the private educational networks. The vast majority of delegates of the Zionist Organization were opposed to this proposal and regarded it as posing a danger to Hebrew education in Palestine. However, except for voicing its disapproval, the Zionist Organization did nothing in terms of increasing the budget.[11] From 1919 to 1925 the amount paid by the local authorities toward the educational budget increased by close to 600 percent. The result was that there were marked discrepancies between those educational authorities which were well-established economically, such as Tel Aviv and the first settlements (e.g., Rishon Lezion and Zichron Yaakov) on the one hand, and poor educational authorities such as the city of Jerusalem on the other.[12] This did not prevent the 29th Zionist Congress from deciding that Hebrew education would be in the hands of the Education Committee and not in those of the local authorities, and it won the strong support of the Teachers Union in this.

The struggle over control of education between the central authority, as represented in the Yishuv era by the Zionist Organization and the National Executive, and the local authorities, in reality persisted even after the establishment of the State.

The Yishuv Era

In the period that preceded the establishment of the State the interaction between central institutions, and secondary ones, shaped educational policy.[13] The central institutions included the Zionist Organization and the National Executive (which, once the State was established, became the Israeli Knesset) as the supreme authorities, and their different departments dealing with education, which included: (1) The Education Committee, which was composed of representatives of the Zionist Organization, representatives of the National Executive, representatives of the Teachers' Union and a representative of the British mandatory authority. Except for the British representative, all the rest were elected by party slate. The topics with which the Education Committee dealt included the education budget, teachers' salaries, policies regarding hiring and dismissing teachers, and approving the curricula of the inspectorate. (2) The various inspectorates of the different systems of education: the general system, the Mizrahi-religious system, and the Labor system. (3) The Education Department, which operated the Hebrew education system in accordance with the directives of the Education Committee. The Department was headed by a single head, who had deputies from each of the school systems. In 1932, in order to prevent the decentralization of the education system, another body was established, the Administrative Committee, whose composition allowed for significant representation by the local authorities, thereby acknowledging their power. This committee did not contain any representatives of the Teachers' Union. The establishment of the Administrative Committee, with representatives of both the National Executive and of the Zionist Organization, paralyzed the work of the Education Committee and the focus of power moved from that committee to the Administrative Committee.[14]

In addition to the central institutions, there were three secondary institutions on the educational–political stage, which in reality were the ones that pulled the strings and affected the direction of educational policy. These institutions included the political parties within the Zionist Organization and in the National Executive (it was these parties which lay behind the different educational systems), the Teachers' Union and the local authorities.

The Political Parties

The Zionist Organization and the National Executive saw the clash of three large ideological–political blocs: the leftist bloc, which included the secular labor parties; the religious bloc; and the centrist and moderate rightist bloc, which maintained a low profile with regard to nationalist education issues.[15] Each of these blocs insisted on its right to formulate educational policy in accordance with its beliefs, which created struggles between the blocs about the character of the education to be offered.[16]

During the Yishuv era such struggles generally ended in a compromise: there was real concern that if the differences were accentuated they would destroy the peace and unity within the nation being created in its land. At the same time, the fear of disturbing the unity brought about a situation whereby, instead of solving problems, they were papered over. In spite of all the evasive decisions meant to preserve unity, it was clear that there were two distinct kinds of nationalistic educational systems, the religious and secular, which differed both in content and in form.[17] The solution to conflicts between the blocs was generally pragmatic: there was unity in fundamental issues and mutual tolerance and autonomy with regard to basic ideology.[18] Given this reality, the 16th Zionist

Congress in 1929 recognized the three educational systems as being equally valid, i.e., the general system, the religious system, and the labor system. It was decided that the general system would be under the supervision of the General Zionists, the religious system under the Mizrahi, and the labor system under the Labor Party.

In 1927 the general system had 105 schools with 11,885 students, the religious had 52 schools with 5,473 students, and the labor system 193 schools with 18,568 students.[19]

This division into different systems was significant politically and educationally. It meant that each of the systems had a permanent representation in the educational administration in the country and was able to express its ideology within its own system. Each system had an autonomous oversight committee consisting of ten people, including teachers, inspectors and parents. These committees established school curricula, set the educational budget, and formulated the educational policy of the particular system. In addition to the political differences between the systems, there were also differences between them regarding the goals and methods of education.[20]

In terms of values, the general school system emphasized liberalism, autonomy in education, the right to vote, progressive education, and individualism in education as primary goals.[21] In terms of methods, it emphasized the study of Hebrew language and literature, the geography of Eretz Israel, and the history of Israel.

In terms of values, the labor school system emphasized cooperation, equality, collectivity, progressive education, self-fulfillment, and physical labor.[22] In terms of methods, these were similar to those of the general school system, with the addition of courses in agriculture and the crafts.

In terms of values, the Mizrahi-religious system stressed the values of the Jewish religion and in terms of methods it laid primary emphasis on religious studies – the Bible, the Talmud, and Jewish thought.[23]

The schools of the different systems received their funds primarily from the Education Department of the Zionist Organization. After the administration of education was transferred to the National Executive in 1932, they received their funds from the latter (its budget coming primarily from funds transferred to it by the Jewish Agency), from support by the British authorities, and from support by the affluent local Jewish authorities. In addition, each system raised funds on its own. The general school system was supported primarily by the local authorities in the towns and settlements. The religious school system was supported by the World Mizrahi Organization, while the labor school system was supported by the Center for Education of the General Workers Histadrut.

In reality, the different systems remained in effect even after the establishment of the State. While they were legally abolished in accordance with a law passed in 1953, the Mizrahi system remained, with its name changed to the State–Religious (SR) school system and it continued to preserve its autonomy, whereas the general system and the labor system were combined into one and became the State school system.

The Teachers Union

The Teachers' Union was only a force in determining educational policy up to about 1914. The Hebrew teachers who belonged to the Zionist renewal movement were the first to seek to formulate a unified educational policy, but were unable to do so, as we shall see below.[24] In 1892, the first convention took place of "the Teachers' Meeting," with the aim of formulating a unified educational policy in terms of school structure, textbooks, curriculum, class times, etc. In spite of the numerous meetings and the goodwill displayed this organization was unable to formulate a unified educational policy. At the initiative of Ussishkin, who was one of the leaders of the Hovevei Zion, the teachers assembled again in 1903. The aim behind Ussishkin's call was "to give the Hebrew teachers the ability to accomplish properly the educational needs entrusted to them";[25] the meetings were meant to formulate an educational policy and to give it concrete expression. In 1907, the Teachers' Center prepared a proposal for an elementary school curriculum in Palestine, which it had decided would be of an eight-year duration. From 1910 to 1914 the Teachers' Union was the focus of authority for Hebrew education. It published books and ran in-service courses for teachers.

In 1914 the Teachers Union began a revolt against the Ezra organization (a philanthropic organization supported by German Jews for education in Palestine), which wanted the studies in the Technion to be conducted in German and not in Hebrew. In its struggle, the Teachers' Union was able to enlist not only the teachers, but the students and parents as well. This debate revealed the need for an organization that would be above those which conducted education and would guide educational policy and mediate between the different groups. This dispute, which was known as "the Language War,"[26] brought about the process of the formulation and nationalization of Hebrew education in Palestine. The heads of the Zionist Organization reached the conclusion that the administration of education could not be left solely to the teachers. From that point on, the Teachers' Union lost its hegemony in the formulation of educational policy, to be replaced by the Zionist Organization and its Education Committee. The transfer of power from the Teachers' Union to the Education Committee of the Zionist Organization was not brought about as a result of the lobbying of the latter, but because the teachers and parents preferred schools that would be administered in a nationalistic vein, and believed that only the Education Committee could guarantee this.[27] Although the Teachers' Union lost some of its power, it nevertheless continued to participate as a representative on the Education Committee. However, when the latter lost its authority in 1933, to be superseded by the Administrative Council, the power of the Teachers' Union was also decreased. The Administrative Council, the new body which would formulate educational policy until the establishment of the State, did not even have any teacher representative. Thus the Teachers' Union, which had been the first organization to seek to formulate a unified educational policy and which had exerted a great deal of effort in this regard, was shunted aside and left the political stage. The Teachers' Union no longer formulated educational policy, a situation which has continued up to the present, and its leaders have had to content themselves with administering a professional union which does no more than protect its members' wages.

The Local Authorities

There were important social and political developments in the local authorities in the 1930s and 1940s. Whereas the labor parties and the religious parties concentrated on national concerns both in the Zionist Organization and in the National Executive, the General Zionists and the Progressives, as centrist parties, focused on the local level. Thus a new power base emerged, consisting primarily of members of the First *Aliyah* waves to Palestine of the end of the nineteenth and the beginning of the twentieth centuries. Many First *Aliyah* immigrants were engaged in farming or commerce, and were to a large extent independent economically and did not need budgetary support from the national institutions.[28] As the local authorities developed economically and socially, they demanded political expression for their economic power, primarily in the realm of education. They wanted administrative and pedagogic autonomy for their institutions, and they organized the parents and residents of their areas in demanding autonomy in setting educational policy. They believed in the old adage that "he who pays the piper calls the tune."[29] Their demands were met with stiff opposition by both the national institutions and the Teachers' Union, both of which feared that the educational system would become fragmented into autonomous units without any guiding hand. The circumstances of the time enabled the affluent local authorities to guarantee themselves autonomy in the administrative realm, an autonomy which they would keep after establishment of the State.

But in the poor local authorities the situation was entirely different. These authorities were generally mixed ones of Jews and Arabs. The Arabs studied in public schools and enjoyed the financial benefits of the British authorities. The Jewish schools, on the other hand, were forced to make do with the meager allocations of the Zionist Organization, because the National Executive did not have the authority or compulsive power necessary to collect funds from the Jewish residents to finance the educational system. But the meager amount of money which reached the schools was barely able to keep the systems going. Teachers were forced to forgo pay raises and in many cases worked voluntarily, just to ensure that the educationsl system continued to survive.[30] A situation arose of clear discrimination in the level of education between the affluent local authorities and the poorer ones because educational funding was now a function of the internal resources of the individual settlements; the obvious consequence was that the affluent local authorities influenced educational policy. The National Executive was finally forced to accede to the demands of the affluent local authorities. At the end of protracted negotiations, a compromise was reached in 1942, whereby administrative autonomy for the local authorities would include the hiring of teachers for their schools and the responsibility for funding the schools, while the determination of educational policy would be left to the central authorities. This situation led both *de facto* and *de jure* to a decentralization of education, with administrative autonomy for the affluent local authorities and pedagogic autonomy for the different educational systems, a situation which would later, after the establishment of the State, lead to uncompromising centralization and the passing of the State Education Law in 1953.

The Establishment of the State

Just before the establishment of the State, elementary school education was primarily public, and encompassed about 80 percent of the students to the age of 14. The high schools were elitist, because they required the payment of school fees and only a small part of the population could permit themselves this "luxury." Most teachers were uncertified and used archaic teaching methods. The education system lacked a real "owner." The education system was fragmented among the administrations of the different educational systems and those of the local authorities, with many power struggles between them.

The educational system did not have clear goals, it had no clear policy and no comprehensive overall plan. The educational system rested on its laurels, as opposed to other sectors of the public services.[31] The elementary school curriculum had not been revised since 1923, whereas the high-school curriculum did not have an overall school curriculum. The limited funding also left its mark: most schools were housed in unsuitable buildings and had meager and outdated equipment, without laboratories or school gyms.

When the State was established in 1948, the educational system finally found itself an owner. On the other hand, it was suddenly assigned tasks for which it had never prepared – the absorption of the mass immigration both economically and socio-educationally. These demographic, administrative, economic and value-oriented changes had profound implications for the educational system. Three interlinked factors brought about dramatic change in the social system: the very fact of independence itself; the security factor, that is the need to protect the country's borders by means of a widespread distribution of the population; and mass immigration and subsequent population growth. In the years from 1948 to 1965, 34 percent of the population growth was attributable to births, while 66 percent was attributable to mass immigration during those years.[32] All these factors had implications for the educational system.

Political Independence was understood to imply the complete responsibility of the State for the educational system, both in terms of the inputs and the outputs of the system. This eventually resulted in legislation mandating compulsory education in 1949 and the State Education Law of 1953.

After the State was declared a Ministry for Educational Affairs was set up. The ministry included a Department for Education (which dealt with formal education) and a Culture Department (which dealt with informal and artistic education). The Department for Education was in reality a continuation of the Education Department of the National Executive. The structure of functionaries and functions which had existed before the State continued to exist for two more years thereafter. The policy-making decisions remained partially in the realm of the Department for Education and partially in that of the local authorities. Only in March 1949, ten months after the establishment of the State, was a Minister of Education appointed.

A prime aim of the Compulsory Education Law of 1949[33] was that there should be an "owner" of the educational system in Israel. It granted legitimation to centralization. All children between the ages of 5 and 13 were required to attend an educational institution, as were all those between the ages of 14 and 17 who had not received an elementary education. Most important of all, the relationship between the three partners in education was laid down: the government was required to supply educational services, including elementary education (schools, teachers, and equipment); the local authorities had to participate in maintaining these services wherever required to do so; and parents were required to register their children and to ensure their continued attendance. The Minister of Education had the power to decide what he wished to reserve for himself and for his ministry and what he would be willing to decentralize and leave for the local authorities. For example, in 1951, the minister at the time, Zalman Shazar – later Israel's third president – decided to concentrate all educational functions in the Ministry of Education, while leaving the local authorities responsible for the buildings and equipment.[34] This policy was in keeping with that desired by the Teachers Union and was against the interests of the affluent local authorities.[35]

The Compulsory Education Law kept all the different school systems as they were, thereby offering support for a choice in education, albeit that another system was added, the Hinukh Atzmai system of Agudath Israel, which was in its own category of "recognized but not official." The question which arises is: Did the leaving of the different educational systems intact detract from the construction and implementation of a unified educational policy? Evidence of members of that era indicates that the continued existence of the different school systems brought about an uncompromising political struggle between the different political parties for the souls and minds of all the new immigrant children, various "ugly" deals, and the establishment of commissions of inquiry.[36] As early as April 1949, the first Minister of Education of the State of Israel, Zalman Shazar, proposed that the Knesset abolish all the different educational systems, but his proposal was of course not accepted.

The continued existence of the different school systems may be viewed as the desire to continue with the compromises which had characterized the Yishuv era and which had prevented a culture conflict. However, given the new reality of struggles and friction over the "educational soul" of each new immigrant family, the State's leaders had no choice but to abolish the systems. In 1950, Zalman Shazar again brought a proposal to abolish the different systems in the immigrant camps (which is where the most fierce battles took place between the different political parties for the souls of the new immigrants). This proposal, and the argument regarding education in the new immigrant camps, brought about a coalition crisis. The Knesset was dissolved and there were new elections, the results of which showed an advantage for those in favor of abolishing the systems over those who wished to continue with them. At the time a decision was made to abolish all the different school systems and to replace them with a single government education system. Kleinberger[37] claims that, in addition to the national factor of preserving the unity of the people and to prevent a schism, there was also a certain degree of self-interest involved. The leadership of the ruling Mapai party was convinced that the abolition of the different school systems would, in the final analysis, serve its interests. By abolishing the different systems, Mapai, as the ruling party, could leave its imprint on the whole of the government school system. Because of the growth in the number of students in the Labor school system and the decrease in the number of students in the general system, Mapai would not lose even if the Labor school system, which it controlled, was abolished. The voices of the founding teachers were ignored. Many new teachers had been added to the system who were not as identified with socialist ideology, so that there was no significance in maintaining a separate Labor school system. The ideologies such as those of the

Mapam and Ahdut HaAvodah parties, both of which were more extreme and were associated with the Labor school system, would serve to strengthen them and not Mapai (which was considered to be a relatively moderate socialist party). Furthermore, all the members of the Teachers' Union had joined the General Histadrut, which was under Mapai's control, so that there was no fear of harming the Labor system.

Just before the different systems were abolished, the general school system had 27 percent of all the students in elementary schools, the labor system had 44 percent, and the Mizrahi-religious system had 19 percent. Another 8 percent were in the Agudah school system and 2 percent in unaffiliated schools. The platforms of most of the parties running for the Second Knesset (except for Mapam, the Communists and the Ultra-Orthodox) were in favor of abolition.[38] As a result, the then-prime minister, David Ben-Gurion, concluded an agreement with the General Zionists, the Mizrahi and the Progressives in December 1952 to abolish the different school systems. Indeed, the State Education Law of 1953 was supported by most parties. Herut abstained while Mapam, the Communists and Agudath Israel were opposed. In order to prepare the law, a committee was set up in March 1953, consisting of 17 members – four representatives of the Ministry of Education, five of the local authorities, a representative of the teachers, two representatives of academia, four representatives of the different school systems, a judge of the supreme court, and a representative of the authors' union.[39] There was almost unanimous agreement about most of the provisions of the law, except for that which permitted parents to have a say in one-quarter of the general curriculum. Those against offering the parents this concession were afraid that the proviso would be used "to introduce the different school systems again via the back door." In the end, the law was passed.

The State Education Law of 1953 thus left two government school systems – the religious and the general one, to which one must add the ultra-Orthodox school system, which is "recognized but not official."

At first glance, the result appeared to be that this was the nationalization of education, leading to a decrease in the autonomy of the secondary units, and a preference for unified centralization and formal equality. But in reality the different systems still maintained a great deal of autonomy, especially in the case of the religious system, as we shall see below. (The law stipulates that education is given by the State without any ties to any political or sectarian group or any organization outside the government.)

It is the aim of the law to base the foundations of elementary education on the values of Jewish culture and the achievements of science, on love of the homeland and loyalty to the State of Israel, on work in agriculture and in the crafts, on Halutzic preparation, on a society based on freedom, equality and tolerance, mutual aid and love for one's fellow-man. However, if we examine all these goals, none of which are spelled out in any operative detail, we see that each political group could find its own aims echoed in these overall aims. Thus, for example, in order to make the goals palatable to the non-religious, the words used were "Jewish culture" and not "the Torah of Israel." For the religious, it states "the achievements of science" rather than "the spirit of science." For the Labor system advocates, there is talk of "Halutzic preparation."[40] According to the law, parents have the right to send their children to either the religious or the general state school system, or to the Hinukh Atzmai school system. In reality, this fact is itself based on a compromise. The religious school system maintained its own autonomy. While it is true that the head of that system is subordinate to the Minister of Education, he is nevertheless able to veto any decision of the minister if the latter intervenes in any area where the religious system is guaranteed autonomy by law.[41] It is true that the autonomy of the Labor school system was abolished, but, through a conspiracy of silence the system managed to implement its ideas through the education department of the Kibbutz movement and by means of the Branch for Settlement Education, which is a unit in the Ministry of Education with inspectors, teachers, and principals of its own.[42]

> These arrangements mark a formal change of structure along with continuity of informal arrangements . . . Agreement at the abstract level and value generalization, along with differences in the level of implementation of educational goals – all these – as they are expressed in the State Education Law of 195, are part of the complex system, replete with contradictions, which the Israeli society developed in order to adjust itself to life with open dilemmas.[43]

Demographic and Social Changes

The demographic changes brought about by the mass immigration of 1948–56 had a tremendous amount of influence on educational policy in Israel both during that era and later. The number of students under the age of 18 grew by 157 per cent. There were also changes in the countries of origin of the immigrants. For example, at the time the State was proclaimed in 1948 Jews who had immigrated from Asia or Africa represented about 15 percent of the total Jewish population, whereas no fewer than 50 percent of the new immigrants between 1948 and 1953 were from these areas, and up to 1957 they represented no fewer than 70 percent of all new immigrants.[44]

The immigrants arrived in Israel from all types of different cultures, with vast differences in their economic and social conditions. They had to be exposed to the Hebrew language and most of all to Israeli culture, which was based on Western culture (planning for the future, advanced technology, etc.). A sizable percentage of the new immigrants came from Asian and African countries – from traditional social structures, from pre-industrial economies, and autocratic regimes.

The question faced by those in charge of education in Israel was how to absorb a population with the norms of a traditional society, which owed its allegiance only to its own immediate environment and not to the society as a whole. Those in charge had two opposing views on this issue: the first was that there was no justification for the socialization and acculturation processes which the educational system wished to implement among the new immigrants, because they had their own unique culture, which should be respected. There was no reason to impose Western culture upon them.[45] Opposed to this view, there were those who held that the Jews of Asia and Africa had no unique distinct pattern of culture, and that the crisis involved in immigration had damaged the ego of the immigrants and impaired their self-image; the communal institutions which had existed in the diaspora and which had served to anchor the individual were no longer relevant. It was therefore imperative for the educational system to act speedily, in order to supply them with a new value system in Israel.[46]

In spite of the differences in viewpoints, all agreed that a society that wished to advance technologically must adopt western criteria, and in order for immigrants from Asia and Africa to attain a suitable social status they needed to attain the level of the society around them as much as possible. The result was that the educational system worked toward socialization and acculturation, attempting to have not only the children but the adults as well learn the Hebrew language and Israeli culture as soon as possible. This meant training a vast number of teachers rapidly and then sending them to border areas. It meant formulating suitable curricula and imparting the basic principles of western culture.

The educational system, not surprisingly, ran into many difficulties, some objective and some subjective. The new immigrants from Asia and Africa were dispersed among various border settlements or were housed in transit camps (*"ma'abarot"*) where the living conditions were extremely harsh. The fact that they were isolated made the acculturation process much more difficult. The new immigrants were content to remain locked up within their own cultures, and were not ready to adopt new social norms with which they were not yet familiar.

The geographic dispersal of the new immigrants meant that teachers had to be sent considerable distances, and in practice the teachers who went to these new settlements were the least experienced. Sixty percent of them had had no pedagogical training but were hired simply because there was the need to find people to teach the students.[47] Because these areas were on the whole poverty-stricken, the children often worked in order to supplement the family income. In a survey conducted in the transit camps in 1954, it was found that the absentee rate was about 40 percent.[48] As a result, some of these children never even completed elementary school. There was a tremendous degree of alienation between the central office staff of the Ministry of Education, most of whose members were veteran Israelis who hailed from Europe, and the new immigrants from Asia and Africa, and that made the absorption process that much more difficult.

Another problem which made it difficult for the educational system to absorb these new immigrants from Asia and Africa was the fact that the elite of these societies, who could have served to aid them in the process, did not immigrate to Israel. Many members of this elite immigrated to either France or Canada. The few members of the elite who arrived in Israel and saw the conditions in the absorption centers elected to move to more affluent areas in the country where there were better educational opportunities available to their children.

The period after the establishment of the State also brought about a change in values. In the pre-State era, the central value had been equality and a rejection of meritocracy (Kleinberger), these having been the values instilled by the Zionist labor parties. The individual was required to dedicate himself to the collective, to the nation, to being a Halutz, while the person's economic status was entirely secondary in importance. Manual labor, including agriculture, was considered as the ideal which would increase the productivity of the Jewish people and would lead to a normalization of the social pyramid, which traditionally had given preference to white-collar workers. Formal education was also of less importance, and differences in salary (besides the differences based on years of experience) were considered to contradict the ideology of equality. The best example was the salaries of government workers on the unified salary scale – where differences between one level and another were minute.

After the establishment of the State, this hierarchy of values began to unravel. In theory, the ideology of equality remained in effect and was even reinforced by legislation (such as equality between the sexes), but in reality a differentiation began to be created between various salaries, the salary becoming a function of the occupation involved and of the role played by the individual. This new reality was a result of technological developments and increased professionalization. The wages in the various professions were no longer uniform, and the value of formal training increased. The process forced a change in the hierarchy of values from one based on collectivism to one based on income, on the prestige of a given occupation and on the power which that occupation was capable of exerting. The result was that the youth began to disparage the hierarchy of values which the different youth movements preached.[49] The socialist government of the time and the Histadrut labor federation fought with all their might against this new tendency by maintaining rigid salary scales within the public service sector. This policy was especially harmful to doctors, engineers, and other professionals employed in the public sector. After 1960, the gap between those with an education and those without it began to increase.[50] Up to that time, only 33 percent of the heads of families without education (and at the time they represented 51 percent of the entire population) were in the lowest income bracket, which meant that one did not need an education to advance. The change from 1960 on did not help the new immigrants from Asia and Africa, because their professional level was low. This was expressed in the high percentage of unemployed among them: 1.5 percent of those from Europe were unemployed, compared to 6 percent for those from Asia and Africa.[51] Simply put, deep chasms began to appear between the social groups in terms of educational level, income, and types of occupation. The differences can be attributed to the countries of origin of the groups. Those from Asia and Africa came from countries which were poor and traditional, and not industrialized, which made it difficult for them to adapt to a modern society. In 1963, those who came from Europe represented 49 percent of all those in the exact and technological sciences; those hailing from Asia and Africa represented but 12 percent of the total, with another 28 percent being native-born. There was also a wide gap in the administrative professions.[52]

Forty-nine percent of those in agriculture, 51 percent of those in the building trades, and 40 percent of those who worked in industry were from Asia and Africa. The transformation of Israel from a relatively equal society to one with various classes, with an ever-increasing percentage of people in the professional, technical and administrative fields, and with the greater need for workers with a formal education, acted to the detriment of the new immigrants from Asia and Africa, who did not have the necessary formal education. The need for skilled personnel was met by new immigrants from Europe rather than by those from Asia and Africa, the latter lagging behind. This inequality was expressed in salary scales, in housing, and in the percentage within each group which were enrolled in the different educational frameworks.

Comparing the formal education of both groups in 1961 and in 1965, while 3 percent of those in the Asia and Africa group in 1961 and 3.5 percent in 1965 had more that thirteen years of education, 12.8 percent and 13.3 percent respectively in the European group had more than 13 years of education.[53] Similarly, while only 3 percent of the European group in 1961 and 2 percent in 1965 had no formal education, this compares with 31.5 percent in 1961 and 26 percent in 1965 among the Asia and Africa group.

The disparity between the two groups with regard to levels of educational attainment can be seen by the median total school attendance of those aged 14 or older, which in 1961 was 5.9 years for those from Asia and Africa and 9.1 years for the European immigrants. The gross under-representation of the Oriental immigrants at the highest educational level is clearly demonstrated by the fact that among those born in Europe aged 20 and over, there were 475 graduates per 10,000 individuals, compared to only 60 per 10,000 oriental Jews of that age. However the most disturbing statistic is the reappearance of these disparities in the second generation, one that has been born and reared in Israel. The median school attendance of native Israelis aged 14 and over varied according to their fathers' origin. In 1961 it was 8.2 years for those whose fathers hailed from Asia and Africa, 9.7 years for those whose fathers were born in Israel, and 11.4 for those whose fathers had immigrated from Europe. The significance of these median values becomes clear when the Israel-born descendants of immigrants from Europe are compared with those from the Asian and African countries in terms of years of schooling. In 1961, 52.4 percent of the Israeli-born whose fathers were from Asia or Africa had between 5 and 8 years of schooling (i.e., a minimal amount of schooling), as compared with only 14.4 percent of those with European fathers. For the higher levels of education, the figures were reversed: 34.5 percent of those with fathers from Asia or Africa had 9–12 years of schooling, compared to 64.5 percent of those with fathers from Europe, and only 4.5 percent of those with fathers from Asia or Africa had some form of post-secondary education or higher education, as compared with 19.6 percent of those with fathers from Europe.[54]

Thus a vicious circle was created, in which educational backwardness breeded social and economic retardation and these in their return generated·a new cycle of educational, social and economic retardation resulting in an educationally, socially and economically disadvantaged status. This vicious circle deprived a large part of the second generation of Asian and African immigrants of the opportunity to rise substantially above their parents' socioeconomic status. Having adopted the more successful Western immigrants as their frame of reference, the younger generation of Oriental Jews felt frustrated and embittered by what looked to them to be flagrant discrimination. These feelings led to the riots of young Asian and African immigrants which broke out in 1959 in Waadi Saleeb, a slum quarter of Haifa, and spread to other urban concentrations of discontented Asians and Africans, who, after their release from army service, found themselves condemned to unskilled, badly-paid jobs or to unemployment. This was a warning signal that alerted both the authorities and the general public to the close and consistent association between one's country of origin and and one's socioeconomic status (SES). It finally induced the authorities to employ the educational system as a major instrument for redressing that socioeconomic inequality of opportunity.

Formation of Educational Policy: the Main Actors

In the Israeli parliamentary system, the Knesset is the legislative body while the government is the administrative body. In other words, the legislative body has widespread legislative powers whereas the administrative body is merely supposed to implement the laws passed by the Knesset. As occurs in other western countries, it is the government which gives its formal seal of approval to educational policy, a policy which is the product of a struggle between ministers, parties, pressure groups, and the government bureaucracy. Because of Israel's unique situation at the time as a State, the primary concern of the government has always been security and external affairs, and matters of educational importance were always of secondary importance.[55] The government would only become involved in educational matters when a strike broke out among the teachers (as occurred in 1970) or among university lecturers, or if the Minister of Education decided to propose a new law, on behalf of the government, to the Knesset (such as the reform in the structure of education in 1965 or the law making high-school education free in 1980, etc.).

The deciding factor in determining educational policy is ultimately the power and status of the Minister of Education. Zalman Aranne pushed through the reform in the structure of education, Zevulun Hammer advocated the free education law for secondary education, and Amnon Rubinstein supported the law governing the regional colleges. The government's avoidance of educational topics was not only due to the fact that security and political issues were more important, but also because the question of education generally aroused fierce disputes. By refraining from dealing with these issues it avoided any potential governmental disruption. The role played by the government in terms of influencing educational policy was thus generally limited to the annual discussion about the education budget (and especially wage policy regarding the teachers) submitted to the Ministry of Finance.

Heated discussions about educational policy often take place within the government in the pre-election period (as happened in 1992, prior to the last Israeli elections, where the left-wing parties

– Labor and Meretz – promised a change in priorities and greater investment in education), or after the elections, in the negotiations with the religious parties about setting up the government, as has occurred with every single Israeli government.

The Knesset

Those scholars who have examined the role of the Knesset in determining public policy in Israel[56] found that there is a gap between its legal status and formal authority on the one hand, and its lack of influence and power on the other. The primary legislation with which the Knesset deals includes bills proposed by the government, which are generally passed, and private members' bills, many of which are not passed. In spite of a great deal of legislation,[57] the implementation of the laws is weak.

Often, the Knesset is asked to delay the implementation of laws simply because there is no administrative or financial infrastructure to implement the law. And this is what occurred with the Knesset law to reform the educational system (1965), with the inspectorate law (1969), and with the youth law (1974), to name but a few. While the Knesset has a very substantial wish list, this often exceeds the ability of the system to deliver. The Knesset has a type of tacit agreement that all legislation which is "good for education" should be supported. This is true for all political parties. The result of this policy is that much legislation is passed but little is implemented. In general, all bills presented to the Knesset are given a first reading there. If the Knesset decides to continue with discussion on the particular bill, it is sent to the Knesset's education committee for substantive debate.

The deliberations about the bill in committee serve to legitimate it, as all the parties of the Knesset have representatives on the committee and the deliberations include representatives of the education ministry, the Teachers' Unions, and others that the chairman decides to invite. However, the committee has no facilities for collecting data and processing it, and it has no special resources to enable it to analyze proposals brought by the Ministry of Education. It is thus forced to rely on whatever appears in the press or on the experience and personal knowledge of the Knesset member who is serving as chairman of the session, or else it must base itself on the data submitted by the Ministry of Education. The importance of the committee lies in the very fact that the topic is discussed and in the fact that the committee can invite any individual or interest group to present various views, even if the final decision adopted by it marks a compromise between various competing interests. Knesset members are able to express their involvement in educational matters by means of the Questions mechanism of the Knesset, where questions addressed to the Minister of Education must be answered by him. But in most cases the Questions mechanism is used as a political tool, to show the electorate that this or that Knesset member is involved in educational matters which concern the public at large.

The Political Parties

Every since the Yishuv period the political structure and organization within the country has been marked by a large number of political parties with differing ideological orientations. In spite of the large number of parties, Israel has generally been marked by stability, with one party dominant, either on the left (the Labor party) or on the right (the Likud), ruling in coalition with other, smaller parties, primarily the religious parties. The religious parties have always been interested in educational matters and have not relegated this issue to a few experts in the field, as have the other parties. The large degree of autonomy granted by the political parties (except for the religious parties) to their members in the area of education often resulted in individual Knesset members adopting a position which was opposed to the ideology of their party. For example, there were Knesset members of the left who supported the privatization of education while some of those on the right were opposed to this. This was especially apparent in the discussion in the Knesset education committee about self-management within the schools. According to Elboim-Dror,[58] the lack of interest by politicians in the school system is due to the fact that, while there are very few differences between the parties as to what is "good for education," there is a wide consensus that what all want is that which is "good for education." It is possible that this neglect is deliberate, because questions dealing with education are very heavily dependent upon one's ideology. As raising the issue can stir up a hornet's nest, it may be better to simply leave certain dilemmas unresolved. The best example which illustrates this was a demand by a member of the Knesset of the Likud for the introduction of an extended school day.[59] This created a dispute and arguments both within the Labor party and within other parties. The result was that the government hushed up the discussion and moved it to a public commission to examine the practicality of such a law.[60]

The Ministry of Education and Culture

The educational system in Israel is a centralized one. This structure was established under the State Education Law of 1953, which decreed that education is given by the State and on its behalf. Every appointment within the system and every curriculum requires the approval of the Minister of Education, either by him directly or by an authorized individual. The result is that education policy is decided upon by the staff of the Ministry of Education and Culture.

The education system is divided into six districts. Each district is headed by a district head, along with a number of general inspectors who work in that district and an administrative staff. The district offices are in actuality extensions of the head office in Jerusalem and are not autonomous units. In 1971, an attempt was made to decentralize the education system but in reality very little authority was granted to the districts, and they did not receive autonomy in determining educational policy at the district level.[61]

The Ministry of Education in Israel is not of one piece. It is composed of various units with different interests, and the power of any particular unit depends on the personal ties its head has with the Director-General of the ministry or with the Minister of Education. For example, in the 1950s and 1960s the educational secretariat had a great deal of power and influence. When Elad Peled (a reserve general of the IDF) became the director general of the Ministry of Education he was concerned about what he considered the excessive status of the educational secretariat and proceeded to limit its powers and to strengthen the administrative units.[62] The status of the curriculum branch in the Ministry of Education was stronger in the 1970s than thereafter, due to the personality and standing of the man heading it, Shevah Eden.

At the top of the hierarchy of those units which influence educational policy is the office of the Minister of Education and Culture.

The office includes the advisers and assistants of the minister, who are generally individuals who have been politically appointed. In most cases, when the minister leaves office these individuals leave office as well. In the first term of office of Zevulun Hammer as Minister of Education (1977–84), it was well known that the office was run by his two top assistants: Orlev and Goldberger (the former would eventually become Director-General of the ministry and the latter the Deputy Director-General).

It is the minister's office which links the political and administrative levels. It is there that the various initiatives are merged into educational policy. This office is subject to pressures by various interests. For example, the concept of a reform in educational structure was proposed in the office of Minister Aranne (who was minister between 1964 and 1970);[63] the idea of an extended school day came up in the office of Minister Hammer, as conceived by his assistants; the initiative to foster the culture of the Jews of the Oriental countries was developed by Yaakov Hadani, the assistant of Minister Hammer. After an idea is formulated in the minister's office, the Director-General and his office are brought into the picture. Sometimes, the initiative itself comes from the Director-General's office, the best example of this being the plan to reform the educational system initiated by the present Director-General, Dr Shimon Shoshani, during his first term (1985–86), under Minister Navon. However, when the minister turned down that initiative, Shoshani left the office. After the idea is formulated as a policy by the office of the minister, the Ministry of Education requests the support of the Ministry of Finance. Sometimes this support is received, such as with the law of free high-school education at the beginning of the 1980s, and with the special enrichment programs for the residents of distressed areas. In other cases support is not forthcoming, such as in the case of the extended school day. Sometimes the ministry administration employs social pressure groups that are involved, and in many cases public commissions are established to examine the topic.[64] There are no known cases in the history of education in the State of Israel where the bureaucracy openly rebelled against the policies of the minister. The way opposition is expressed is by private discussions about the functioning of the minister (the most striking instance of this was the case of Minister Navon);[65] or else by bringing in an outside body to protest against the minister's policy, the best example of this being the utilization of academics to oppose the Judaic studies curriculum in the State (non-religious) school system by Minister Hammer, who was the head of the National Religious Party.

As mentioned earlier, the Ministry of Education is composed of units. Up to the beginning of the 1970s, the ministry was divided up into departments according to age level: kindergarten, elementary school, high school, and staff units such as personnel, budget, etc. At the beginning of the 1970s, a reform was instituted in the structure of the ministry, and it was divided into pedagogic units and administrative units, the division between them being functional. Operatively, it meant that there was a branch for institutions, which embraced all levels of education, a branch for curricula, one for developing educational systems, one for in-service training, and others for youth, planning, budget, etc. Some of these branches were under the supervision of the pedagogic secretariat, while others were under the educational administration branch.[66]

The Branch for Religious Education has, by law, a totally autonomous status. While the head of the branch is formally subordinate to the Director-General of the Ministry of Education and Culture, in practice he has total autonomy in those areas within his jurisdiction. He has, to assist him, the religious education council, composed of public figures, and this aids him in determining educational policy in the religious sector. The religious education administration has its own inspectors, principals and teachers, curriculum, and teaching methods.[67] Kleinberger states that the administration is a ministry within a ministry.[68]

One of the important sections of the Ministry of Education is the pedagogic secretariat. According to government regulations it is defined as the highest authority in educational matters. It is composed of the heads of those units which are subordinate to it, such as the curriculum branch, the national inspectors, the evaluation unit, and units subordinate to the educational administration (such as the units that deal with teacher training and in-service education in the ministry or the educational institutions unit).

In the 1950s and 1960s, the secretariat had a great deal of influence. It dealt with formulating the pedagogic work in the different educational institutions, curricula, teacher training and in-service, guidance, registration, accreditation examinations, etc. Its directives had operational significance.[69] Its membership was composed of the Deputy Director-General as chairman and representatives of various units within the ministry. All its members came from the educational field. From the beginning of the 1970s, people entered the ministry in key positions who came from other administrative fields, without having a background in education. For example, the Director-General and the head of the planning branch both came from the army. The result was that the educational administration department and the budget branch became stronger, while the pedagogic sections, led by the pedagogic secretariat, became weaker.

Along with the transfer of power to the administrative and budget sections, new autonomous professional units developed in the Ministry of Education, which enjoyed prestige due to the quality of the programs they produced, such as the educational television network, or because of political agreements reached, such as the Branch for Religious Education.

The Ministry of Education expresses in the clearest possible form the political and social changes in Israel. When the National Religious Party received the ministry, it made sure, using various methods, to introduce personnel changes in the ministry staff, and positions were filled by members of the new party.[70] When the parties in power changed and the ministry was transferred to the Meretz Party (a left-wing Israeli party), the entire staff in the ministry was changed, and the religious members of the staff, who had arrived there during the time the National Religious Party had the helm, were forced to leave the ministry. They were replaced by members of the Meretz Party or the Labor Party.[71] This is a clear politization of the educational system. The increased strength of the scientific and technological fields in Israeli society has brought about changes in all realms of the economy, including the Ministry of Education. Educators are being replaced by scientists in the physical and social sciences and experts in the technological world.

The Local Authorities

The standing and influence of the local authorities with regard to formulating educational policy underwent changes after the establishment of the State. An examination of the legislation which determines the status of the local authorities with regard to education shows that the compulsory education law of 1949 stated that the duty to maintain official educational institutions devolved upon both the State and the local authorities. The law did not define how this cooperation was to be achieved, how authority was to be apportioned, or how education was to be financed. It only stated that the education budget would be established by the Minister of Education in consultation with the Minister of the Interior.[72] The developments and changes that took place over the years were never entrenched in any law, but were arrived at through various special agreements.[73] In other words, the Knesset left considerable freedom of action to both sides in arriving at an agreement between them. The result was that there was nothing preventing political considerations from playing a role in determining educational policy. The ministry and/or branches of the ministry maintained independent ties with the local authorities and made agreements with them, and the different agreements entered into by the various branches often contradicted one another.[74] The 1953 regulations also stated that it was within the authority of the Minister of Education to set regulations for the local authorities regarding the allocation of funds in their budgets, and that each budgetary allocation needs the approval of the Minister of the Interior.

In a study conducted in 1980[75] it was found that there were marked differences in the perceptions of the central government and of the local authorities as to how they viewed the relationship between them. It is these differences in perceptions which explained the gap between the setting of educational policy by the central government and the poor implementation of this policy by the local authorities. The local authorities, rather than being regarded by the Ministry of Education as one of the levels of government with a responsibility in determining educational policy, were regarded as an interest group intent on expanding its own influence by means of resources received from the government. The local authorities regarded themselves as entitled to set educational policy, not only in the administrative realm but in the educational realm as well. The central government, on the other hand, preferred to regard them as implementers of its policy, leaving to them the duties of establishing and maintaining educational buildings, registering and transferring students from one institution to another, supplying services approved by the Minister of Education in the field of first aid, offering supplementary classes for new immigrants, psychological guidance, and extra-curricular activities.

The compulsory education law of 1949 was primarily concerned with elementary education; it left high-school education in the hands of the local authorities. Even during the Yishuv era, the affluent settlements had transformed their high schools into city institutions. This situation was reinforced after the State was declared. The result was the development of a strongly, centralized elementary school system, alongside a decentralized high-school system. This situation developed even though the percentage of the high-school budget paid by the central government kept increasing. The different governmental commissions appointed to examine the financing of the local authorities[76] stated clearly that the central government should pay 70 percent of the costs of required educational services and 50 percent of the costs of those added courses that the central government insisted be given by the local authorities.

Even though there have been no changes in legislation regarding the power and influence of the local authorities, the fact is that their power has grown and their involvement in education – at the administrative level as well as the pedagogical level – has continued to increase, for a number of reasons:

1. The reform in the structure of the educational system which brought about the introduction of junior high schools added a tremendous burden to the Ministry of Education, which was simply unable to carry it. It was clear to those in charge that the reform could only succeed if the local authorities were involved, and that was indeed what happened.[77]

2. A change took place in the perceptions of the heads of the different local authorities, who began to appreciate the importance of the development of education in their area as a means for economic and social development. It was clear to them that the way to attract an affluent population to their area was to have decent educational standards. At the same time, a revolution took place in the leadership of the local authorities. More and more second-generation immigrants from Asia and Africa, who had been educated in Israel, ran for election in various local authorities and won. Their platforms uniformly called for making education the highest priority. When they were elected, they had to honor their campaign pledges. This occurred in Yavneh, Carmiel, Kiryat-Gat, and other places.[78]

3. Changes took place within the administration of the education departments of the local authorities. Young, educated and dynamic principals entered, who sought to give expression

to their potential. They coalesced into the Union of Heads of Education Departments and became a power group which has forced the Ministry of Education to involve them in formulating educational policy.[79]

4. A change has taken place in the perceptions of the Ministers of Education and their Director-Generals. There is greater readiness on their part to deal with affluent local authorities in terms of decentralizing their authority. The best example of this was the establishment of the Education Administration in Jerusalem both *de facto* and *de jure*, and the same *de facto* in Tel Aviv.

There is no doubt that the weak legal structure also encouraged, indirectly, a policy of decentralization and the growth in the power of the local authorities.

The Teachers' Unions

During the Yishuv era the teachers played an important role in the founding and development of the educational system; some even set educational policy. Toward the end of the Yishuv era, at the beginning of the 1940s, there was a decline in the status of teachers as full partners in establishing education policy. After the establishment of the State, the decline in the status of the teachers continued, even though professionally the quality of teachers improved.

The Teachers' Unions changed from seeing themselves as responsible for the formulation of the education system and setting its goals to a body which regards itself as in charge, first and foremost, of improving the working conditions of its members. It was transformed from a body which determined policy to a professional association. In order to understand this change, it is necessary to examine the stages in the development of the Teachers' Unions. Two distinct phases can be discerned: 1920–47 – before the independence of Israel, and 1948 to the present.

The Histadrut Hamorim, the first and the biggest Teachers' Union, started losing power as the chief educational policy-maker in 1920. World War I and the lack of resources led to the transfer of the 27 primary schools which were under Histadrut Hamorim control to the Zionist Federation, which had money.[80]

Instead, the union turned its attention to the physical needs of teachers.

In 1942, the teachers went on strike for an improvement in the conditions of their employment, an effort that received little public legitimacy even though teachers had not been paid for three months.[81] The economic situation grew grave, and the British governing Palestine under the mandate of the League of Nations refused to provide more sources to the Jewish schools. Teachers were split between those working in wealthy schools, who were a small fraction of the teachers, and the majority working in poor schools.[82] This led Histadrut Hamorim to become a trade union, aggressively pursuing its self-interests and calling for strikes.[83] Since statehood in 1948, the nature of Histadrut Hamorim changed. The number of union members has increased eightfold to some 86,000 members.

In 1950, because the then prime minister, David Ben Gurion, wished to integrate manual workers with intellectuals, Histadrut Hamorim joined the general federation of Israeli workers, Histadrut Haovdim. The significance of this fusion is that the Histadrut Hamorim is now purely a trade union, which perceives its main task as being to defend teachers' economic interests.

The second major event occurred in 1958. The secondary-school teachers, disenchanted with their representation in Histadrut Hamorim, fought to disassociate themselves, a process that took nearly two years of struggle against Histadrut Hamorim and its backer – the government led by Mapai – the Labor Party. Finally, the secondary-school teachers formed Irgun Hamorim because they wanted a special division of high-school teachers with policy-making autonomy and recognition of their special status as professionals.[84]

An analysis of key documents on school reform in Israel since 1960 demonstrates that teachers overall have had only a limited impact on school reform. In the policy process which led to the great reform of the Israeli educational system in 1965, the biggest teachers' union, Histadrut Hamorim, was not involved. The decision made then to create junior high schools and to attach these to the secondary schools was completely against Histadrut Hamorim policy. The Minister of Education did not even agree to take into account the teachers' reservations.[85] However, the Teachers Unions' main power has remained in the field of labor withdrawal. They have succeeded through their strikes to improve their economic and social conditions. Obviously, these changes have had an impact upon the budget and upon the allocation of resources in the educational system.

The Parents

The involvement of parents increased greatly between 1958 and the end of the 1970s, in comparison to the Yishuv period. And the level of involvement has further increased since the beginning of the 1980s. The abolition of the different educational systems in 1958 removed much of the ideological basis for parental involvement. The abolition of the different systems lessened the ideological tension of living in Israel, along with a decrease in the feeling of living "sacred mission" which the parents had felt before. If we add to this the change that took place with the founding of the State in the ownership of education, it is understandable that the processes of centralization decreased the feeling of personal responsibility of the individual citizen and strengthened feelings of helplessness and apathy.

The State Education Law gives parents the right to determine one-quarter of the supplementary program, while the regulations of the Director-General of 1974[86] grant legitimacy to their activities and even emphasize the importance of regarding the parents as full partners in formulating the pedagogic life in the school. Indeed, the regulations of the Director-General regard parents' organizations as legal entities entitled to financial support by the State and as representing the parents to the State, the local authorities and the teachers. Until the end of the 1970s there was little evidence of deep parental involvement. Even though the ideological tension of the Yishuv era did not repeat itself, the actions of parents from the end of the 1970s onwards has shown marked drive. This change is only noticeable in affluent settlements. In the poor areas, the principals have succeeded in halting attempts of parental intervention which went beyond the limits the principals had set.[87] The early 1980s saw a cut of between 7 to 8 percent in the schools' budgets (see chapter 5). This cut meant a decrease in hours of instruction, which parents in affluent areas made up for by paying for teachers to teach after the official school hours. The growth of this "gray education," and the fact that parents were required to pay more for their children's education, intensified their desire to be involved in the life of their children's schools. As long as the government had paid all education costs, parental involvement had been limited to aiding the school administration in technical and administrative matters as decided upon by the administration. But when the parents' share in the cost of their children's school increased, their involvement also grew in extent and in frequency.

Ellen Goldring's[88] found that most of the reciprocal actions in the relationship of parents and the school (up to 80 percent) involved the operation of special programs, bringing innovations into the schools, and raising funds; only a small part of their activities (up to 20 percent) involved classifying children, hiring teachers, or evaluating teaching methods and school curricula. In a review of educational columns in the daily press, parental involvement found its expression in different forms. This included striking a school to force the dismissal of a principal[89] or as a way to show opposition to a new curricular offering. It has also involved appealing to the Supreme Court to prevent the integration of "strong" schools with "weak" ones. The national parents' council prevented the cutting down of schooling to a five-day week.

One can also explain the increase in the involvement of parents by the fact that involvement in a school committee and a demonstration of activism is a path for advancement to a political post, and there are, indeed, many examples which illustrate this new reality.[90] For example, the head of the parents' committee in Givat Shmuel (in the Tel Aviv area) became the head of the local council. In Ramat Gan, the chairman of the parents' committee ran for mayor on a slate which included six members of the parents' committee. In Haifa, the parents' committee called upon voters to support a specific slate in the elections, as one of members of that slate came from that committee. The Teachers' Unions and many of the inspectors of the Ministry of Education are very much concerned about the growth in parental involvement in the schools. For the Teachers' Unions this is a clear threat to their professional status. For the inspectors it is a threat to proper administration in the educational system. The two groups have been working together to foil excessive parental involvement in education. The head of the central district of the Ministry of Education refused to support the dismissal of a principal in Rishon Lezion, in spite of threats by the parents.[91] The inspectors of the Tel Aviv district supported a school principal in spite of parents' demands that she be dismissed. Even though the principal won in court, the parents refused to give in.

This phenomenon of parental involvement in the educational system will continue to grow as long as specialized schools continue to be opened and developed. It is probable that the legislature will at some time in the future take steps to determine the limits of parental involvement, because in the present situation the dialogue between the parents and teachers will be a "dialogue of the deaf," with the parents fighting for what they think is good for their children and the teachers for their professional status.

The Social Lobby

The involvement of parents is but one facet of the growth of involvement of bodies outside the educational system which wish to exert influence on it. This book is not the forum to examine these bodies (scientists, Jews of the diaspora, various religious groups, etc.), but it is worth mentioning the group of heads of development towns (i.e., towns that need development – the non-affluent towns), and Knesset members who hail from Asia and Africa, who personally felt the discrimination against them and who wish to establish an educational policy by means of a body known as "the social lobby." The factors leading to the increased power of this group lie in the significance of the term the "social gap" in terms of equality and integration in Israel. Zionism has always stressed the values of equality and social justice, the need to change values and to create a new society, and these were important identifying marks of the State of Israel. When these values were not realized and a gap emerged between declared norms and actual conduct, feelings of guilt and of being ill at ease emerged. And these feelings were instrumental in shaping the way the affluent population regarded the population from distressed areas, and in an increased desire to meet their needs.[92] Social equality in Israel also has a national and religious base. Those who have immigrated from all the different countries have added their own personal, social and cultural contribution to the shaping of the nation. Therefore, the more the correlation between one's ethnic origin and failure, the more intense their sensitivity to the problem.

There are three cases where the decisive influence of the "social lobby" for the distressed population was apparent: the first case is their support of the parents' committees to prevent the cutting down on the length of the school week. The second, which almost brought down the Israeli government, was the demand by the head of the Labor Party Knesset delegation head, Eli Dayan, to lengthen the school day in the distressed areas, which was totally opposed by the government, and especially by the Minister of Finance. Eli Dayan managed to push the government to establish a state commission to examine the topic. The third case was the success of the "social lobby" in forcing Tel Aviv University to decrease its entrance requirements from those coming from distressed areas who wish to study law in the faculty (the faculty has the highest admission requirements, except for the faculty of medicine).[93] There is no doubt that in the future the "social lobby's" increased strength will be a challenge to those who formally determine educational policy.

Summary

This chapter presented and analyzed the development of the education system from the viewpoint of those who are involved in the decision-making process, and of the characteristics of the decision-making. In the Yishuv era, it is difficult to speak about a unified educational policy and about a clearly defined educational system. The educational system suffered from serious financial difficulties, from division into competing school systems, and from decentralization of the power and decision-making centers. Yet, in spite of this, the system succeeded in educating many students, strengthening their Zionist consciousness, and teaching the Hebrew language and culture. This was primarily due to the motivation and sense of idealism among the teachers.

In the period after the establishment of the State there was a revolution in education. It is true that for the first two years of the State the old administrative patterns still remained, but thereafter the State took control. Decentralization was replaced by centralization. The system grew to an extent unknown before due to the waves of immigration. The educational system changed not only in terms of size, but also in terms of the composition of the student population. There were many more students from culturally deprived homes, more students whose parents were illiterate. The social situation created an unexpected load on the system – teachers were trained in a superficial and speedy manner, and educational institutions were built up quickly but not always wisely. Segregated institutions remained, and very few of the disadvantaged received a secondary education. There was also a high drop-out rate in the elementary schools. Socially, the situation was unbearable.

The centralized nature of the system gave a great deal of power to the bureaucracy of the system, including the Ministry of Education and Culture and its different units. The power of the local authorities was weakened when compared to the Yishuv era, and similarly the Teachers' Unions and parents' organizations had less of a say than before

4

Education Policy Landmarks

To understand the trends of education policy in Israel in the past decade and the way this policy has coped with its conflicting goals (equality versus excellence, equality versus educational choice, the upholding of the principle of efficiency), it is worth noting several milestones in the development of this policy from the time Israel was established up to the late 1980s.

In the period before Israel proclaimed its independence, and during the first three decades thereafter, the clash of coexisting educational goals mirrored the dilemmas that Israeli society faced at that time. In the Yishuv period primary education was meant to be egalitarian, and uniform in structure and content. This modality of primary schooling, however, coexisted with post-primary schooling that was elitist and offered a diversity of curricula (academic, agricultural, vocational). Primary education was centralized, its funding controlled by the Education Committee of the World Zionist Organization; post-primary schooling was decentralized and funded by parents and local authorities, which sought to translate their economic clout into policy-making influence. Furthermore, despite its proclaimed uniformity, primary education had four distinct "streams": general, proletarian, religious, and independent (*haredi*) – each with its own curricula, educational emphases, and criteria in choosing teachers. This curricular diversity was not contrary to the existence of uniform, egalitarian primary education. In other words, the education system in the Yishuv period stood for egalitarianism and uniformity, but nevertheless allowed for elitism at the post-primary level.

This reality expressed the dilemmas with which the education system had to cope even before Israeli independence was achieved: how to respond to conflicting political and ideological interests, how to contend with egalitarian values and a social orientation that lacked deep class or ethnic differences, and how to adopt elitist values in order to prepare an infrastructure for the future society.[1]

The challenges that the education policy-makers faced in the Yishuv period became more acute after the State of Israel was established and immigrants from Asia and Africa flooded the country. These immigrants, strongly predisposed to traditionalism, were unlike Western immigrants in terms of formal educational level and technical skill; this was due to the conditions of life in their countries of origin. Lacking the necessary skills and knowledge to integrate into all levels of Israeli society, the immigrants of Asian-African origin fell behind those of European-American origin. Over the years, Israelis' countries of origin began to overlap with socio-vocational indicators such as formal education, occupations, and income.[2] The education system was instructed to integrate the diverse immigrant groups and eliminate the disparities between them. To carry out this task, the education system chose three strategies, each characterizing a stage of development of the education system in independent Israel.[3]

The First Strategy: Formal Equality

The first strategy – formal equality in and nationalization of education – manifested itself in the first decade of Israeli independence (1948–58). In view of the demographic and social upheaval that the country was experiencing, the policy-makers in education decided to make the uniform, integrated primary school into a melting pot, in which immigrant children's initial identity would be shaped in the light of Jewish-Israeli culture. The decisions were based on the assumption, subsequently shown to be mistaken,[4] that uniform administrative and pedagogical mechanisms and equality in allocation of inputs would cause the pupils to adjust to the system and its demands, leading to equality in educational results.

This policy led to pronounced manifestations of centralization, bureaucratization, and formality in the education system. Substantiation of this trend is found in speeches by the Minister of Education at this time, Benzion Dinur, in the Knesset. The pattern of his speeches reveals the emphasis on the need to render all Israeli children equal in intellectual and cultural status.[5] Benzion Dinur regarded Israeli children as cut of one kind of cloth; he believed that all should be given a uniform educational load, irrespective of their sociocultural background, personal inclinations, and talents as individuals. According to this philosophy, which was widely held, each pupil was entitled to a certain minimum input, with no serious regard for the results.

Paragraph 2 of the State Education Law (1953), which provides further evidence of this trend, sets forth the goals on which the future education system should be based: values of Jewish culture and of scientific achievement (the achievement principle), equality (the equality principle), and liberty (the choice principle). The achievement principle manifested itself in the selective policies of academic secondary programs and higher education. The equality principle was translated into formal equality in primary school, including uniformity of inputs for pupils and equality in class size, length of school year, curriculum, and teaching methods, irrespective of individual differences and the heterogeneity of the student body. The freedom principle, by contrast, was reflected in parental choice of the educational "stream" that they desired – general, religious, or *haredi* – and their right to introduce supplementary (special-purpose) curricula up to one-quarter of the total curriculum. Elboim-Dror argues that the achievement principle was the one that ruled in the field.[6] The equality principle was only given lip service. The choice principle was fulfilled only in its ideological sense: namely, the choice of educational stream and the right of parental involvement in the curriculum as legally detailed.

As time passed, however, the policies of uniformity in inputs and formal equality, which consumed much of the education budget, created inequality among pupils, because those of affluent origin made better use of the inputs than the less affluent. The education policy rooted in formal equality did not enable pupils of Asian-African origin, who were culturally deprived and whose scholastic achievements lagged, to improve their standing. Their achievements remained low and their dropout rate relatively high. Post-primary schooling remained as elitist as ever; primary schooling did not meet expectations. Only a small percentage of students of Asian-African origin passed the survey examinations administered at the end of eighth grade, and only those who passed these examinations secured an opportunity to enroll in post-primary schooling and qualify for a discount on tuition. In view of their difficulties in accessing formal education in the higher grades, coupled with their poor scholastic achievements relative to their peers of Western origin, youngsters of Asian-African origin were excluded from upper-echelon positions in fields that required high formal-education attainments. The Wadi Salib incidents in 1959, in which protesters rioted against the system, alerted the politicians. The organizers of these protests sought to prevent the formation of a consensus that would accept the inferior status of social groups originating in the Muslim countries.[7]

Addressing the Knesset on the education budget for 1959/60,[8] the late Education Minister Zalman Aranne acknowledged that the combination of ethnic homogeneity in the schools (including schools in development towns), poor teacher quality, and a policy of formal equality, had rendered the education system incapable of coping with its own needs and those of society. Remarks by the next Education Minister, Abba Eban, the following year, also reflected recognition of the need for change. During the 1960/61 debate on the education budget, Eban described improvement of the level of the Asian-African origin groups as the most important social mission of the education enterprise. "Starting this year," he said, "efforts to cope with the fact of identity among social distress, poor scholastic achievements, and ethnic origin will be the central feature of activity in the education system."[9]

The Second Strategy: Differential Resources

Thus from the policy establishment acknowledged the need for change in education policy – a change that would facilitate the realization of two values: equal opportunity in education and achievements in education. The late Education Minister Zalman Aranne, who had returned to this office at Ben-Gurion's request, formulated new principles:

1. Governmental favoritism, in which the disadvantaged would be given substantive advantages by means of differential inputs and compensation mechanisms in areas in which the disadvantage was relatively severe, would be enacted. This manifested itself in the building of small classrooms, addition of teaching positions, and augmentation of other inputs for schools that had a high proportion of disadvantaged students as defined. These actions were meant to make up for all the disadvantages of the culturally deprived.[10]

2. Patterns of educational action were to be commensurate with differences in ability among pupils.

3. Expansion of the democratization principle to post-primary education was to be achieved by: (a) "Head-start" mechanisms (special textbooks and curricula, enrichment programs, individualized instruction). (b) Development of new post-primary education settings (two-year and three-year post-primary schools) and the fostering of vocational education. (c) Introduction of a two-tiered new norm system in the survey tests given at the end of eighth grade,[11] in order to facilitate the admission of disadvantaged students to post-primary education and to give them greater access to the reduced tuition scale. (d) Special attention for gifted pupils of Asian-African origin, by setting up special residential schools for this population group (e.g., Boyer and the Amalia Academy in Jerusalem).

The four principles – (3(a)–(d)) – formulated by the late Zalman Aranne were implemented in schools around the country. They attested accurately to the public's concern for the special needs of disadvantaged pupil groups. They also pointed to the intentions of the government, which adopted a policy of deliberate preference of children in this population group by means of generous budget allocations meant to eliminate disparities between them and children from affluent social strata. Nevertheless, the gap remained. The "head-start" and differential-input policy failed to break the correlation between ethnic origin and scholastic achievement.[12] Academic post-primary education still screened out youngsters of Asian-African ethnicity. Even Israel-born teenagers whose fathers were of Asian-African origin were under-represented in the academic streams.[13] The size of the achievement gap between pupils of Asian-African and European-American origin did not narrow, neither on the survey tests nor on the matriculation exams. Kleinberger found that 38 percent of pupils in the Asian-African group who had passed the second-tier norms test enrolled in academic high-school programs, compared with 52 percent of pupils of European-American origin who had scored equally well.[14] Twenty-one percent of members of the Asian-African group earned matriculation certificates, as compared to 37.5 percent of European-American origin students in the same age group. Smooha *et al.* found that in 1970 the percentage of Asian-African origin pupils who scored 59 or below was three times that of the European-American origin group.[15] The percentage of outstanding students of Asian-African origin, i.e., those earning scores of 80 percent or more, was one-third that of the European-American origin group. In 1968/69, the percentage of students of European-American origin in higher education was seven times that of those of Asian-African origin.

Because the final reckoning with respect to the differential-inputs method seemed to be negative, the late Minister of Education Zalman Aranne reached the following conclusion: "It will be hard to accomplish more than this in education using the existing structure. To achieve more, the existing structure must be changed."[16]

The Third Strategy: Reform and Integration in Education

Heading into its third decade of independence, Israel faced the urgent need to deal with the correlation that had taken shape between ethnic differences and economic, educational, and political disparities, which persisted among second- and third-generation offspring in the independent State. Educational economist Shmuel Amir believes that the measures taken in the 1950s and the 1960s were not vigorous enough or efficient enough to break the intergenerational vicious cycle.[17] In this context, it is worth noting the findings of a survey by Minkovich et al.[18] on educational achievements in primary school. The study found that affluent schools offered more enrichment programs, took more pedagogical initiatives, had a more active library, and made more rooms available to the secretarial staff, nurse, and guidance counselor. Furthermore, even those advancement programs which had been instituted primarily for the disadvantaged, such as the psychological and counseling services, were used most frequently in high-income schools. Similar patterns were found with respect to quality of teaching staff, modalities of management, the quality and diversity of educational programs, and innovative initiatives taken in the schools.

The education system stood at a crossroads. Policy-makers were aware that Israeli society had to seek ways to cope with the two urgent challenges, even if meeting both concurrently might be somewhat detrimental to each of them. The Education Minister at the time, Abba Eban, expressed this well:[19]

> What judgment would be visited on a state such as ours, that strives simultaneously for intellectual advancement and social quality, when there is objective tension between the two? The most

complicated aspect of the matter is just that: the impact of the two goals, the intellectual and the social, on each other. All we can do is look for solutions that will meet, to the extent possible, both of these intentions at once.

The education-system reform was meant to attain this objective in two ways: administratively, by restructuring the system and establishing integrated post-primary schools, and pedagogically, by creating heterogeneous home room classes, pupil tracking by scholastic subjects, greater use of electives, and encouragement of social education in the school.[20]

The way the decision to implement the education-system reform was made is an indication of how the education system struggled with a sensitive issue that represented a focal point of public polemics. The system seems to develop unique ways of coping when it needs to address itself to fundamental issues, some bearing internal contradictions, on which society is at odds and that do not lend themselves to easy and satisfactory solutions. With respect to the equality/elitism dichotomy, the education system chose to seek consensus on equality at the declarative level and to eliminate equality at the practical level. Thus, for example, the old school structure, i.e., eight primary grades and four secondary grades, coexists with the new school structure created by the education-system reform: six–six or six–three–three. Similarly, the reform has been implemented in three stages in view of resistance on the part of the teachers' union, affluent parents, and local authorities. Even though these features of the decision-making system have caused inefficiency and inflated costs, they did help to reduce friction, maintain consensus under conditions of conflict, and prevent alienation under circumstances of unresolved dilemmas.[21]

The reform law[22] sought to achieve two goals by means of this structural and content change:

1. To expedite the social integration of students of various ethnic groups.
2. To raise and enhance the scholastic and educational level.

The reform sought to achieve its first goal by automatic promotion of all children from primary to post-primary education, by demarcating enrollment districts that would create junior high schools with an ethnically-mixed student population, by organizing heterogeneous home-room classes, and by encouraging social education in the school. To achieve the second goal, comprehensive (academic/vocational) schools were set up, in which children with different talents and fields of interest might be catered to properly. Remedial care for low-achieving pupils, and encouragement of high achievement as one of the values of a modern society based on the achievements of science and technology, were considered major objectives. The reform mission was entrusted to the Curriculum Division of the Ministry of Education and Culture. Special curricula stressing achievement in science were developed to meet pupils' different needs. Efforts to upgrade the academic requirements of the teaching profession began, as did attempts to improve pupil counseling and guidance.

An analysis of remarks by members of Knesset shows that progress in implementing the reform and evaluating its accomplishments was far from satisfactory. Below are several quotations from Knesset plenum meetings in which the issue was debated. A report on the reform by the Knesset House Committee, chaired by MK Yitzhak Yitzhaki,[23] asserted that by 1981 (13 years after the reform law had been enacted) it had been fully applied in only 46 urban jurisdictions, had not been applied at all in 75 urban jurisdictions, and had been applied only partially in 28 local jurisdictions, including Tel Aviv and Jerusalem. The committee acknowledged that efforts had been made to improve scholastic and educational levels and to effect social integration, but systematic care of the disadvantaged had not become more intensive and little had been accomplished in the field of social education. The committee found a substantial disparity between the quality of teachers in affluent areas and that of their counterparts in disadvantaged regions. The committee also ruled that integration should begin at the primary-school level.

In 1983, the issue came up again for discussion in the Knesset plenum. Again the legislators asserted that the reform was ebbing away. All the changes made under its auspices had been beneficial for the well-off, but not for the underprivileged.[24] In that year, MK Yehuda Perah of the Likud[25] (a former Central District inspector with the Ministry of Education) sought to halt the establishment of new junior-high schools, arguing that the reform had failed to attain its objectives. "In junior high, the [student] of Asian-African origin finds that he is a second-class citizen. You'll find him mainly in the lower tracks." MK Perah's findings led him to reach the following conclusions:

1. Offspring of affluent parents had neither lost nor gained from the reform.
2. Within the Asian-African origin group, members of strong socioeconomic strata had come out ahead.
3. Within the Asian-African origin group, members of socioeconomically weak groups had come out behind.

The issue of reform and integration remained on the parliamentary agenda. In 1984, for the first time, a slight retreat from the reform idea was made in the Knesset Education Committee – of all places![26] The committee recommended a moratorium on the establishment of new junior-high schools and ordered the Ministry of Education to stop making the transfer of development budgets to local authorities contingent on their adoption of the reform (as had occurred in Ashqelon). Concurrently, the committee recommended the reinforcement of primary education and application of the principles of integration there. The intensity of retreat from the reform rose and fell like a pendulum in education debates in 1987 and subsequent years. In 1987, MK Sartani of Mapam[27] asked, while making a motion for the agenda: "Has integration succeeded or failed? Is integration truly inimical to high educational quality?" In the same debate, the chairman of the Knesset Education Committee, Nahman Raz of Labor, added: "Has integration really reduced motivation among the strong? Does the fact that, 17 years after the Knesset passed the reform law, only 50 percent of the communities have adopted the reform not attest to a sense of discouragement with it?"

The response of the then-Minister of Education and Culture, Yitzhak Navon, points to his awareness of the problems of the integration, even though he supported it. The 1987 Knesset Education Committee report on primary schools urged the Minister of Education and Culture and local authorities to uphold the principles of integration.[28] This very call indicates that some were indeed retreating from this ideal. In January 1990, MK Perah of the Likud, in a debate on education in the Knesset plenum, said that integration had succeeded only in places where there were no scholastic disparities among pupils. In the same debate, MK Hagai Meirom (Labor) noted that integration was being undermined from many quarters.[29] The report of a public committee that investigated the implementation of the reform noted clearly that the reform had been only partially realized.[30]

Many studies on the reform have been conducted and published. The most salient of them are:

1. A study of junior-high schools, commissioned by Yigal Allon, the late Minister of Education and Culture, and conducted by research teams from the Hebrew University of Jerusalem and Tel Aviv University[31] between 1972 and 1975.

2. A paper by a public committee established in late 1977 and headed by Professor Amir of Bar-Ilan University.[32]

The research findings indicate that structural change is important to promoting social integration. It was also found that junior-high schools, which link primary and post-primary education, promote educational continuity and more years of schooling for students overall. However, the findings do not indicate any substantial, fundamental improvements in the academic achievements of disadvantaged pupils. The researchers noted that the performance of the junior-high schools was affected by tracking and by teachers' negative attitudes toward pupils in low-level classes. Despite these flaws, the committee recommended continuing with the reform.

Professor Amir's committee examined the extent to which the objectives of the reform had been achieved. The committee lauded the special impact of the pedagogical input in the junior-high schools with regard to new curricula, equipment, in-service courses for teachers, and intensification of the academization trend in teacher training. The committee emphasized the rise in pupils' scholastic level as a result of the increase in years of schooling and a reduction of the dropout rate after tenth grade. On the downside, the committee accused the system of failing to make a concerted effort to find ways to teach effectively in heterogeneous classes and to ensure the advancement of weak pupils in such classes. Action taken to expedite integration on the organizational and pedagogical levels was inadequate. Interestingly, both research groups recommended continuing the reform and downscaling parallel systems. Additional research reports that considered this question,[33] as well as rulings by the Supreme Court,[34] called for continuation of the reform. However, implementation of the reform continued slowly for the following reasons:

1. When the late Zalman Aranne decided to set the reform process in motion during his tenure as Minister of Education, he waived his legal right to advance it by administrative means. He wished to achieve a consensus among all political factions in the Knesset by making concessions to various political parties. As a result, the Knesset passed a vaguely worded piece of legislation with loopholes that made it possible for groups with differing interests to avoid implementation.[35]

2. There were unclear instructions for implementation. Regulations issued by the Ministry of Education and Culture made the local authorities responsible for establishing integrated junior-high schools and placing students in them. This role is part of the responsibility of local government to set up and maintain schools, define enrollment districts, and transfer pupils from school to school. Each local authority had its own attitude to the reform in its area, and their responses ranged from total willingness to categorical opposition.[36] Local authorities that opposed the reform noted in support of their position that the ministry preferred to recommend the reform rather than to implement it by force.[37]

3. Opposition of the Teachers' Union[38] and affluent parents made implementation of the reform very difficult.

4. The Israeli geo-demographic situation – the division into two school systems, large towns populated mainly by people of Asian and African origin, and kibbutzim that preach ideological unity – also made the reform difficult to implement and encumbered the achievement of genuine equality. The Ministry of Education was in a state of conflict – it wanted to implement the reform and, consequently, achieve integration as part of its policy, but it was also unable to force the reform on the country.

Summary

True equality and social integration were not major issues in official education policy in Israel's first five to ten years of existence. It was clear that equal rights for all citizens, guaranteed in the Proclamation of Independence, would apply to the education system as well. This equality was given a formal interpretation that emphasized standardization of input. Only in the early 1960s did the first signs appear of attention to the problem of true equality and integration in education, based on awareness that the general social problems arising intrinsically from the country's ethnic composition could not be ignored. The first stage, which lasted from 1963 to 1968, may be defined as a time of coalescence of the concept of bolstering and enhancing weak social strata by means of an extended school day, tracking, and programs for gifted students.[39]

In the 1970s, the focus was on implementing the reform law and expediting integration. The discussion among ministry officials in the mid-1970s (seven years after the law was passed) on imposing the reform and integration by law is evidence of the ministry's impotence in instituting the reform. Consequently, the minister decided not to press for legislation at this stage, but rather to instruct district directors to use their powers under enrollment rules to increase the mix of pupils and notify local authorities in advance that they would do so.[40] In the late 1970s, the Ministry of Education decided to adopt the idea of equal results and integration, not only as a means of furthering educational objectives, but as a national objective per se. This policy was supported by Klein and Eshel,[41] who showed that all integrated groups made noticeable achievements in locations where the reform was accompanied by appropriate educational activity. Thus, the 1970s can be defined as the years in which the reform became accepted in educational policy.

The 1980s and 1990s underscore even more clearly the pressures and conflicting objectives that the education system will face. On the one hand, the Ministry of Education remains committed to the reform and its policy of narrowing gaps by means of the following steps: the Free Secondary Education law, upgrading the professional status of teachers, extending the school day, and offering activities for parents of disadvantaged children. These efforts, however, are countered by the economic realities of cuts in finance ministry budgets for education services and back-door privatization.[42] Parents are being asked to shoulder a larger share of education expenses, schools are being encouraged to specialize, and the development of specialized schools (nationalist, science, music, Labor-movement values, supplementary Jewish studies [TALI], etc.) is being encouraged. Schools are also being given more responsibility and autonomy in choosing curricula, using budgets, and hiring teachers. This is a move away from centralized education in favor of community-based education. The question that arose in the early 1980s and still remains is: is it possible to continue integrating and simultaneously foster excellence and specialization?

5

The Past Decade: Conflicting Aims

An analysis of the speeches of ministers of education in the Knesset, the reactions of Knesset members, and items placed on the Knesset agenda by legislators, elicits a picture that the Minister of Education and Culture, Zevulun Hammer, expressed aptly on the Knesset podium in 1986: "The considerations for setting priorities in the education system are intricate and complicated. They require an understanding of our social realities, which are riddled with internal contradictions, and an assessment of our national needs and goals in the short and long terms. Sometimes they even compete and clash with each other."[1] This statement characterizes the education policy of the past decade – the wish to pursue conflicting educational objectives in order to satisfy different education interest groups: teachers, parents, local authorities, academia, and industry. The education system is supposed to meet the expectations of each of these groups. Under such circumstances, policy-makers have to maneuver between public support for continued educational integration, and support for the existence of selective, supra-regional, and specialized schools.

In 1982, Hammer was asked why the Ministry of Education and Culture, which espoused a pro-integration policy, was funding the busing of children from two kibbutzim (Ma'ale Hahamisha and Qiryat Anavim) to non-integrated schools. Hammer's response provides the best possible illustration of the dilemma that he faced. Every local education authority, he said, is entitled to decide on the structure of education in its area of jurisdiction, and the kibbutz movement has this right as well.[2] If this is so, one may wonder about the role and status of the central government. If the central government is the source of power, and if it has its own policy on the matter, why does it not use its prerogatives to enforce implementation? Why does it pay to bus pupils to non-integrated schools? In another speech the same year, Hammer could not conceal his desire to satisfy everyone, despite the intrinsic conflict of interests inherent in such an approach. According to Hammer, the Ministry of Education would continue to operate simultaneously on several tracks: promoting weak population groups without rejecting excellence and achievement, i.e., uniformity coupled with variegation and parental choice of schools. In 1983, in his annual policy speech in the Knesset, Hammer described the intentions in his ministry is activity as advancement of integration and equality along with excellence, centralization alongside community systems, and parental choice.

The Free Secondary Education Law

The best example of the response of the education system to these conflicting demands is the Free Secondary Education Law, sponsored and brought to the legislature by the Minister of Education himself. Hammer regarded his bill as a way of enabling every Israeli child to complete high school at state expense, following the practice of many Western countries. Educational economists in Israel warned that the socioeconomically advantaged (rather than the disadvantaged) classes would be the main beneficiaries of this law, since the taxation that would fund the reform, to be collected by the National Insurance Institute (social security), would apply to all taxpayers equally. Consequently, the new law would not solve the problem of inequality in education. The Knesset passed the law over the economists' objections.[3] It is true that the law enabled more disadvantaged pupils to enrol in post-primary education, but the increase was not significant when compared to the period preceding the legislation. As predicted, the new legislation undermined equitable income distribution between the poor and the rich. MK Arbeli-Almozlino expressed this well during a Knesset debate on the law.[4] Before the law was implemented, she stressed, 70 percent of pupils received tuition discounts on the sliding scale; now, 100 percent of the pupils were totally exempt, including those with high-income parents who had previously paid full tuition. These parents would have additional disposable income that they might use to reinforce their children's education with private lessons. In the same debate, MK Ora Namir expressed astonishment at the nature of a law that guaranteed free education while children attending a junior-high school of the Mateh Yehuda

Regional Council had to pay NIS 1,114 ($370) a year for miscellaneous school expenses (activities, supplementary education, "class betterment levy," and so on). Namir's remark reveals once again that the mainstream interest groups are the beneficiaries of legislation that ostensibly seeks to improve matters for peripheral groups.

Gray Education

Education policy-makers have shown similar behavior toward the spread of the so-called gray education (i.e., parentally financed supplementary classes) in schools. Gray education and the establishment of specialized schools are two additional examples of policy-makers' responses to conflicting pressures. In a 1989 Knesset debate on gray education, MK Michael Bar-Zohar warned of the expansion of gray education concurrent with a widening of social disparities: "We'll have one form of education for the rich and another for the poor."[5] In contrast to MK Bar-Zohar's apprehensions, MK Dedi Zucker (Citizens' Rights Movement) expressed understanding of the new circumstances in the education system. Gray education did exist, he said, but only because of the system's mediocrity, which caused parental dissatisfaction with their children's education, and because 150,000 classroom hours had been cut from the education budget.

In view of the legislators' conflicting attitudes, Education Minister Yitzhak Navon responded that his ministry's own position on the issue was unequivocal: the hours that had been cut had to be restored, because budget cuts in education had led to the development of gray education. However, he added, "let us not forget that gray education is essentially a supplementary curriculum, recognized by the 1953 State Education Law. As long as it is confined to supplementary subjects instead of compulsory ones, it isn't illegitimate under the present circumstances." Navon said nothing about how his Ministry would recover the classroom hours that had been taken from the education system. It is not clear from his statement whether he agreed with the Treasury's policy of slashing education budgets. Moreover, Navon explicitly supported the existence of gray education as an outgrowth of the State Education Law. Because there is no authorized interpretation of the 1953 State Education Law, anyone may interpret it as he or she wishes – as Navon did. The minister added that no supplementary school curriculum should be approved if it barred pupils from participation because of their parents' inability to pay.[6]

Little research has been done thus far on the magnitude of gray education in Israel. The limited information that we possess suggests that gray education is offered in 38 percent of primary schools. It is especially prevalent in the central and Jerusalem districts, and less so in other areas (Haifa, the north, and the south). This type of education, operated by parents' associations largely in affluent areas, is meant to provide experiential enrichment and reinforcement in basic subjects such as English, computers, and mathematics.[7] A study comparing the extent of gray education in Rishon Lezion, a city in which the integration reform was implemented, with that in Bat Yam, where it was not,[8] found that even though the cities were similar in population size and composition (in 1987/88, when the research was done), private lessons were more common in Rishon Lezion than in Bat Yam. Gray education was on the rise in both cities and was especially prevalent in the upper secondary grades – not only in enrichment subjects but in basics such as mathematics, English, and Hebrew. The study showed that the integration reform had made the education system accessible to a population group that had not subscribed to it in the past, but had increased competitiveness and the desire of children from affluent homes to keep their disadvantaged counterparts disadvantaged by using the private-tutor system.[9] Devotees of gray education based themselves on Section 8 of the 1953 State Education Law, which authorizes the Minister of Education to accede to a request by parents to offer a supplementary curriculum in their school, i.e., on top of the official curriculum, provided that the supplement is funded by the parents or the local authority.

Although the legal infrastructure for gray education was created in 1953, it was not widely used until the early 1980s. American educational economist Estelle James, in a comprehensive study of the distribution of gray education in 50 industrialized and developing countries, found that the phenomenon was common in all the countries in the sample, and expressed, more than anything else, a differential demand for quality.[10]

If we regard James's findings as universal, we may argue that the spread of gray education in Israel is a manifestation not only of citizens' wishes to realize the opportunities offered by the State Education Law, but also of a differential demand for education. The fact that gray education is more common in affluent areas may tip the scales of the pro-equality/ pro-excellence dichotomy in the direction of the latter. Summing up, one may expect gray education to grow further as long as the education system fails to meet consumers' demands for higher quality. This may be detrimental to the equality policy that the education system has advocated so strenuously.

Autonomous Schools

Another trend that has surfaced in the education system over the past decade, and which points to substantial changes in the Ministry of Education policy, is the establishment of autonomous schools.[11] The drive for educational autonomy actually began in the early 1960s. The inability of a rigid centralized system to satisfy the varied needs of a pluralistic society and meet specific local requirements, coupled with the demands by professionals in various countries for education systems to be decentralized and community involvement promoted, have influenced Israeli government policy as well. Thus the Ministry of Education and Culture has made an effort to give district administrations additional powers and teachers greater autonomy. This has not been a one-time operation; it has continued for years and developed in stages.

The first stage was one of educational initiative. Policymakers believed that allowing teachers to take pedagogical initiatives would increase their job satisfaction and reduce burnout.[12] Teachers were given three hours per week to devise special educational activities, and the innovation indeed proved to be useful. The second stage, termed the stage of flexibility,[13] took the democratization process one step further. Its goal was to "elasticize" the hours of instruction within schools in order to meet students' special needs, commensurate with curriculum development in the schools. In the late 1970s the Ministry of Education took two more steps toward school autonomy by introducing a degree of pedagogical autonomy.[14] In practice, this meant endorsement by the establishment of administrative and teaching teams to develop curricula on the individual school level. Another step toward autonomy was the encouragement of parental participation in setting educational policy for the schools.[15]

The most recent stage in the democratization process was the provision of full school autonomy. For the 1981/82 school year, the Ministry of Education and Culture made a direct, intensive effort among primary school principals to make autonomy a reality. This measure transcended the encouragement of educational initiatives and flexibility; it transferred budget planning, selection of teachers, and internal organization to the school.[16]

How effectively has school autonomy been implemented? Although the central system conceived the idea, it did not liberalize its supervision mechanisms and actually reduced classroom hours overall, thus reducing maneuverability and narrowing the options available. The Teachers' Association withheld its support of the idea of school autonomy because of the lack of practical means of implementation. In 1992, however, then Minister of Education Shulamit Aloni decided to continue this policy[17] and appointed six committees to consider how to implement and improve it.[18]

Special-Curriculum Schools

Another step toward education system democratization was the promotion of special-curriculum schools. If most of the opposition to school autonomy was expressed by professionals (principals and teachers), opponents of the formation of special-curriculum schools – and the unexpressed intentions behind this enterprise – include not only professionals but also legislators representing peripheral social groups (the "social lobby," led by MK Rafi Alloul [Labor]). These circles fear that this change will harm the social-integration policy, strengthen mainstream social strata at the expense of the disadvantaged, and make social mobility even less possible for peripheral groups. We will list the reasons for these apprehensions below.

The special-curriculum schools were formed in response to the parents' right to choose different forms of education for their children, one of the basic goals of education in a democratic society. The issue became the subject of public controversy; studies were performed and, pursuant to them, several policy documents were issued: a memorandum by the Knesset Education Committee,[19] a memorandum by the Unit for Sociology of Education and Community at Tel Aviv University,[20] and a report by a committee[21] appointed by the Minister of Education at the time, Yitzhak Navon, to explore the matter. The committee was known as the Kashti Committee, for its chairman, Professor Yitzhak Kashti of Tel Aviv University.

The Knesset Education Committee held a special debate on the special-curriculum schools. Ministry of Education and Culture officials who participated in the debate expressed the familiar platitudes of officials forced to explain the contradictions of their policies. Their answers were general, vague, and non-committal; they willfully overlooked the contradiction between the Ministry's democratization policy and the intrinsic danger it presented to the government's integration policy. The committee members, listening to the Ministry officials' remarks, acknowledged that changes in Israeli society, coupled with the Ministry's own budget cutbacks, had created a change in public opinion. However, the committee members understood that the scholastic accomplishments of the education system, as reflected in national achievement tests sponsored by the Office of the Chief Scientist at the Ministry of Education, had caused parental dissatisfaction with the education system. This, the legislators realized, was the main reason for the turnabout in Ministry of Education policy. The change manifested itself in encouragement by the Ministry of the opening of special-curriculum schools (such as schools for the arts, sciences, supplementary Jewish studies, and Labor Movement values). The Knesset Education Committee admitted that the special-curriculum schools were open-enrollment institutions; there were no district lines and anyone might register. This breached the rule, derived from the government's integration policy, that required compulsory enrollment districts, but the Education Committee was convinced that such schools were needed. To pay lip service to the principles of integration, the Education Committee handed responsibility for honoring these principles, at the time of enrollment, to the local authorities.[22] Since the local authorities had no mechanism that might ensure the discharge of this duty, the upshot of the Education Committee's decision was the effective abrogation of the integration policy.

The Ministry of Education administration, under Yitzhak Navon, was aware of the internal contradiction in Ministry policy. Apprehensive of public opinion, in December 1989 Navon appointed a public committee to consider how to keep the special-curriculum schools "special" while upholding the principles of integration, i.e., how to resolve conflicting intentions.[23] The committee was chaired by Professor Kashti; members included representatives of the Ministry of Education, the teachers' unions, academia, and the National Parents' Association.

The committee was apprised of the situation: between 35 and 40 open-enrollment special-curriculum schools, with a total enrollment of 10,000–15,000 students, existed at the primary and junior-high levels within the state (secular) system. Most of the schools were supported by parents and/or local authorities. Their areas of special emphasis were diverse: the arts, science, supplementary Jewish studies, Labor-Movement values, and schools for the gifted, to name only a few. Furthermore, there were 138 special classes in State–Religious schools, and roughly half of the State–Religious student body was enrolled in special settings: high-school yeshivot, *ulpenot* (religious high schools for girls), Ne'emaney Tora va-'Avoda, Habad, and the No'am system (sponsored by Yeshivat Merkaz ha-Rav). The Arab education system had 28 open-district primary schools, most affiliated with Christian denominations, with an enrollment of 8,400. The *haredim* had two systems of their own: Independent and Ma'ayan (the latter sponsored by Shas, Shomrey ha-Tora ha-Sefaradim, Sephardi Torah Guardians). Precise data on the *haredi* systems were unavailable.

The conclusions of the Kashti Committee[24] indicated that in recent years Israeli society has shown an increasing tendency to be amenable to cutbacks in resource allocations for social welfare, has been less strongly motivated to advance disadvantaged social groups, and has been less committed to the goal of a cohesive, just society. Other trends – liberalism, competitive economic entrepreneurship, the quest for individual rights and self-fulfillment – have gathered momentum. Self-imposed segregation along community lines has become stronger. These trends did not bypass the education system. Primary schools had implemented the decentralization policy of the early 1980s,[25] had become more responsive to the needs of pupils and communities, and had taken the initiative to diversify and reform curricula at the school level. The conflict between integration and equal opportunity on the one hand, and selection and competition on the other, had become more acute, especially in junior-high schools. True, the growth of open-enrollment schools had encouraged the pursuit of excellence, but it also threatened the education system policy of equality and integration. The expansion of enrollment districts and the introduction of the principle of parental choice are liable to force the education system into social segregation. It appears that interest groups in the social mainstream have been encouraging a trend that might force peripheral groups from the center.

After considering all this, the committee recommended, by majority vote, that the activities of open-enrollment schools be endorsed, provided that these schools adhere to the integration policy. A study monitoring the implementation of the integration policy in the field should be performed every three years. A public committee should also be formed to authorize the establishment of new open-enrollment schools. The committee also suggested that regional special-curriculum schools be established to cope with the dilemma that the committee had noted when it accepted its assignment. This would enable parents living within a given region to choose the school best suited to their children's aptitudes. Every child would be entitled to attend the school of his/her choice without entrance exams. The Ministry of Education and the local authority, jointly, would monitor compliance at the time of enrollment, and action would be taken to prevent the emergence of ethnically homogeneous schools.

The committee also recommended the development of counseling and guidance programs for parents and students, in order to apprise them of the significance and consequences of their choice.

Comparing the Kashti Committee conclusions to the position paper issued by the Unit for Sociology and Community of the Tel Aviv University School of Education (of which Professor Kashti was a faculty member), one can see that the ideas and rationale were nearly identical in each case. Both documents recommend school autonomy in pedagogy and administration, in order to improve the status of schools as the foci of education. Both favor the establishment of schools with different educational ethos; both favor controlled "parental choice" that would make parents genuine partners in fashioning the educational views of individual schools. Both favor the retention of enrollment districts (there is no support for the establishment of true open-district schools). Finally, both recommend the formation of supervision mechanisms to keep population groups balanced, in order to assure social integration.

The conclusions of the Kashti Committee and their underlying rationale certainly bring quite a few questions to the fore. Will the education system really create the supervision mechanisms needed to ensure integration? What will happen to local authorities that reject the integration policy and instead promote the development of special-curriculum schools using the familiar pattern of selective open-enrollment? Will the state be entitled to intervene in schools that are fully funded by parents? There is no doubt that the conclusions of the Kashti Committee offer no solution to the dilemma which it faced. The response of the Director-General of the Ministry of Education and Culture to the committee conclusions[26] leaves no doubt that the Ministry's policy orientation had indeed switched from equality and integration toward parent choice, specialization, and excellence – contrary to the minister's assertion that, "We are committed to continuing the integration policy."[27]

Will the regional schools indeed continue to implement the integration policy and ensure the development of special curricula and excellence? Time will tell. What we know of the Israeli experience thus far comes from the findings of Shapira and Haymann,[28] who examined two types of special-curriculum schools: those based on ideology (Labor Movement values, supplementary Jewish studies) and those based on special course content. The findings show that the threat of elitism and social selectivity does indeed exist in schools of the latter type. To overcome this, the schools involved can be required to enroll a certain percentage of disadvantaged students who show aptitude and take an interest in the relevant areas of specialization. The Municipality of Tel Aviv has chosen this course with respect to the special-curriculum schools in its jurisdiction.

In the ideology-based schools, the question of integration never arose because these schools had never been selective. In schools that offered supplementary Jewish studies, however, a vast majority of students came from socioeconomically advantaged groups, including many from Anglo-Saxon countries. The researchers believe this may be overcome by means of suitable advertising among the disadvantaged.

Despite these problems, the researchers conclude that the special-curriculum schools justify their existence because of their high educational and scholastic quality, their teaching methods, the identification by the teachers and students with the school's goals, parental participation, strong teacher involvement, and a favorable social climate. In an article in *Haaretz*, economist Mickey Gur reinforced these ideas: "The results of parental involvement in special-curriculum schools show that this method should succeed throughout the education system."[29]

The findings of Shapira and Haymann support the contention that there is considerable danger that special-curriculum schools will further the interests of mainstream groups at the expense of those that are marginal. The case study of Shapira and Haymann notes explicitly that despite intervention by the Municipality of Tel Aviv, only 30 percent of students in special-curriculum schools belonged to disadvantaged groups, and the admission of students from disadvantaged areas on the basis of a percentage quota has a stigmatizing effect on these students. In the supplementary-Judaism schools, the share of the disadvantaged failed to reach even this level. Consequently, one can only ensure integration in special-curriculum schools by installing efficient control mechanisms to prevent social selectivity. Such mechanisms require special budgets, and municipal officials who rely on the mercies of the electorate are unlikely to invest funds in this controversial topic. Chapter 6 considers this development in terms of conclusions for action in the future.

State–Religious Education

State–Religious (hereinafter: SR) education is an integral part of the general education system and is meant to serve that segment of the population that desires it. The 1953 legislation defines SR education as state education that has a religious character manifested in the way of life, curriculum, and special traits of the teaching staff. Because SR education is state education, it identifies with the goals of education expressed in the law and undertakes to further them.[30] However, even though it is governmental, the SR system was given autonomy in shaping its policy. The head of the SR education administration is a government appointee who works with a council that helps him or her formulate policy.

The ideology of SR education is not set forth explicitly and has no compulsory practical manifestation.[31] Even though SR education serves a relatively small sector of the population and is characterized by what appears to be religious unity, the SR system is nevertheless markedly polarized with regard to basic issues of education. The major dichotomy is between those who favor religious schooling for all-comers and those who espouse religious excellence. The crux of tensions and conflicts in this system is the inconsistency of a statist approach with an educational mindset that caters to a narrow sector of the population, yet wishes to satisfy everyone. The public that subscribes to SR education is not religiously monolithic; it represents a broad spectrum of religious behavior, ranging from *haredi* (such as the Habad schools) to semi-observant. SR education policy-makers believe that religious education can exist only if all sectors of the religious population take part in it and cooperate with each other.[32] Consequently, there is a place for specialization and diversification within SR schooling, provided that everyone accept certain religious requirements. The second director of SR education, Yehuda Kiel, expressed this well: "Religious schools should be open but not *wide* open."[33] This policy, compatible with the ideological underpinnings of SR education, expressed a perspective of outreach. This policy was disputed by the population groups that subscribed to this form of education, which regarded it as a prescription for religious compromise and even a retreat from religious excellence. In pursuit of the latter goal, graduates of Yeshivat Merkaz Ha-Rav in Jerusalem established a rival system at the primary level, which they called No'am.[34]

Understandably, the establishment of the No'am system was sharply criticized by the SR education administration and various groups identified with national-religious education. This criticism stemmed from the selective practices of No'am in choosing its pupils. Few children of Asian-African origin were admitted, because their religious way of life was too compromising for the tastes of the No'am administration. The No'am policy collided with that of state education, which espouses equality and integration. Indeed, Education Minister Yitzhak Navon, reviewing the operations of his ministry in the Knesset, stressed the great difficulties that had arisen in the implementation of integration principles within the SR system. There were indications of erosion and student flight to the special-curriculum schools of the SR system.[35]

The SR education administration came under several kinds of cross-fire that affected its policies. The No'am constituency (known as the *torani* [Torah] camp) insisted on religious exclusivity and autonomy; Ne'emaney Tora va-'Avoda, on the other hand, pressed for equality and outreach. The administration also had to contend with the system-wide structural reform. Ostensibly, the structural reform and its corollary, social integration, were consistent with the SR administration policy that encouraged pupils of all types to enroll; the reform also coincided with the interests of principals of religious post-primary schools, who complained that good students were fleeing to the selective high-school yeshivot. Indeed, the pairing of junior-high and high schools helped principals persuade parents to leave their children in school until the end of twelfth grade, and had the effect of stanching the outflow of good students to the yeshivot. The reform was nevertheless an impediment in the religious education system, and only some SR schools actually implemented it. There were several reasons for this:

1. Socio-educational research shows[36] that educational integration succeeds only if at least 60 percent of pupils in an integrated class are non-disadvantaged. Because the share of non-disadvantaged in the SR system was only 27 percent, genuine integration was out of the question.

2. When junior-high schools were established alongside high school yeshivot, parents had to send their children to distant schools and pay for their dormitory accommodations. As it turned out, most parents of Asian-African origin were so reluctant to do this that they preferred to enroll their sons in nearby non-religious junior highs. Fear of a large outflow of students to non-religious schools reinforced resistance to the structural reform.

3. The SR education administration understood that ethnic integration meant religious integration as well. Ostensibly, integration should have gathered Orthodox Jews of all kinds into a single rubric. However, differences in ethnic heritage ruled this out. It became necessary to choose between preserving diversity of traditions (pluralism in customs and liturgy) and uniformity in customs and prayer (at the expense of pluralism). Many construed the structural integration as an abandonment of the religious traditions of Asian- African Jewry, which accounted for a majority of SR enrollment.[37] Indeed, the European-American tradition became the preferred and dominant rite in the SR system.[38]

4. The geographic dispersion of the SR population made it necessary to establish small, inefficient junior-high schools. The possibility of merging religious and non-religious junior-high schools in small localities was untenable. The option of gathering pupils from different localities into regional religious junior-high schools was similarly unworkable because of objections presented by leaders of the localities themselves. The best example of this was an attempt to implement such a merger between Ofaqim, the Merhavim Regional Council, the Azata Regional Council, and Sederot. The working experiment was unsatisfactory because each local authority wished to keep

its children within its own jurisdiction.[39] The result was an outflow of strong students of Asian-African origin from local post-primary schools to high school yeshivot and *ulpenot*. This left post-primary schools in development towns with a disadvantaged student body that was channeled from the very start into lower-level programs and into vocational education. Teachers expected little of these demoralized students. It is therefore no wonder that, despite the massive investment, allocations, head-start programs, and abundant classroom hours, these schools' educational and scholastic achievements were meager.

5.   The numerical ratio of advantaged to disadvantaged pupils in the SR system is not the only noteworthy factor; the extent to which one is disadvantaged is also important. Disadvantaged students in SR schools belong to weaker social strata than disadvantaged students in general schools.[40] The most salient manifestation of this, of course, is the disparity between the advantaged and the disadvantaged in scholastic achievements and basic skills. The numerical ratio and the extent to which students are disadvantaged have a cumulative impact on the scholastic level of a given class. Consequently, when a majority of pupils are disadvantaged, the favorable scholastic impact of the advantaged students is less than that expected under optimal conditions of integration. Despite its vacillations and reservations, and despite the implementational difficulties that arose, the SR education administration went ahead with integration as instructed.

A public committee that examined the implementation and achievements of the structural reform found that segregation was more prevalent in SR education than in the general state system.[41] Chen, Levy, and Adler[42] explain this segregation in religious schooling (which was corroborated in studies on the SR junior-high schools) by citing the educational philosophy of the SR administration, which segregates talented students from others in order to give them more comprehensive and intensive religious instruction.[43] If this allegation is accurate, Coleman adds,[44] it is contrary to the principles of integration. Nevertheless, Chen and Kfir conclude that this policy has no practical adverse effect on weaker students.[45] "One cannot state flatly that inequality among pupils throughout their school years . . . is greater in SR schools than in regular state schools" (p. 70). The SR administration has never denied that it encourages competition and exclusivity, in nearly deliberate disregard of the integration policy that had been forced upon it. One expression of this competition is the opening of separate Torani (intensive Torah study) programs in religious post-primary schools; these classes are meant to compete for good students with high-school yeshivot and *ulpenot*. This policy has proven itself. For example, the Zeitlin Municipal Religious High School in Tel Aviv, once considered prestigious, lost many of its good students to high-school yeshivot because of the structural reform, and recovered its primacy because it opened Torani programs. In the 1960s, 5–10 percent of the enrollment at Zeitlin was of Asian-African origin; today this group accounts for roughly 50 percent of the enrollment.

The SR education administration favors open enrollment and academic (science, music, arts) and religious specialization in its schools. The tendency within the SR system to support competition and exclusivity is the result of cross-fire between *haredi* and secular circles, with SR education in the middle. When the *haredim* accused the SR education system of religious compromise, the system responded by establishing high-school yeshivot for boys and *ulpenot* for girls. Secularists criticized the weak scholastic achievements of the SR schools and challenged the justifiability of the very existence of a separate state system for the religious. To counter these charges, the SR system stressed its schools' commitment to Zionist ideology (which the *haredi* schools lacked) and the accomplishments of the high-school yeshivot and the *ulpenot*.

Summary

The SR education policy is clear and well-defined. It cultivates the image of the *talmid hakham* – the well-versed Torah scholar – the integration of religious and general erudition, a combination of religious excellence and love of country and performance of the duties flowing from this allegiance. The open-door policy of the SR system entrusted this system with the task of educating many of the country's disadvantaged pupils, most of whom came from traditional homes. This was not necessarily good for the SR system. The SR administration was caught in a vise – maintaining the ideology of turning out *talmidey hakhamim* (elitism) and dealing with disadvantaged population groups (equality). Some within the state school system regarded SR education as an unnecessary drain on the budget, citing small class size and supplementary manpower that they regarded as unnecessary (e.g., school rabbis). In fact, some education officials have never been at peace with the existence of the SR education system.

The participation of the National Religious Party (NRP) in nearly every coalition government in Israel's history has undoubtedly benefited SR education and sweetened the bitter pill of opposition to the system itself. In 1992, however, the NRP joined the opposition. Upon taking office, (now former) Education Minister Shulamit Aloni swiftly reduced the standard SR allocation by 15,000 classroom hours.[46]

The SR system has had to defend itself against a two-pronged attack, from opponents in the non-religious education system and from *haredi* circles. The delegitimization of Zionist-religious education is expressed in the pungent rhetoric of Rabbi Ovadia Yosef, leader of the Sephardi *haredi* movement, against the "compromising" SR system.[47] The *haredi* struggle against SR is also reflected in efforts to persuade parents of Asian-African origin to enroll their children in *haredi* schools by offering negligible tuition and extending the school day into the late afternoon. Confronted with this reality, the SR system, supported by the Religious Teachers' Association, embraced a policy of "selective integration." In this "integration cum exclusivity," SR schools countrywide are encouraged to strive for an exclusivity and excellence from which the disadvantaged, too, will profit. Consequently, disadvantaged pupils in development towns from Yeroham in the south to Qiryat Shemona in the north have shown significant scholastic improvement. Teachers' efforts to convince their students that even a development-town school can achieve excellence have proven themselves.[48] Without abandoning its policy of excellence, the SR system has undoubtedly invested in mitigating its students' scholastic shortcomings. One of the most interesting initiatives in this regard is a program encouraging outstanding socioeconomically disadvantaged students in development towns to finish high school.[49] The pro-excellence policy of the SR administration has had the additional result of downscaling technological education in SR schools, thus reducing the prevalence of a framework that had been accused of perpetuating the poor achievements of students of Asian-African origin and impeding their access to higher education. As for whether this pro-excellence policy can maintain social integration, only time will tell.

SR education policy, from the origin of the SR system to the mid-1990s, is the most convincing support for the argument that the ideological basis of mainstream interest groups effectively dictates SR educational policy. SR schooling has been elitist from the time of its inception, favoring its outstanding students, most of whom are socioeconomically advantaged, in prestigious settings such as high-school yeshivot, *ulpenot,* and prestige religious schools (such as Zeitlin in Tel Aviv or Ma'ale in Jerusalem). Students who are less talented or unable to afford the favored SR frameworks are referred to vocational programs or academic programs in comprehensive schools. The structural education-system reform, and the integration policy derived from it, threatened the basic values of SR policy. State–Religious education, loyal to statism, accepted the reform for lack of choice, but developed its own way to handle it – a way that provides a certain measure of integration without relinquishing the educational philosophy of promoting excellence.

Technological Education at a Crossroads

Vocational/technological education in Israel developed recently, when compared with other subsystems of the education system. Until the late 1950s, this type of education was a marginal player in the system and was in little demand. The reasons have to do with Jewish tradition and the structure of Jewish society in Europe, which encouraged intellectual study, and the economic circumstances of early Israel, largely an agrarian country with little industry and slow modernization.[50] Consequently, most immigrants in the country's early years entered an education system that stressed academic studies over technological education, the latter meant chiefly for disadvantaged groups.

In the late 1950s, the emphasis in education began to shift from the primary to the post-primary level. When a compulsory education law went into effect in 1949, increasing numbers of youngsters, of all social strata, enrolled in post-primary settings. Between 1949 and 1956, enrollment grew by a factor of five while the population grew by a factor of only three.[51] In response, Ministry of Education policy-makers, led by the late Minister of Education Zalman Aranne, understood that the system had to treat urgently the problems caused by the steady increase in the percentage of adolescents of Asian-African origin who had completed post-primary schooling, and by the growth in the number of disadvantaged students who sought post-primary education. "From now on, a young generation of ingathered exiles, who will demand the concern of the state for their continued study, is mounting the national stage."[52] Just the same, the academic high school system remained selective and elitist, turning many applicants away and experiencing a high dropout rate among those admitted.

After pondering this reality, education policy-makers developed vocational-technological education as an alternative for the disadvantaged. This system opened its doors to the disadvantaged and refrained from creating excessively tough obstacles, stiff requirements, and rigid admission terms. Vocational education, which had thought of itself as inferior to academic education and, until 1960, actually was inferior in share of enrollment and other quantitative criteria, now began to develop rapidly.[53] Since the 1960s, vocational education has been advancing both quantitatively and qualitatively. Enrollment has risen substantially, new programs have opened, and modern curricula have been developed. During this period of momentum and development, vocational education has been given favorable treatment in government budget support.

Until the Free Secondary Education Law went into effect, students in development towns were fully exempt from tuition fees, and a large majority of them enrolled in vocational-technological programs. The massive intake of pupils of Asian-African origin, coupled with the material benefits for which these students qualified, were for many a conduit to social mobility at a time when social status was determined largely by formal education and scholastic achievements. As, however, most enrollment in technological education (63 percent in 1977) originated in disadvantaged groups, the system was stigmatized, forcing it to seek ways to lure socioeconomically advantaged youngsters as well. Policymakers in the technological system therefore diversified the syllabus. Four-year programs leading to matriculation were created, allowing graduates to advance to higher studies and achieve vocational certification.[54] Sophisticated curricula were introduced and advertised in appropriate fashion. Graduates who stayed on to pursue the two-year degree of *handasay* (practical or civil engineer) were given extra privileges, and hours of vocational study, especially in "practical" subjects, were reduced. Students in the regular vocational program were encouraged to switch to the matriculation track, and classes within the matriculation track were differentiated in each subject, commensurate with the students' level.

The policy change paid off: the number of socioeconomically advantaged students aged 14–17 in technological education rose. This increase, coupled with the opening of the matriculation track, created ethnically integrated (Asian-African/European-American) classes.[55] However, it also led to polarization between the prestigious matriculation track, favored by socioeconomically advantaged students of whatever ethnic origin, and the non-diploma "practical" and "guidance" vocational classes, which were attended by weak students, mostly of Asian-African origin.

Technological Education and Education Reforms

Neither the 1968 structural reform nor the 1979 matriculation-examination reform has been good for technological education.[56] After the structural reform, which attached the junior-high level to the upper echelon of post-primary education, principals persuaded good students to stay on and referred the less proficient to technological education. The matriculation reform allowed a larger number of mediocre students to enroll in the matriculation track and pass the matriculation exams.[57] Consequently, as the Minister of Education noted in the Knesset in 1990, 5,000 students moved from vocational matriculation programs to academic high schools.[58] Technological education reverted to its former status as a refuge for mediocre and weak pupils. Another factor has contributed to enrollment stagnation in the vocational matriculation track since 1990: the Technion did not give preference in admission to vocational matriculates over academic graduates.[59] Consequently, many students who might have done well in technological education preferred to enroll in academic high schools; the academic programs were much less strenuous. They lacked the burdensome laboratories and workshops that proliferated in the vocational programs, and they offered greater opportunities for continued study.

Aware of the need to fight this development, technological education policy-makers responded in the following ways:

1. They persuaded the Technion to change its policy toward graduates of technological education, i.e., to give graduates

of the vocational matriculation track preference over graduates of academic schools.[60]

2. They reduced the hours of vocational study and created clusters in which vocational subjects were combined.
3. They deferred vocational specialization until grades 11 and 12.[61]
4. They increased the number of classroom hours devoted to academic and theoretical study.

It is too early to assess the success of this reform.

Technological Education – Coping with Dilemmas

Documents on technological education policy in Israel make it clear that this system is vacillating on several issues that illustrate better than anything else the difficulties the system faces. The first of these dilemmas may be defined as equality versus excellence. The economy expects technological education to provide high-quality, skilled human resources, with which it may turn out quality products that will compete internationally. To meet this expectation, technological education needs suitable inputs, including highly talented students. Most applicants for technological education do not meet this requirement. Turning these applicants away, however, would violate additional social expectations and needs. The education system is expected to fulfill the wishes and aptitudes of every teenager to the greatest possible extent; thus it must prevent the rejection of any applicant for lack of a setting that would serve him or her as a conduit for social and occupational mobility.

The second dilemma may be termed utility versus prestige. The public stigmatizes technological education, considering it a refuge for the rejects of academic schooling and, chiefly, for the socioeconomically disadvantaged. It is hard to support this allegation with respect to "rejects of academic schooling," but the second part of the allegation is a fact. It is true that technological education policy-makers have strived over the years to improve the public image of vocational schooling by the means already described: recruitment of talented students and, especially, the apportioning of more classroom hours for intellectual subjects and fewer for technological studies. In the wake of this policy, however, a new gap took shape: the vocational skills of the graduates of the technological schools failed to meet industry's expectations for trained vocational workers. By striving to meet the expectations of socioeconomically advantaged parents to reduce vocational hours and increase academic teaching hours,[62] the technological education system began turning out graduates who failed to satisfy the economy's expectations. The economy gains nothing from such a policy, and neither do the graduates, who risk finding themselves unemployed.[63]

The third dilemma may be termed efficiency versus effectiveness. Economist Ruth Klinov found that Israel has one of the highest percentage rates in the West of enrollment in technological education, surpassing the United States, Japan, and several European countries.[64] If so, how can one explain that technologically and economically advanced countries such as Japan and the United States have not seen fit to develop technological education as Israel has? Does academic education outperform technological education in cost-benefit terms? If it does, then Israel, too, should downscale its technological education system. However, economic considerations are not the only factors. For some people, technological education is the only path to a vocation and a job. This deserves consideration, too.

Cost-benefit studies in the West[65] and in developing countries[66] leave no doubt that academic education is preferable to technological education for both individuals and society. Unlike technological education, academic education creates opportunities for further study. Furthermore, in an era of rapid technological change, general education is preferable to the specific, narrow education given to those who seek their occupational future in industry. Technological education is more costly than academic education because it requires expensive equipment, lengthy hours of study, and small classes. Its utility for society and individuals, however, appears to be low relative to the large financial investment required, because many technological education graduates do not find suitable jobs, and many others take up occupational fields other than those that they studied in school.

In the Israeli case, however, Neuman and Ziderman,[67] in a comprehensive study, found that the value of investment in technological education exceeds that of investment in academic education, but only if graduates of technological education programs indeed practice the occupation they acquired in school. The study found that only 50 percent of technological education graduates in Israel remain in their fields. Consequently, technological education is of considerable utility to individuals but of little utility to society. Neuman and Ziderman do not prescribe the downscaling of technological education, since it is not clear whether every youngster completing primary school is qualified for academic schooling. Comparing the cost and the benefit of vocational/technological education in its various tracks with those of technological education in industrial schools, Ziderman found that the latter have a clear-cut economic advantage over the former.[68] Ziderman does not consider the social implications of a technological education policy based mainly on industrial schools. Shutting down some vocational high schools and opening new industrial schools may widen the disparity between students of Asian-African origin, who would gravitate to industrial programs, and those of European-American origin, who would choose academic tracks. A flow of this kind would exclude the former from the path to social and occupational mobility and eliminate options that the existence of vocational high-school education makes available to them today.

Another dilemma that the technological education system faces is its definition as a framework committed to meeting the economy's labor needs and ensuring its graduates an occupational future, as against the criticism that the system has attracted as a setting in which the social gap is perpetuated.[69] Technological education officials claim that this form of education, as presently constituted, is meant to meet the economy's labor needs and ensure vocational training for youth who have no chance of admission to academic schools. Opponents of this argument note that students referred to technological education feel stigmatized, thus diminishing their expectations of social advancement. Because most students in the non-diploma and guidance tracks of technological schooling are of Asian-African origin, their prospects of future access to higher education and social mobility decrease progressively. If this is so, the technological system indeed perpetuates the ethnic gap.[70] Even if it does not, an unanswered question still remains: the fate of those who, because of their poor learning skills, cannot handle the academic track and may be harmed by the downscaling of technological education.

In fact, many unanswered questions remain with respect to the best policy for technological education. Technological schooling, more than other levels of education, is trapped in the vise of the conflicting goals of education in a democratic society – especially in the variegated Israeli society, with its numerous and clashing expectations.

Technological Education: New Challenges

The criticism of technological education in its present form led to the establishment of a committee under physicist Haim Harari.[71] In his letter of appointment, Minister of Education Zevulun Hammer informed the committee members that they were to subject scientific and technological education in Israel to thorough inquiry and propose new programs and projects that might advance these fields of schooling. The changes Hammer had in mind were more than incremental. Notably, the committee's brief was to examine scientific/ technological education, with emphasis on scientific; technological education was a poor relation. This phrasing points to a change in ministry orientation. The meaning of a transition from vocational/technological education to scientific/technological education is the reinforcement of academic study and the downscaling of the vocational component. A plurality (45 percent) of committee members were academicians in the natural sciences and were known to oppose technological education in its present form. Thirty percent of the members were Ministry of Education officials, most of whom represented academic education. Thirteen percent were public figures, and 12 percent taught science in post-primary schools. Technological education, in whatever setting (ORT, Amal, Amit), was not represented at all. Technological education officials were able to make their views known to the committee, but the committee's recommendations, listed below, clearly add up to a proposal that would revolutionize scientific/technological education in Israel:

1. Science should be studied from kindergarten through the highest secondary grades, and should be taught by qualified science teachers even in primary schools.
2. A major effort should be made to promote the use of computers in all schools, primary and post-primary.
3. Technological subjects should be made part of the academic syllabus.
4. The Technological Education Division of the Ministry of Education and Culture should be reoriented and reconstituted as the Scientific Education Division.

5. Hours allotted for practical vocational education (workshops) should be reduced substantially, and hours devoted to academic study should be doubled.

6. Students in the non-diploma vocational/technological track should be offered a special program meant to improve their math and science achievements and permit them to take matriculation examinations in several subjects.

7. Practical vocational training should be deferred until twelfth grade or the end of post-primary studies.

8. The committee accepted the industrialists' basic attitude that secondary studies should focus on strengthening students' basic command of science, with practical training provided in-plant.

These recommendations reinforce the argument that technological education, for both advantaged and disadvantaged population groups, is heading in the direction of less traditional vocational schooling and greater emphasis on modern scientific education. Unconditional acceptance of the Harari Committee report would undoubtedly give scientific education in Israel a significant push forward, remove a social and scholastic barrier faced by the disadvantaged, and fulfill the untapped potential of many students. However, there is a risk of which the committee may not have been aware: what will become of students who fail to cope with the new scholastic challenges and cannot find a suitable setting in the milieu of future technological education? Such students account for 35 percent of technological education enrollment today. If the practical tracks, those commensurate with their skills, are downscaled or eliminated, these students may be sent into the job market at an early age or take refuge in the youth employment projects run by the Ministry of Labor and Social Affairs.

Implementation of the Harari Report may resolve several of the dilemmas that the technological education system faces, as listed at the beginning of this chapter. Technological education would acquire prestige and attract students of all socioeconomic classes. The downsizing of practical training in schools would reduce the high cost of technological schooling, and the resources thus released could be used to strengthen scientific education for the disadvantaged. If technological education succeeds in advancing these groups, it will have also fulfilled the goals of equality and social integration.

Summary

The development of technological education in Israel points to changes in its objectives, scholastic orientation, and composition of the student body. Initially, technological education was indistinguishable from traditional vocational education; it prepared students for manual trades by offering a curriculum including a few hours of academic study and many hours of technological and practical training. It was designed to sweep up the rejects of elitist academic schools and provide them with vocational training. This purpose served both the interests of mainstream social groups and the needs of peripheral groups, who viewed the acquisition of a trade as the path to a job – irrespective of social mobility. In the era of structural education reform and integration, technological education placed disadvantaged students in the diploma and non-diploma tracks alongside socio-economically advantaged students who were headed for matriculation. This tracking actually amounted to social tracking, even though the matriculation track attracted some strong students from peripheral social groups as well. This new trend continued to serve the purposes of the mainstream social groups, because it served social goals and determined who would go on to higher education.

The differentiation trend has gained strength since the mid-1980s. The technological matriculation track has moved even more emphatically to reduce vocational study hours and increase academic ones, so its graduates might enroll at the Technion. Reality indicates that the trend of social and track differentiation will continue to gather momentum if the Harari recommendations are implemented only in part. However, if the Ministry of Education and Culture implements the recommendations in full, the scientific/technological model will create a vehicle by means of which the disadvantaged may advance.

Arab Education: Evolution or Revolution?

The formal principle of equality, which we encountered in the Jewish sector, was applied to the Israeli Arab sector under the 1949 Compulsory Education Law. The state determines and defines the goals of education for Arab children in Israel and educates them following a curriculum that it devises. The Ministry of Education and Culture inspects Arab schools, textbooks, and ancillary literature, and pays the teachers. Arab local authorities provide schools with miscellaneous services including maintenance. Israeli education laws and regulations apply to the Arab education system, the structure and operation of which mirror those of the Jewish system.

However, the Arab sector also has private schools, most affiliated with church denominations and largely independent of government support. Although the Jewish and Arab education systems are ostensibly uniform, several factors set them apart:

1. Most Arab citizens of Israel live in totally Arab areas.
2. The two peoples are differentiated by ethnicity, religion, and culture, and both wish to avoid proximity and assimilation.
3. The Government of Israel has a democratic attitude that takes into account the minorities' special needs.[72]

Although the two education systems are separate, the Arab sector is not independently budgeted; its allocations come from various divisions of the Ministry of Education and Culture, via the Ministry's Arab Education Department. Sa'ad Sarsour, a researcher in questions of Arab education, believes that resources for Arab education are allocated arbitrarily, without objective guidelines.[73] But there is no evidence for this allegation. However, a ministry planning team appointed to deal with the Arab education system for the 1980s found that the Arab Education Department had, for 20 years, provided this system with nothing but the minimum services required by the Compulsory Education Law, with no thought given to additional fields such as post-primary and supplementary education.[74] These findings triggered reactions from leading education system officials. The Director-General of the Ministry at the time (1977), Eliezer Shmueli, stated:

> We can't be calm if the Ministry of Education and Culture, as a system that espouses the equality of Jewish and Arab citizens in Israel, is at peace with what's happening today in our Arab sector, for whose education we are responsible.[75]

An internal Ministry document circulated by the Ministry Director-General, Elad Peled, contained the following statement:

> Because of historical circumstances, the disparity between the Jewish and the Arab education systems is profound and wide in all respects:

contents and curricula, number and quality of teachers, physical infrastructure, and education services. Without analyzing the reasons and factors that led to this, one may state that this sector should not be dealt with in the conventional way.[76]

Although the ministry made efforts to solve the problems of the Arab education system, formal equality was not sufficient and an input–output gap took shape between the two systems.[77] It is note worthy that Arab school enrollment has grown by a factor of 15 since 1949, while the Arab population of Israel has merely tripled. Scholars who have traced the reasons for the disparity between Arab and Jewish education cite the following facts:[78]

1. The two systems began from different "starting lines"; the Arab education system lagged behind the Jewish system at the time Israel was established.
2. Overall ministry policy toward the Arab sector is unclear. This is an outgrowth of the protracted conflict between Israel and the Arabs, including frequent wars. The Arab-Israeli conflict has made the two sectors mutually suspicious and insular. It has also created an acute dilemma of identity for Israeli Arabs, who waver between loyalty to the Zionist Jewish state and identification with its people on the one hand, and allegiance to the Arab world, to which they are bound by language, culture, and religion, on the other. The wars and the domestic incidents that led to "Land Day," first marked on March 30, 1976, honed the dilemma and the confrontation between Israeli Arabs and the Jewish population, hinting at dangerous trends of separatism and challenging of the status quo.[79]
3. When the Knesset formulated the State Education law in 1953, it gave no thought to the goals of education for the Arab population. Young Israeli Arabs were unable to identify with some of the goals of the state education system, such as allegiance to the values of Jewish culture. The young found it difficult to identify with Israeli Arab schools and therefore preferred to avoid them. The identity crisis has also slowed the integration of young Arabs into Israeli society.[80]
4. The Arab tradition – conservative, patriarchal, authoritarian – seriously impeded the introduction of modernization processes into Israeli Arab society. Consequently, Arab schools accepted few of the pedagogical innovations that the Jewish sector had embraced.[81]

5. The quality of teachers in Arab schools was affected by the fact that most of the Arab intelligentsia fled the country during the War of Independence (1948), leaving the teaching profession in the hands of persons whom the traditional leadership "recommended." Even Arab graduates of Israeli teachers' colleges or universities found it quite hard to obtain jobs in the Arab education system because of the structure and power centers of Arab society.[82]

6. Involvement of leadership and parents was lower in the Arab sector than in the Jewish sector.

7. Arab local authorities have one of Israel's lowest levels of municipal tax collection. When total government spending for education was reduced and the share of private funding rose, one would have expected households in Arab localities to assume a greater share of funding for education. This did not happen, and development of the local education system was adversely affected. In 1990 the Ministry of Education and Culture covered 77.8 percent of Arab education outlays, compared with 62 percent in Jewish localities.[83]

Arab Education – The Advancement Committees

The Ministry of Education and Culture appointed a series of ministerial committees to propose ways to improve education in the Arab sector.[84] The first such committee was named in 1981; after three years of work it determined that Arab education lacked various components without which it could not catch up with the Jewish sector. Specific needs included more classrooms, much more study equipment, better technological education, and a major investment in teacher training. The committee also mentioned the need for a special head-start program for disadvantaged Arab pupils and recommended the development of a second-chance program for those who had failed matriculation examinations.

Pursuant to the recommendations of the first committee (1981), the Director-General of the Ministry of Education appointed another committee (1985) to plan and monitor implementation of the first committee's recommendations. The second committee repeated some of its predecessor's arguments and recommended that budget allocations for education in non-Jewish localities be increased. In September 1986, the Director-General of the Ministry of Education formed a third committee to examine and pinpoint problems and needs in the Arab sector, for policy-making purposes. The committee presented its conclusions, which offered new directions to follow in assessing the situation. Its report contained the following recommendations:[85]

1. Goals and objectives in Arab education should be redefined. "The goal of state education in the Israeli Arab sector is to provide education based on the fundamentals of Arab culture, the achievements of science, the aspiration for peace between Israel and its neighbors, love of the homeland that all citizens of the state share, allegiance to the State of Israel with emphasis on shared interests, and encouragement of the singularity of Israeli Arabs and familiarity with Jewish culture."

   This definition acknowledges the uniqueness of Arab culture and seeks to foster it in the Israel-Arab school. However, it stresses allegiance to the state, familiarity with Jewish culture, and participation in the modernization processes that the Jewish sector is experiencing. This definition undoubtedly facilitates identification by the young with the Israeli Arab school.

   The committee added several practical aims in order to narrow intersectoral disparities: gradual development of preschools, provisions for the instruction of mothers to enable them to help in their children's education, development of academic and scientific course programs in post-primary schools, extensive development of technological education, and improvement of teacher quality.

2. The administrative functions of the Arab Education Division at the Ministry of Education should be decentralized and transferred to district-level management.[86] This measure should make district officials more attentive to developments in Arab education, make them intimately familiar with problems in the field, and facilitate immediate remedies. This decentralization should be supported by an increase in the district offices of administrative and pedagogical job slots earmarked for Arab education. The Arab Education Division should keep only its pedagogical functions, and should serve as the Arab sector's representative at the Curriculum and Youth Divisions of the Ministry. Decentralization should be used to achieve greater equality in handling the problems of the Arab sector and promoting the correct apportioning and use of resources.[87]

3. Allocations for Arab education in both sections of the State
    budget – development (investment) and ongoing (operations)
    – should be increased, in order to finance new enrollment,
    pre-service and in-service teacher training, and the upgrading
    of schools.

In March 1987, the Director-General of the Ministry of Education
and Culture appointed a fourth committee to monitor implementation of the previous committee's recommendations. This committee
found that the policy of delegating the functions of the Arab Education Division to the district level was being implemented. The
committee then recommended that a five-year plan for education in
the Arab sector be prepared. In response, the Ministry of Education
put together a five-year plan for the years 1988–1992. A special
Ministry circular on the subject contained the following points:[88]

In order to improve the performance of the Arab education system
within a five-year period and to narrow the educational disparities
that had built up over many years, the goals and objectives of
education in the Arab sector should be adjusted in the spirit of the
third committee's recommendations. In other words, the administrative decentralization proposed by previous committees should
be upheld, and standard classroom hours should be increased in
accordance with the extent of remedial action needed. An extended
school day should be introduced in some schools, and for this
purpose 2,100 classroom hours should be added for the 1991/92
school year.

Another 855 classrooms should be built during the five-year
period of the plan: 500 to accommodate natural increase, the rest
to replace existing facilities. The curriculum should be fleshed out
with subjects relating to Arabic language and culture. To accomplish
this, the Curriculum Division should be given another eight job slots
solely for this purpose. The budget for teacher in-service activities
should be increased. Prestigious technological tracks should be
opened, with the intent of increasing the share of technological
enrollment from 19 percent to 35 percent. Fifteen new inspectors'
positions should be created for subjects such as computers, Islam,
educational television, and music. Ten new positions should be
created for truant officers and five for educational psychologists.
Each year, five outstanding Arab students should be given scholarships for master's degree studies.

Careful examination of the five-year plan in comparison with the realities of education in the Arab sector suggests that the plan, if carried out, will transform the development of education in the Israeli Arab sector, as manifested in a greater share of government funding of education expenditures. The Arab education system is experiencing a paradox. The state is reinforcing educational decentralization and autonomy, yet it is not decreasing its share of education funding or passing on the financial burden to residents who use the education services (either through direct payment for education or by means of municipal taxes). In fact, the government is increasing its own share in outlays. This paradoxical process is unquestionably part of an inclusive policy designed to narrow the educational disparities that have built up over the years between the Jewish and the Arab sectors. These are manifestations of a government policy meant to blunt the Arab residents' sense of deprivation, which, in turn, has generated growing support of Arab political parties and radical Islam.[89]

Summary

Several factors have contributed to disparities in education between the Jewish and Arab sectors: (1) historical circumstances: the Arab-Israeli conflict and its side effect, the identity crisis of Israeli Arabs, have impeded Israeli Arabs' integration into Israeli society;[90] (2) the traditional structure of Arab society, which impedes innovation and change in the education system; (3) the country's economic difficulties, which have reduced total inputs for education, with the Arab sector enjoying no exemption; and (4) the practice of Arab local authorities to earmark a very small share of their budgets to education.

Nevertheless, considerable effort is being made to change the situation, in the following ways:

1. A substantial increase of inputs to be invested in the Arab sector (the five-year plan is a palpable manifestation of this).
2. Acknowledgment of the educational and cultural uniqueness of the Arab sector and modification of the goals of Arab education in order to help young Arabs identify with the goals of the curriculum and whet their scholastic motivation.
3. Decentralization of and autonomy in the Arab education system, in order to increase parental and community involvement in the system's activities.

Israeli educational policy in the past decade has been characterized by a proliferation of clashing goals. Notwithstanding this,
policy-makers – Ministers of Education and their senior officials on
the one hand, and the Knesset Education Committee on the other
– have strived to attain all the clashing goals simultaneously. To
meet the conflicting expectations and interests of pressure groups
in Israeli society, the education system leadership adopted a policy
that reflects its own initiative in some ways and the effects of outside
pressure in others.

The leadership's "endogenous" policy manifests itself in maintaining the system as it exists: ensuring continued integration by
channeling budgets to disadvantaged schools, extending the school
day in disadvantaged localities (770 classes thus far), implementing
the Free Secondary Education Law, reinforcing religious education,
developing Arab education, reinforcing Jewish studies in the state
(secular) schools, and encouraging schools to act autonomously.
The exogenously inspired policy manifested itself most saliently in
acquiescence to the education budget cuts, tacit acceptance of gray
education, consent for the opening of special-curriculum schools
and special curricula in regular schools, and benign neglect of
localities that refuse to implement the integration reform policy.

6

Budget and Curriculum

This chapter will consider the extent to which the education decision-makers' declared policy has been reflected in the budget and the curriculum. To what extent did the policy of educational equity and integration manifest itself in larger budgets for disadvantaged areas and weak students, the establishment of suitable schools for educationally disadvantaged children, and improvement of teacher quality in disadvantaged communities? Does the decrease in the State contribution to educational financing, coupled with an increase in the households' share, point to a policy that promotes excellence and elitism? To what extent is the declared policy of greater efficiencies in the education system implemented in practical ways, such as the formation of classes with an optimal ratio of students to teaching position and the optimal use of teaching personnel?

The curriculum questions to be investigated are the following: to what extent does the curriculum reflect the pro-integration education policy. To what extent is the declared policy of decentralizing the school system reflected in schools' freedom to design curricula (more elective and fewer compulsory programs)? In other words, in what ways does the education policy manifest itself in the curriculum?

Education Policy in Terms of Numbers

The budget is the best reflection of education policy.[1] Every change in policy should express itself in an increase or decrease of resources allocated for various sectors and disciplines of education. Therefore an education policy that strives for greater equality among population groups should express this goal tangibly, by means of higher government expenditures that compensate the disadvantaged and increase the economic burden on affluent families.

Statistical data for Israel in the past decade – growth of school enrollment, growth of national expenditure on education as a percentage of the Gross National Product, public expenditure on education compared with household expenditure, the number of schools built, the increase in the number of teachers, and growth in the number of teaching positions – point to several changes. In general, the education budget did not stagnate in the 1980s. Major changes occurred, each for its own reasons. These included increased enrollment (caused by immigration in Jewish schools and by natural increase in Arab schools), growth of compensation mechanisms for disadvantaged areas (extension of the school day), changes in teachers' remuneration (implementation of the Etzioni commission agreements), and larger development budgets (renovation of old buildings and the construction of new ones).

However, several contrary trends are evident. National expenditure on education (spending by public institutions, nonprofit organizations, and families), expressed as a percentage of the GNP, increased in real terms between 1970 and 1979. From that time until the mid-1980s, however, national expenditure on education dropped from 9.5 percent to 8.7 percent of the GNP, and most of the decrease was explained by a decline in the government's share of this expenditure.

In 1988, national expenditure on education as a percentage of GNP began to rise again, although at the time of writing (1994) it still remains 6.5 percent lower than in the base year of 1980. In other words, the upturn in national education spending over the past few years has not regained the ground lost since the 1970s.[2]

The share of the central and local governments in national expenditure on education dropped from 84 percent in 1979/80 to 77 percent in 1987/88. The difference was made up by nonprofit organizations and households, i.e., by private financing. Household expenditure on education as a percentage of family income has almost doubled since 1984. In other words, the government adopted a mixed-financing model, in which both the public and the private sectors take part.[3]

The decrease in national education spending was reflected mainly in cutbacks in central-government education budgets and a percentage decline in the overall share of educational funding within the total civilian (nondefense) expenditure. Education expenditure accounted for 17.7 percent of total government civilian expenditure in 1979, plunged to 13.6 percent in 1981, and continued to slump until 1986. A slight recovery then ensued: 14.2 percent in 1987 and 14.7 percent in 1988. Since then, the level has remained at around 14 percent. Consequently, education spending as a percentage of civilian expenditure has decreased by about 28 percent since 1979.

When the change in government spending on education is compared with spending on other social services, we find that the government's share in funding welfare services has increased four-fold in the last decade. Most expenditure in this category is for immigrant absorption and income maintenance for the indigent.[4] The education budget was slashed because of government efforts to stabilize the economy, reduce inflation rates, and narrow the balance-of-payments deficit. According to economist Ruth Klinov,[5] the decrease in the public budget, including the share reserved for education, was caused not only by economic constraints but also by a change in the structuring of expenditure: more "welfare spending" (chiefly income payments), at the expense of "in-kind" services" (education, health, and personal social services).

The Downscaling of the Education Budget

The downscaling of the education budgets brings several questions to the fore:

1. How deep has the cutback been in real terms?
2. How has the cutback affected classroom hours per class and classroom hours per pupil, and how has it manifested itself at each individual level of education (primary, junior high, post-primary)?
3. How has the cutback affected class size and density at each level of education (in the Jewish and the Arab sectors and at different grade levels)?
4. How has the budget cut affected enrollment and dropout rates at each level of education and in each sector?
5. What have been the trends in the development (investment) budget?
6. How has the cutback in government expenditure on education affected per-capita education spending at the local-government level?

The Budget Cuts in Real Terms

Sharkansky[6] estimates the real decrease in education budgets between the late 1970s and the mid-1980s at 24 percent. Central Bureau of Statistics figures set the inflation-adjusted erosion in per-capita expenditure on education between 1980 and 1987 at 8 percent, from NIS 0.64 to NIS 0.59. Even though per-capita expenditure on education rose in 1988, the level achieved was lower than that of 1979. Total civilian spending in the State budget increased by 35.8 percent in real terms during the aforementioned period; real spending on education rose by only 8.5 percent.

While national expenditure on education rose 3 percent between 1986 and 1987, it only rose 2 percent between 1988 and 1989. Only in 1990 was there a significant increase in national education spending (7 per cent), in per-capita education spending, and in the government's share of education expenditure (a rise of 10.45 percent in 1990, as against 6.52 per cent in 1985).[7]

Manifestations of the Budget Cuts at the Different Education Levels

All levels of education were affected by the budget cuts. The effect was greatest, however, in primary and junior-high education and less at the post-primary (high-school) level. Pre-schools were not affected. Expenditure for nursery schools ("pre-compulsory kindergartens") is borne by parents in affluent areas and largely by local authorities in development towns and disadvantaged areas. Budgets for pre-schools have been rising as part of a systematic policy.[8] The brunt of the cuts was borne by primary education: a dramatic 15 percent decrease in per-class hours of study during the period reviewed, and a 7 percent decrease in average hours per pupil. Primary-school enrollment increased by only 11 percent during the period discussed (with most of the growth in the ultra-Orthodox and Arab sectors). At the junior-high level, in contrast, the decline in education expenditure caused average classroom hours per class and per pupil to contract by 7 percent and 18 per cent, respectively, even though enrollment rose by nearly 30 percent during the period.[9] Consequently, the budget cut affected not only the number of classroom hours but another equally important factor: class size.

In the higher post-primary grades (10–12), the budget cut did not cause a reduction in classroom hours, because budgeting in these grades is more flexible and computed on a per-capita basis. High schools also have private revenues that give them flexibility. Another reason for the negligible impact of the education budget on the high post-primary grades is the structure of the syllabus, which typically is more varied than in the lower grades. By switching to subjects which cost less per classroom hour, post-primary schools are able to maintain a fixed number of hours even with a lower budget;[10] the lower grades do not enjoy this flexibility.

The Effect of the Budget Cuts on Class Size and Density

The education budget cuts also affected both class size and density. The State Comptroller's Report[11] shows that the relatively slow growth of enrollment at the primary level prevented a significant increase in the number of classes with over 30 pupils between 1980 and 1990. However, the number of classes with over 20 pupils, and the number of classes with 20 or fewer pupils, each increased by 6 percent.

At the junior-high and post-primary levels, the findings point to a different trend. The number of classes with 30 or more pupils rose by 13 percent; classes with 20 pupils or over grew by 8 percent. Consequently, class density increased. The higher post-primary grades show the same trend, albeit to a less pronounced degree than at the junior-high level: a 6 percent increase in the number of classes with 30 or more pupils and those with 20 or more pupils. In vocational education, class density increased by a modest 4 percent.

Comparing educational sectors (Jewish versus Arab) and streams (State, State–Religious, Independent), density is highest in the Arab primary schools (30.7 pupils per teacher) as against 28.8 in Jewish schools in the State system (without any significant change since 1989), 25.6 in State–Religious schools (no significant change since 1989), and 22.7 in the Independent system. The intersectoral differences in class density reflect rapid enrollment growth (caused by natural increase) and relatively few classrooms in the Arab sector. The differences in class density among the streams of Jewish education are explained by Ministry of Education and Culture rules that allow State–Religious (SR) schools to open a new class if at least 11 pupils need one. If no nearby facility offers religious education, and if State–Religious education is in demand locally, classes must be opened to meet this need.

However, the highest ratio of pupils to teaching positions is found in the Independent system (29.9 as against 23.3 in the State system, 18.4 in the SR system, and 26.6 in the Arab sector). It follows that Independent education makes the most efficient use of its manpower. The SR system has the lowest ratio of pupils to teaching positions, followed by the State system and the Arab sector.

The growth of enrollment in Jewish post-primary schools is especially apparent in the State system (from 30 percent to 32.5 percent) and the Independent system (from 22.7 percent to 24.6 percent). The share of SR enrollment slipped from 25.6 percent to 25 percent. This points to an increase of enrollment in State, as opposed to State–Religious, post-primary schools (apparently inspired by the Free Secondary-Education Law). The decrease in SR enrollment, coupled with the growth in that of the Independent system, indicates religious radicalization among certain groups in the SR system, who now prefer ultra-Orthodox to SR education. Comparing the Jewish and the Arab sectors, there is a significant rise in Arab post-primary enrollment. This rise, which is most evident in vocational schools (43 percent growth since 1989), attests to a growing awareness among Arab families of the importance of post-primary education.

The Effect of the Budget Cuts on Enrollment and Dropout Rates

The data in Ministry of Education publications[12] point to several trends. In primary education, the enrollment rates are growing steadily in both the Jewish and the Arab sectors, reaching 96 percent and 85 percent, respectively, in 1990. These enrollment rates in Jewish post-primary education rose by 14 percent since 1989. Relative to the 1970s, the growth rate, for both boys and girls, was 34 percent on average. Arab enrollment rates also increased during this period: by 8 percent for boys (reaching 66 percent in 1990) and by 15 percent for girls (reaching 60 percent in 1990). The enrollment rates in Christian schools approximate those in the Jewish sector. It is not surprising that the enrollment rates are lower at the post-primary level than at the primary level, because although post-primary education is free, it is not compulsory for those older than 16 years of age. Some youths choose to find jobs and earn a living at this age. This is why enrollment rates of the 16–plus age cohort are lower for boys than for girls in both sectors.

Dropout rates, as shown in Ministry of Education publications, have declined in both the Jewish and the Arab sectors. The post-primary dropout rates, however, show a wide intersectoral disparity: 17 percent of Arab pupils dropped out in the period reviewed, as against 6 percent in the Jewish sector.[13]

Trends of Change in the Development Budget

The figures for the education development budget indicate significant increases in both the Jewish and Arab sectors.[14] The development budget is meant for the construction of new classrooms and the renovation of physically dangerous classrooms. Between 1980 and 1988, the development budget increased by a moderate 10–13 percent on average. The rate of increase has accelerated since then: by 40 percent between 1989 and 1990, and sevenfold between 1990 and 1992. The last increase unquestionably reflects efforts to absorb immigrants and meet educational needs in new settlements. The data also show the following itemization in the 1991 development budget: 9 percent for new pre-schools and 5 percent for continued building, 40 percent for new primary schools and 38 percent for continued building; 33 percent for new junior-high and high-school facilities, and 26 percent for continued building; 9 percent for new schools and 24 percent for continued building in the Arab sector. The other development outlays, which were smaller, were for agricultural schools and community centers, for Educational Television, and for the replacement of flammable buildings. In other words, most of the effort was invested in pre-school and primary education, in new and continued building in the Jewish and Arab sectors.

The Effect of the Budget Cut on Per-Capita Education Expenditure by Local Authorities

The slashing of education budgets also impacted on the education budgets of local authorities.[15] While education in Israel is a service provided by the State, local authorities help finance schools within their jurisdiction. Most of the financial burden is borne by the central government, which provides the local authorities with funds to cover their education expenses. The salaries of pre-school and primary-school teachers are paid by the Ministry of Education, but maintenance expenses, including the salaries of the clerical, cleaning, and other administrative staff, are covered by local authorities. At the post-primary level, in contrast, local authorities are responsible for most payroll expenditures (especially in junior-high schools). Most funding of these expenses is provided by the central government, in the form of "transfers" to local authorities, and by parental contributions.

The data indicate[16] that total outlays through the local authorities' regular budgets (the "current" or operations budget) have increased since 1989 by 6 percent on average in real terms. The highest rate of growth in the regular budget was found in Druze and Arab local authorities (107.4 percent and 61.5 percent, respectively). In the Jewish sector, noticeable increases in budget outlays occurred among smaller local authorities (27.4 percent), municipalities (13 percent), and large regional councils (11 percent). The regular budget outlays of large municipalities declined during this time.

Even though the regular budgets of most local authorities increased, per-capita expenditure on education decreased in real terms by 5 percent on average. The share of total local authority expenditure devoted to education decreased by about 5 percent in the period 1980 to 1988. In the Jewish sector, the decline was most conspicuous in large local councils (approximately 15 percent). Municipalities and regional councils showed an average decrease of 5 percent, and the share of per-capita education expenditure in the outlays of small local councils increased by 8 percent. This parameter increased by 64 percent in the Druze sector and 30 percent in the Arab sector. The increase was caused by two factors: a 47 percent rise in revenue earmarked for education, originating mainly with the central government, and the desire of Druze and Arab local-council chairmen to pledge much of their regular budgets to education. In the Jewish sector, this effort is most strongly evident in small local authorities. This unusual development is obviously the result of changing awareness of the importance of education for social advancement among the minorities and the weaker Jewish population groups. The new awareness is expressed in a changing order of priorities and a reapportionment of the budgetary pie. Another factor is the wish of the Druze and Arabs to narrow the education gap between themselves and the Jewish population. The intersectoral gap has indeed narrowed, from NIS 227 ($76) per capita in the early 1980s to NIS 150 ($50) by the end of the decade, i.e., a 34 percent decrease. Figures from the Central Bureau of Statistics also show that the highest average expenditure rate for education services is that of local authorities whose residents are in the lowest socioeconomic decile. This confirms the findings of previous studies on this subject.[17]

The data show[18] that even though the small local authorities' total revenues for education decreased by 1 percent (the central government's contribution to education expenditure dropped by 17 percent), the percentage of their budgets devoted to education increased by 8 percent. The education revenues of municipalities grew by 10 percent (some from central-government sources), but their per-capita expenditure on education decreased by 5 per cent. The education revenues of regional councils rose by 7 percent (mostly from private sources), but their education outlays dipped by 4 percent.

Summing up, the last decade was characterized by declining education budgets at both the central-government and the local-government levels. In the Jewish sector, only the small local councils made an effort to increase their education outlays beyond their revenues. The revenues of Arab local councils rose by 63 percent, while their education expenditure increased by 47 per cent. It is therefore evident that the Arab and Druze sectors significantly enlarged both their revenues (mainly through central-government allocations) and their outlays on education.

Those Jewish localities which failed to expand their education budgets increased the parents' financial burden for education expenditure and channeled local-authority resources to other services, such as welfare, Project Renewal, and culture. While trimming their education spending by 5 per cent, the municipalities increased culture outlays by 37 percent. Large local councils spent 15 percent less on education and 5 percent more on culture. The truly surprising figures pertain to the Druze and Arab local authorities, in which outlays on education and culture increased by more than 100 percent. Examination of the share of the central government in the cultural expenditure by local authorities reveals that the share of the central government in financing outlays categorized as "culture" decreased by 51 per cent between 1980 and 1988 – 56 percent in municipalities, 63 percent in large local councils, and 46 percent in small local councils. By deduction, this shows that the increase in expenditure on culture, which was evident in all types of local authorities, was caused by direct payments by the "consumers" of culture, i.e., the residents. The growth trend in local outlays for culture is also evident in the development budgets. Notably, however, the trend under the present administration is the opposite. The then Minister of Education, Shulamit Aloni, declared her intention to increase significantly the share of the central government in financing culture.[19]

Summary

The cuts in government education budgets have led to cutbacks in classroom hours, especially at the primary and junior-high levels, and have had a moderate impact on classroom density at the primary level. The slashing of education budgets for local authorities affected the large local councils (–31 percent) but spared the other local authorities. Although the education revenues of the small local councils decreased by 17 percent, they made a perceptible effort to increase expenditure and did so by 8 percent.

The central government significantly increased its share in the education outlays of Druze and Arab local authorities (by about 50 percent on average) and allowed the development budgets for education to grow appreciably. In other words, although the government cut the regular education budget – forcing households to take on an increased burden in educational expenditure – it reordered its priorities and increased its investment allocations for education. The share of the central government in the education expenditure of the Druze and Arab local authorities also rose considerably. The crucial question is: are the changing trends in the education budget, as reflected in the data for the period 1980 to 1990, consistent with the declared policy of Israel's education policy-makers?

The Education Budget and its Effects on Educational Equality

Since the 1970s, education policy in Israel has revolved on one major axis: equal opportunity in education. This policy was reflected in the 1968 structural reform, which had the following major aims:

1. To replace the 8–4 education structure with a 6–3–3 structure, in order to improve secondary-level graduates' readiness for higher studies. (Students with four years of post-primary education under the old system cannot be compared to students with six years of post-primary schooling under the new system.)

2. To remap the enrollment districts, and to form schools designed to integrate socially and scholastically diverse pupils, as well as to promote comprehensive schools that offer a choice of different educational tracks.

The overarching purpose of these changes was to help disadvantaged groups and decrease social disparities. The reform entailed tremendous expense: the expansion of existing schools, the construction of new schools, the retraining of seventh- and eighth-grade teachers for junior-high work, the preparation of new textbooks, and so on.

In the 1970s, as Klinov shows,[20] total national outlay on education was 8.5 percent of the GNP, and most of it was funded through the public system. In the 1980s, this changed. Public funding was slashed by 28 percent, and families' share of education funding rose from 7 percent to 26 percent at post-primary level and from 19 percent to 31 percent in higher education. It is hard to estimate the share of households in funding primary education, but we know that gray education has been on the increase, despite expectations of an increased government share in education expenditure following the reform. In other words, the education budget shows a trend opposite to the declared policy of the education policy-makers.

How can disadvantaged population groups be helped if there is less public and more private funding? The question is even more valid in view of the data on cutbacks in teaching hours per class. The data show that teaching hours per class at the primary level have been reduced by 15 percent. This has induced parents to hire private tutors to improve their children's performance on the national achievement tests.[21] Moreover, the junior-high schools, which were supposed to have pursued a policy of integration with the help of supplementary classroom hours, had to cut classroom hours by 7 percent for lack of funds. Class density at the junior-high level rose as well, even though the educational philosophy favored smaller classes as the avenue to integration.[22] Rotem showed that recourse to private tutoring was actually greater in integrated schools than in others.[23] Although the cutback in classroom hours was more moderate in the higher grades, the percentage of private financing reached as much as 26 percent (a 53 percent increase) at this level of schooling. If we recall that the education budgets of the local authorities, which bear the financial brunt of post-primary education, were cut by 5 percent, we will understand why.

The Free Secondary Education Law was legislated, according to
its sponsors, in order to give the socially disadvantaged, most of
whom were of Asian or African origin, an opportunity to advance.
The data show that since the law was passed in 1981, the enrollment
rates in the upper post-primary grades increased slightly, but by
only 14 percent for boys and 10 percent for girls.[24] This means that
the academic high school, meant to serve as an instrument of social
mobility, has, by utilizing a selection mechanism, drained the law
of its ideological content and circumvented the new policy,[25] even
though there was an increased demand for academic education.
Pupils who cannot afford private tutoring drop out of the system
and enter the labor market, the Ministry of Education vocational
programs (the *masmar* and *masmam* tracks), or the Ministry of
Labor apprenticeship settings. The conclusion to be drawn is that
the educational equity policy has not passed the test of reality.

The trend toward inequality in education, caused by cuts in
public funding, has been gaining strength because of the growing disparity between input and output. The per-capita education
outlays of socioeconomically disadvantaged local authorities exceed
those of affluent local authorities. (One of the country's highest
levels of per-capita education expenditure – NIS 2,588 ($863) per
capita in 1987/88 – is found in Mitspe Ramon, a disadvantaged
development town in the Negev.) Achievement tests, however,
show that the pupils' performance in these localities is substand-
ard.[26] These findings can be explained in the following way: the
foremost resource for improving school input is the staff (principal
and teachers).[27] High-caliber teaching staff is expensive, but local
authorities and school boards are not allowed to exceed wage
agreements by paying teachers higher salaries commensurate with
their abilities, and are thus forced to spend their increased revenues on equipment rather than on salaries. This prevents them
from attracting superior teachers by offering attractive salaries.

Furthermore, Dan Davis of the Hebrew University and his colleagues of the Ministry of Education Remedial Education Department found that disadvantaged schools have been giving preference
to Jewish studies, homogeneous grouping, extracurricular activities, and an extended school day.[28] However, no differences were
found in the number of classroom hours devoted to arithmetic,
Hebrew, and English. The researchers conclude that the disadvantaged schools have made considerable improvement in the
utilization of available input. However, contrary to expectations,

they showed no increased use of modern teaching methods and special curricula, and these are two of the main factors in improving scholastic achievements.

In contrast to the greater inequality in the Jewish sector, the gap between the Jewish and the Arab sectors has narrowed significantly. The Ministry of Education policy, which seeks to narrow the intersectoral input differentials that have existed since the establishment of the State, is reflected in the education budget. In the Arab sector, development budget allocations have grown by 9 percent for new construction and 24 percent for continued construction. Post-primary enrollment rates have soared by 113 percent; dropout rates are down. Even the number of truant officers has doubled. The share of the central government in the education outlays of the Arab local authorities ranged from 67 percent to 97 percent. The increase in public education funding in these local authority jurisdictions has narrowed the intersectoral gap in per-capita expenditure. The policy of narrowing the intersectoral disparity is even more evident in the Ministry of Education budget for 1993.[29]

Summary

The foregoing analysis of statistical data on the Israeli education system in the period 1980 to 1990 shows a tendency toward mixed funding, i.e., an increase in the share of private funding. If mixed funding becomes entrenched, low-income families that are not presently defined as disadvantaged[30] but cannot afford the school-imposed parental contributions will need to have special arrangements made for them. Will the share of public input for poor families increase and that routed to affluent families decrease? Only time will tell. Will today's tendency in education policy, which favors the establishment of special-curriculum schools, enhance equality or have the opposite effect? It is hard to draw an unequivocal conclusion on the basis of the scanty knowledge presently available, though chapter 6 attempts to deal with future trends in light of present developments.

The Education Budget and its Effects on Educational Efficiency and Effectiveness

The data show a decrease in total government expenditure on

education, in contrast to the continuing growth of enrollment and enrollment rates, i.e., a decline in real average expenditure per pupil. The higher the class density, the greater its economic efficiency, although, on the pedagogical level, the reverse is generally true. Klinov, who studied class size in various countries, reached the conclusion that the conventional class size in Western countries peaked at 35 pupils.[31] Using this figure as a basis for comparison, it can be argued that the State–Religious (SR) and Independent schools are much more efficient than State schools in the Jewish sector and all the schools in the Arab sector. However, the highest ratio of pupils per teaching position is found in the Independent schools, meaning that Independent schools use their manpower most efficiently. State and SR schools have a lower ratio of pupils to teaching positions, meaning that they use their manpower less efficiently. The previous conclusion is valid only if one disregards the fact that the State and SR schools use special-subject teachers for individual subjects, whereas teachers in the Independent schools teach a variety of subjects. The data show that the teacher/pupil ratio is smallest in vocational schools and that, for this reason, these are the least effective schools, at least in this respect.

Klinov's comparative data show that the Teachers' Union allegations of overcrowded classes are not backed by sufficient evidence. Moreover, literature on school effectiveness[32] shows explicitly that pedagogical factors (teaching methods, school curricula) have a stronger effect on pupils' achievement than do demographic factors such as the size of the school or the class.

Thus far the adverse influence of mixed public–private funding on educational equality has been demonstrated. If, however, its impact on educational efficiency and effectiveness is examined, it is found that precisely this type of funding may improve the cost/effectiveness ratio and improve school quality. A higher share of private funding may make the system more responsive to pupils' needs and improve the quality of educational services offered. Private funding increases parental involvement and supervision of school performance. However, the efficacy of such supervision is significant only if the schools are autonomous. Educational economists are of the opinion that private funding may be more advantageous if schools are given discretion in the apportionment of their resources.[33] Greater flexibility in the use of school budgets would make it easier for a school board to modify class size and curricular emphases in response to needs, to recruit better teachers, and to pay them commensurate with their marginal output and comparative advantage. Education system decentralization would also stimulate competition between schools and force them to become more efficient.

The trends in the technological education budget point to budget growth in an educational field of disputed efficiency and effectiveness. The scale of vocational education has grown substantially over the past two decades, against the prevalent Western trend.[34] The difference between Israel and the West is that Israeli educational policy-makers considered technological education a vehicle for economic development and the advancement of socially disadvantaged groups that had been barred from an academic high-school education. This policy quickly proved erroneous, for the Technion did not prefer graduates of the prestigious *masmat* track in technological schools over graduates of academic high schools. Only in the past year (1993) has a change taken place in this regard. Moreover, graduates of the *masmar* and *masmam* tracks were not accepted by the higher education establishments, which, from the students' point of view, were their passports to social mobility.

Furthermore, industry preferred to train its future pool of vocationally skilled staff on the job, and expected vocational schools to provide students with a broader basis in theoretical science. Thus, technological education helped its graduates neither socially nor economically, unless they went on to higher education. The data also show that technological education is not efficient; its cost is extremely high (workshops, laboratories, expensive equipment) and the classes are underpopulated. Moreover, graduates who are able to continue in higher education prefer to take vocational retraining.

Although the efficiency and effectiveness of vocational schools run by the Ministry of Labor and Social Affairs has not been compared here with those of schools sponsored by the Ministry of Education, Klinov[35] found that the industrial schools were less effective both in economic terms (erosion of graduates' vocational know-how due to army service, unless they served in units that made use of the knowledge they acquired before induction) and socially (the industrial-school curriculum is scanty in general education and, for this reason, reduces graduates' prospects of achieving social mobility). It would seem, then, that the efficiency and effectiveness of technological education may be raised by modifying the emphases in the syllabus (greater attention to academic and scientific aspects, less emphasis on vocational workshops), changing class size, and improving teaching methods for the disadvantaged.

Summary

State education is the most efficient educational stream in one respect: the pupil/teacher ratio. The Independent system is the most efficient in its ratio of pupils to teaching positions. The Independent and State–Religious systems are the most effective in the pedagogical sense of a small number of pupils per teacher. Academic education is more efficient and effective than technological education.

Education Policy as Reflected in Curricula

Although teachers and educationists construe the term "curriculum" in different ways, policy-makers in the Ministry of Education and Culture consider its meaning unequivocal.[36] It pertains to the official, approved document issued by the Pedagogical Secretariat that is responsible for formulating the program of studies for a specific subject throughout the pupil's stay at a State or State-Religious school.[37] In an era of educational policy that favors school autonomy, some attribute special importance to this "curriculum," which, more than anything else, expresses uniformity within the education system and ensures the country's socio-national goals in education.

Silberstein argues that the Israeli curriculum has always reflected the ideal level (the viewpoints and ideas of education policymakers) and the formal level (the action needed to realize these ideas), but has not taken account of other aspects of scholastic planning, such as how the curriculum is perceived by teachers.[38]

The curriculum in Israel is set by a committee appointed by the Director of the Curriculum Division of the Ministry of Education and Culture, in coordination with the chief inspector and subject committee of each individual subject. The curriculum committee formulates the curriculum in accordance with principles set forth by the subject committee, together with a specification of aims, major topics, and specific subject matter. The curriculum committee is also responsible for offering general guidelines for the development of study materials. The committee is headed by a specialist in the discipline or an educational specialist, and its members are representatives of the Ministry of Education and Culture, academics, and teachers (two subject teachers, according to the age group). Proposed curricula require endorsement of the subject committee and the chairperson of the Pedagogical Secretariat. When this is obtained, the curricula are forwarded to the inspectors, principals, and teachers who are responsible for implementing them.[39]

The curriculum document is divided into two parts. The first provides a general frame of reference and spells out the aims and principles. This part reflects the policy-makers' perception of the subject and its epistemology, i.e., its place *vis-à-vis* the needs of society and the student. The second part of the curriculum document specifies the subject matter, contents, skills, and expertise that teachers should impart when teaching the subject, bearing in mind the continuum of subject matter and its distribution across the student's school career. The curriculum also specifies a time framework and the number of hours that should be devoted to each particular subject.

Perusal of these documents, which reflect changes in curriculum policy in Israel, points to three main turning points: (1) the first period, from the establishment of the State to 1966, which we shall call the first generation of curriculum-planning policy; (2) the second period, from 1966 to the early 1980s – the second generation of curriculum-planning policy; and (3) the period 1980 to 1992, or the third generation.[40]

It is worth noting that, for principals and teachers, any change in curriculum planning indicated a change in overall educational policy. Such a change was evident both in terms of the curriculum objectives (emphasis on the needs of society as opposed to those of the students) and of principle, involving the identity of the agency entrusted with implementing the policy (center or periphery, Ministry of Education and Culture, or school and community). Each of the policy generations defined above was noted for different emphases on both levels: that of objectives and that of the agencies responsible for carrying them out.

Despite the changes in emphasis in the various periods, education policy-makers were careful to maintain an equilibrium between the conflicting aims of the curriculum (individual versus society) and the clashing agencies (center versus periphery) that were to implement it.[41]

The Curriculum and Education Policy: Complement or Contradiction?

From a socio-historical point of view, curriculum planning is regarded as one of the expressions of the way society and its education systems interrelate. These interrelations are studied and analyzed at various levels, and compatible conceptual frameworks are adopted. At the macro level, Oliver believes that a distinction should be drawn between an industrially oriented social organization, characterized by a predisposition to technological achievement, and a community-oriented organization, based on the values of human relationships.[42] Each of these forms of social organization has effects on the type of education and the curriculum offered by the school. Whereas an industrial-organizational society would probably emphasize children's cognitive abilities and encourage social stratification over scholastic achievement, the community-oriented paradigm would generate educational frameworks that take students' personal needs into account. A study of the relationships between the nature, values, and educational policy of a society would help one understand the processes of educational planning and the phenomena that accompany such processes over time.

If we accept the foregoing arguments, we should expect a curriculum at any particular period to be affected significantly by socio-educational policy. Shevah Eden, a curriculum policy-maker in the 1970s, wrote that the ground-rules for curriculum planning in Israel are based on theories set forth in the professional literature and influenced by the interplay of expectations and curricula on the one hand, and reality and social constraints on the other.[43]

Curriculum researchers discern three periods in the development of curriculum planning in Israel.[44] The first starts with the establishment of the State and ends with the formation of the Curriculum Division in the Ministry of Education and Culture in 1966.

The major purpose of the curriculum in the first period was to· effect an inter-generational transmission of the cultural heritage, a socialization that implied the imparting of the fundamental values of Israeli society to all its social strata, with emphasis on themes to which all were committed. Most of the curricula were uniform and homogeneous; they took no account of the different social needs of the essentially heterogeneous Israeli population. The authors of the curricula were inspectors and senior officials of the Ministry of Education and Culture. The curriculum-planning process was not based on curriculum theories and made no use of formal evaluation strategies. Most curricula lacked detailed guidelines, since teachers were given major responsibilities in teaching. The teachers were expected to plan and devise suitable teaching activities on the basis of textbooks written by inspectors who specialized mainly in instruction, not necessarily in curricula.

These curricula were unquestionably consistent with the elitist educational policies of Israel's first decade. One corollary of this policy was visible in the strict selection procedures used in the transition from primary school to high school, and from class to class within high school. Elitism was evident not only in the characteristics of the curriculum but also in the matriculation examinations. Six external matriculation exams that high-school graduates had to take (depending on the track being tested) created a situation in which only 13 percent of students of Asian-African origin managed to earn the certificate that constituted a passport to university, as compared to 77 percent of European-American origin.[45]

Structural reform and the educational integration policy influenced the curriculum and matriculation exams and ushered in the second period of curriculum planning policy. The declared objectives in this period, which lasted until the late 1970s, were the development of curricula that took into account the differential needs of pupils in a heterogeneous society and the development of curricula on a professional basis, focusing on the "epistemic structure" of the individual subjects. The main manifestations of the social trend in curriculum planning were acknowledgment of the need to teach the cultural creativity of the Jewish people on the basis of the nation's ethnic groups (teaching units in literature that included selections of cultural works by individuals of Asian-African origin) for all Israeli youth,[46] and the desire to improve the scholastic achievement of disadvantaged students by devising suitable study material.

Various curriculum initiatives were invoked to implement the objectives of the education policy: alternative formulations for teaching a specific subject in heterogeneous classes; the publication of booklet-form modular material geared to age groups rather than specific grades, so that identical material could be used in different classes as needed; and finally, the use of the material itself, coupled with the correction of distorted thinking that impedes the learning process.

Significant changes took place at the professional level of curriculum planning. The formulation of curricula was reassigned from inspectors to scholars, who, together with the educators, assumed that the best way to teach a given subject was by using research methods.

Curriculum planning was entrusted to special teams that included American-trained epistemologists and curriculum-development experts. The development process typically attempted to adhere to a planning model based on the approach of Tyler[47] and Bloom,[48] which emphasized the following elements: defining the objectives of the curriculum, developing teaching materials, piloting the teaching materials in the classroom, and formal evaluation of the curriculum. The planners adopted the "epistemic structure" approach and research-based teaching, and attempted to tailor requirements to various target population groups and match the curricula to students' differential needs and aptitudes. The curricula they turned out included a specification of aims, curricular content, and teaching methods, and came with teachers' guides and special in-service training programs in order to ensure sound and successful implementation.

No significant change occurred in the status of teachers when compared to the first period, except for a diminution of teacher discretion due to new developments in the Israeli social situation and in the professional field of curriculum development. In the first period, teachers were handed curricula as finished products that were to be applied in class using the teaching methods that they deemed suitable. In the second period, teachers faced restrictions in both respects: subject matter and teaching methods. From then on, teachers were asked to teach material that the Curriculum Division experts had set forth, using methods that the Curriculum Division experts had set forth. The teachers' latitude in their choice of both the curriculum and the teaching methods was decreased. Consequently, the school inspectors became the agents of change and assumed responsibility for apprising teachers of the change that had occurred. Special guidance publications appealed directly to teachers in an attempt to influence them to adopt the new curricula. "Sometimes I think that the planners are afraid the teachers will become too independent; that's why they ask the teachers to do as they're told."[49]

This development in curriculum planning was perfectly suited to an education policy that espoused integration, heterogeneous classes, and involvement of academic experts in curricula and teaching methods. "Everyone knew that in order to meet pupils' different needs in the best way possible, the aggressive intervention of curriculum development experts was required; [this] could no longer be left to the sole discretion of the teachers."[50]

The era of social openness and the desire to advance the disadvantaged was reflected not only in the curriculum but also in the structure of the matriculation exams. In 1965, the matriculation examinations were restructured again, and two changes of significance to students of Asian-African origin were made: a matriculation certificate in vocational education was introduced, and a State diploma was issued for twelfth-grade graduates who were unable to pass all the matriculation exams. These two innovations were undoubtedly meant to increase the number of secondary school graduates among the disadvantaged.[51] The year 1965 belongs to the transitional period between the era of elitism and that of educational integration. Therefore, alongside measures favoring the disadvantaged, one can find additional strictures that made it difficult for students to complete their high-school studies and earn a matriculation certificate.

The disadvantages of the change seem to have outweighed its advantages. The number of external matriculation exams was reduced from six to five, but two additional internal exams were introduced, and the number of compulsory matriculation subjects did not change. Another problem that encumbered both students and teachers was recognition by the Ministry of Education and Culture of schools' internal evaluations of their pupils, as reflected in report-card marks. Each school that was interested in such recognition (which constituted 50 percent of the final matriculation score) had to demonstrate that at least one-third of its students were eligible for a full matriculation certificate. Consequently, schools would accept only the most promising students and would assign their best teachers to coach the matriculation students. Schools became exceedingly selective and private tutoring in critical subjects such as mathematics and English flourished. The results, however, were contrary to expectations.[52] Perusal of contemporary sources shows that this paradigm came under scathing criticism.[53] It was clearly necessary to modify the matriculation format in order to align it with an educational policy that stressed integration and equal opportunity in education.

Thus, in October, 1972, the late Minister of Education, Yigal Allon, appointed a committee to recommend changes in the spirit of the educational policy of the period.[54] The Ministry received the committee's recommendations in August, 1973, and accepted them. They served as the basis for the following reform principles:

- a distinction between compulsory and elective subjects;
- gradation of the newly formulated curriculum (low, medium, high);
- elimination of the "track" paradigm and introduction of the possibility of combining compulsory and elective subjects at various levels;
- limitation of compulsory subjects to Hebrew, mathematics, and a foreign language;
- spreading the matriculation examinations over the last three post-primary grades;
- downscaling the compulsory material for matriculation exams; and
- award of matriculation certificates to pupils who passed examinations on a minimum level of 20 credits.

The reform undoubtedly aroused hope among many disadvantaged youths of receiving a matriculation certificate. The elimination of tracks, the introduction of electives, and the possibility of choosing the level of difficulty of the examinations, expanded the circles of matriculates and gave many young people access to education settings that promoted social mobility. In response to this liberalization, the universities tightened their entrance requirements, seeking to keep the social interest groups in balance despite the educational integration policy.

The universities began to use a psychometric test, which attracted much criticism for its cultural bias.[55] This test protected the universities from an "undesirable invasion" of students who would not be able to complete their bachelor's degree. A study of the ethnic distribution of students who entered the universities after the reform shows an increase in the number of students of Asian-African origin. However, the linkage of their admission to the results of the psychometric test caused these students to gravitate to disciplines in which a psychometric score of 400–500 points was considered sufficient (the highest possible mark being 800).[56]

In the third period of curriculum planning, which began in 1980 and has continued up to the mid-1990s, significant changes occurred in terms of both the objectives and the agencies meant to implement them. The third period represents the humanistic period in curriculum development, due to its cardinal stress on tailoring curriculum development to the needs of the participants in the educational process: the students, teachers, and parents.

The focal point of curriculum planning in the first period, by virtue of its resources, expertise and comprehensive overview of the system, was the Curriculum Division of the Ministry of Education and Culture; the teacher was responsible for putting theory into practice. Since 1980, the focus of curriculum planning has shifted to the teacher, pursuant to several paradigms that will be examined below. This change coincided with changes in the overall educational policy, which, since 1980, has emphasized teachers' professionalism in the following ways: the adoption of the decisions of the Etzioni Commission;[57] the school autonomy policy, which gave teachers a central role in formulating curricula;[58] and acceptance of the decision of the Reshef Commission,[59] which favored the encouragement of creativity among teachers and pupils by promoting teaching methods that encourage active learning and individualized instruction. One outcome of these changes was the shift of curriculum planning to the teacher. Research findings in Israel and abroad indicate that the quality of teaching materials prepared by teachers was deplorable in most cases, due to the teachers' ignorance of the subject matter. Materials prepared by the teachers cannot be compared to those prepared by experts.[60] The researchers admitted that in view of the insufficient curriculum-development training that teachers had been given in colleges and universities, they could hardly be expected to fulfill the assignment entrusted to them.[61] Dory[62] examined the views of 113 junior-high science teachers concerning the way they viewed their roles as developers of curricula. He found that almost 90 percent preferred ready-made materials to the option of developing their own.

The question facing policy-makers was how to make teachers part of the curriculum planning process without affecting the quality of their product. This question led policy-makers toward the adoption of various versions of the integrated approach. This approach was consistent with a very important principle of an Israeli educational policy that now stands at a crossroads: the principle of equilibrium, the imperative of keeping the needs of the subject and the needs of teachers, and the individual's needs and society's needs, in balance. Any violation of this balance would cause the system to malfunction.

When the Ministry of Education and Culture held all the power, the teachers regarded the monopoly as a slight to their professionalism. When the ministry tended toward a change that would transfer the center of power to the teachers, not only in classroom work but also in curriculum planning, the academics – the subject specialists, joined by the high-ranking officials in the Ministry (who were interested in preserving the Ministry's power) – objected vehemently, arguing that the teachers turned out poor-quality material. Consequently, the curriculum planning policy in the last decade has maintained a basic equilibrium in the relative share of each of the actors involved in curriculum development. All the proposed paradigms regard teachers as partners in curriculum development; the difference between the approaches focuses on the teachers' share in this activity.

With this in mind, the Ministry of Education and Culture set forth three levels of autonomy in curriculum planning:[63] a compulsory curriculum, an elective curriculum assembled from a list drawn up by the Ministry, and an optional curriculum that is implemented in keeping with the discretion of the school administration. Consequently, one may note different degrees of teacher involvement in curriculum development.[64] The teachers' involvement in the compulsory curricula manifests itself in their selection of teaching materials and teaching methods. In other words, the Ministry of Education and Culture is the principal author of the curriculum; teachers use materials that have been elaborated, choose solutions that they deem suitable, and transform these into teaching and learning situations. In the elective subjects, teachers present curricula developed by external agents but are able to carry on a dialogue with the curriculum developers, make comments, and tailor the curricula to their needs.[65] The teachers of optional curricula are able to select ready-made programs or develop subjects and topics that are not connected to existing available material. The optional curriculum permits and fosters local curriculum-development initiatives meant to meet the special needs of schools and communities.

Since 1995, the Ministry of Education and Culture has promoted school autonomy and has encouraged school staff, aided by experts in the relevant subjects, to develop school curricula. Because only a few schools have taken up this challenge thus far,[66] several avenues of curriculum development have taken shape: the autonomous teacher-consumer, who, after reviewing existing curricula and packages of teaching materials, chooses several and fashions them into his or her own personal curriculum that meets students' needs; or the teacher who develops teaching materials independently, especially in subjects for which off-the-shelf material has not been prepared. Such teachers follow the curriculum orientations, principles, and objectives set forth by the Ministry of Education and Culture. The third path is followed by teachers who devise and develop curricula of their own, on the basis of which teaching materials are prepared.[67] Schools that have chosen this third path (as a growing number have, according to figures provided by the Ministry of Education and Culture) are thereby expressing their willingness to take responsibility for the results of their actions, and tackle the changing needs of their surroundings.

The educational policy of shifting the focal point of curriculum development from the center to the periphery has also been evident with respect to matriculation exams. In July 1979, the then Minister of Education Zevulun Hammer, appointed a committee to submit recommendations on the contents and status of the matriculation exams.[68] The committee, chaired by Professor Ozer Schild of the University of Haifa, reached the conclusion that the matriculation exams should not be abolished but that the number of external exams should be reduced. In 1986, another step toward reducing the importance of the external exams and increasing that of the internal exams was taken.[69]

In 1992, the Minister of Education appointed two committees to deal with this matter: an internal committee headed by the Chair of the Pedagogical Secretariat, and a committee under Professor Ben Peretz of the University of Haifa. The two committees are considering a further reduction in the importance of the external matriculation examinations and may recommend the separation of success in matriculation examinations and admission to university.[70] If the committees reach the conclusion that the number of external matriculation exams should be reduced to a maximum of three and that schools should be allowed to draft their own exams in the other subjects, the implementation of such a policy would be consistent with the school autonomy policy that has existed since the start of the decade.

Conclusion

The policy of maintaining equilibrium among the contradictory goals of the Ministry of Education and Culture policy-makers is also evident in curriculum policy. Compulsory curricula remain, but they are coupled with elective and optional curricula, which are innovations when compared with the policy in Israel's first two decades. There is a "center" that wishes to ensure that all important subjects are taught to all segments of the population, but there are subjects that this "center" is prepared to allow the school and school staff to develop by themselves, thereby bolstering the teachers' professional power. The "center" is willing to serve as a service agent that advises schools in the development of their own curricula and markets these curricula, insofar as it accepts them, to other schools.[71] Contrary to the trend toward openness that characterizes the policy of the Ministry of Education on this issue, there has, since 1988, been a reverse process in England and the United States, which are famous for their decentralized structure. In these countries, education policy-makers are reclaiming control over the curricula, much to the teachers' displeasure.[72]

7

Education Policy in Israel: Toward the Millennium

Israeli education policy has wavered between change and continuity, with the guiding principle being the desire of policy-makers to keep the expectations of various social interest groups in equilibrium. This equilibrium is between devotees of the egalitarian approach to education and proponents of elitism, between the needs of State education and the needs of State–Religious education, between the demands of advocates of academic and advocates of technological education, between supporters of centralization and supporters of decentralization in curriculum planning.

The desire to maintain equilibrium is an outgrowth of the pluralistic nature of Israeli society: different ethnic groups, different values, and different beliefs. Education policy-makers regarded this as the only way to protect the country's delicate social fabric from the pressures of diverse interests. As long as the social equilibrium was maintained without significant disruption (as in the 1950s and the early 1960s), education policy-makers did not believe that the system required major structural changes. However, when the social equilibrium was thrown off significantly (as manifested, for instance, in major disparities in scholastic achievement between those of Asian-African and those of European origin), and the education system did not deliver a suitable remedy for the socioeconomic problems that arose, a crisis erupted, at which point the policy-makers decided to reform the education system.

Reform in education means radical change, possibly by means of legislation, in the structure of the system, the curriculum, and the social power relations within the system, in an effort to improve achievements. Even when the decision to carry out a reform by going to a 6–3–3 structure was made, social interest groups made sure to introduce checks that would keep the reform from tilting the pendulum in the opposite direction. The purpose of these checks was to prevent a situation in which the side that had faced discrimination (the weak, peripheral classes) would benefit from advantages that would lead to discrimination against the other side (the mainstream social classes), in other words, to make sure that the reform, which was supposed to help the disadvantaged, would not harm the advantaged. The policy-makers introduced two checks of this type: granting local authorities the discretion to choose the timing (if any) and methods of implementation of the reform, and allowing tracking in junior-high schools, which made social and scholastic integration difficult to achieve.

Chapter 4 explained that the decision to carry out the reform met with much displeasure. The Teachers' Union complained that it had not been included in the decision-making. It also feared loss of membership, because seventh- and eighth-grade teachers, now facing reassignment to post-primary education, would join the rival Secondary Schoolteachers' Union. The kibbutzim were not happy with the decision for reasons of ideological elitism. The religious school system had objective reasons to dislike the decision, but it also opposed the reform for reasons of ideological elitism. A majority of State–Religious (SR) students were disadvantaged, and the significance of the integration policy for the SR system was the busing of students to out-of-town schools. Busing was opposed by parents, who preferred to enroll their children in State (secular) schools rather than in religious schools far from home. This would reduce enrollment in the religious school system. The State–Religious system also opposed the reform for reasons of ideological elitism, as shown by its tacit acceptance of the growth of the No'am network and the accelerated development of yeshiva high schools and *ulpenot*. Groups of elitist parents opposed the reform for fear that it would lead to mediocrity in the education system.

Because of the many opponents, the education policy-makers at the time settled for a vaguely-worded decision, in which commitment to carry out the reform was not unequivocal and differing interpretations were given much latitude. By granting local authorities freedom of action in carrying out the reform, the central government showed that it would rather let them be the ones to fight it out with the opponents of the plan. Out of an obligation to their constituents, the local officials preferred not to rush to carry out a controversial policy. The 1975 law prescribing the direct election of mayors[1] caused even more problems for local officials who wanted to support the reform, because they were afraid that their voters did not favor the new policy and would express their disagreement on election day. (Consider the incident involving Hananya Gibstein, attorney and former mayor of Rishon Lezion.)[2]

Opposition to the reform decision, which led to a vague policy, explains better than anything else why the reform was implemented in only half of Israeli localities, and why several junior-high schools introduced special classes[3] and tracking as ways of circum-venting the integration decree. The SR system evaded integration by lending its tacit consent to the existence of the selective No'am school system. However, the education budget for junior-high schools, the jewel in the crown of the reform, was slashed by 7 percent instead of being increased as the reform policy warranted.

The director of the Educational Welfare Division of the Ministry of Education and Culture found that Ramat Hasharon, a town with a very low share of disadvantaged, was given a larger welfare budget than the strongly disadvantaged Ajami quarter of Jaffa.[4] However, the research teams that evaluated the reform did not recommend eliminating it. The reform actually managed to increase the enrollment rates of some Asian-African origin groups. Furthermore, in localities where the reform had been carried out as prescribed, it led to impressive matriculation scores. The best example of this is Kefar Sava, where the municipal education administration decided to scatter graduates of primary schools among four local junior-high schools on the basis of scholastic achievement, while upholding the principle of integration. The students expressed satisfaction with this policy, and their scores on matriculation examinations indicated that it was a success.[5]

Nevertheless, two questions remain to be answered: How can we explain the fact that, despite the funds invested in development towns to improve scholastic achievement (indeed, per-capita expenditure on education did rise), the achievement-test scores there were among the worst in the country? The results of matriculation examinations painted a similar picture, which was confirmed by the former chief scientist of the Ministry of Education and Culture: "In the development towns, two-thirds [of students either] do not make it to the matriculation examinations or do not pass them."[6] According to another statistic, the gap between the number of matriculation-certificate eligibles of European-American origin and Asian-African origin failed to narrow even after the reform was carried out.[7] This finding makes the questions posed above even more salient. In interviews with twenty senior officials in the Ministry of Education and Culture, some (25 per cent) explained the situation in a way consistent with the findings of Coleman (1966) in the United States, asserting that ethnicity and home life have a greater influence on children's achievements than does the school. Others (20 percent) had no explanation. The majority (55 percent), however, were convinced that scholastic results depend on many factors, including how the resources given to the schools are used. Most of the respondents said that numerous studies done in the United States provide a research basis for this.

American studies indicate clearly that schools perform well in terms of scholastic achievement when their budgets are invested directly in improving teaching and learning, and in hiring good teachers – and vice-versa. When the education resources are used to cover administrative expenses and are not spent directly on the quality of teachers and teaching, scholastic achievement is poor.[8] In a nutshell, these findings tell us that the success of education reform depends not only on structural changes and added resources, but also, and mainly, on how these resources are apportioned within the education system. The more that is spent on higher-quality teaching and learning, the more productive the school will be. Several examples from the Israeli experience that reinforce this argument follow.

The general comprehensive school in Hatsor Hagelilit (a small development town in the Galilee) was known for poor scholastic achievements in biology. A joint initiative by the school administration and the district facilitator located a good teacher; as a result of her efforts and collaboration with the facilitator and the school administration, the school became the country's leading achiever in this subject.[9] Mathematics achievements in the comprehensive schools of Sederot, Ofaqim, and Netivot (development towns in the south of Israel) were among the worst in the country. After the Science Teaching Department at the Weizmann Institute introduced a special intervention program for teaching of mathematics in these schools, the number of pupils who passed the matriculation examination in mathematics tripled.[10]

Nevertheless, because the structural reform did not meet all expectations, it attracted public criticism led by those who had opposed it from the start. Education policy-makers have listened attentively to the criticism. The poor achievement test results, the stagnation of matriculation success rates, and the gap between implementation of the reform and its shapers' intentions led to the conclusion that the integration policy was merely lip service for the cause of equality, a fig leaf that did nothing for the classes that it was meant to help.[11] The Ministry of Education and Culture administration did not have the courage to accept reality and undo the reform, since the public would have construed such a step as an admission of failure and a breach of the principle of social equilibrium. However, continued support of the reform at any price seems ridiculous in view of its social and scholastic results. The Ministry of Education and Culture administration therefore chose a policy of inaction, comprised of numerous assertions about continued integration, along with tacit consent to local or school initiatives that did not conform to the reform policy. In this fashion, the ministry tried to satisfy everyone. We observed something similar in chapter 4; the following examples substantiate this assertion.

Former Minister of Education Zevulun Hammer, sponsor of the Free Secondary Education Law, wished to aid the weak social classes and increase the post-primary enrollment of students from these classes. Hammer was aware that the socially advantaged would also benefit from the law and that, for this reason, the scholastic gap between the social classes would not change. Nevertheless, he asked his cabinet colleagues to support his bill, if only out of loyalty to the policy of trying to please everyone.

Hammer, who initiated the extended school day program and provided a budget to implement this policy in disadvantaged areas, continued to accept the cutbacks in public expenditure on education (including the integrated junior-high schools) and the increase in families' share in education funding through the gray education mechanism. Hammer even supported the coexistence of integrated junior-high schools, new special-curriculum schools, and special classes in the integrated schools. He favored the reinforcement of technological education, but took the initiative to appoint the Harari committee and instructed it to promote scientific-technological education, even though the committee's recommendations might spell the nullification of technological education in its present form. In an attempt to preserve the principle of equilibrium, Hammer unveiled a five-year plan to promote education in the Arab sector, entailing a substantial increase in education budgets for this sector to equalize its level with that of the Jewish sector. Here, too, a gap developed between policy and implementation.

The "satisfy-everyone" education policy was also manifested in the curriculum. The policy stipulated compulsory curricula, designed by the Education Ministry, in order to satisfy inspectors who advocated centralization and uniformity, and optional courses, designed partially or completely by schools, in order to satisfy the devotees of decentralization and school autonomy. Hammer's violation of the principle of equilibrium between the State and State–Religious school systems, by reallocating funds in order to reinforce the teaching of religious subjects in the schools, elicited a counter-reaction with the change in government. The new Education Minister, Shulamit Aloni, set out to harm the essential interests of State–Religious education by recomputing budgets by number of classes rather than number of pupils (even though pupil-based budgeting is more efficient).[12] Following pressure on the Prime Minister by the Meimad movement, this policy was suspended.[13] It transpires, then, that most changes in education policy since the establishment of Israel have been incremental and gradual, because any revolutionary change that might move the pendulum in any given direction would subsequently move it back to the point of equilibrium.

The foregoing makes one ask: Does the policy of satisfying everyone and preserving the status quo not, in the end, make the system less efficient and less able to meet society's future needs? Doesn't society pay for this equilibrium by having an education system that operates at a lower level, a system less capable of coping with worldwide economic changes? Is it not possible to have all three: socio-educational integration, scholastic excellence, and system efficiency? I shall examine these questions below, in view of trends that are already visible in the education policies of the present Government, and in view of developments in education policy in the Western world.

It is no secret that the education systems of the West are on the verge of collapse, having failed to keep up with the pace of technological, economic, and social change. Evidence of this includes poor scholastic achievement, ineffective schools, and high rates of teacher burnout and student dropout. Educational disparities between the socioeconomically advantaged and disadvantaged are widening, and many countries are groping for remedies.[14] Various countries have tried frequent education reforms, but no unequivocal solutions have been found. The quest for a good solution embraces all the Western countries, including Israel.

Policy Trends

Examination of the policies of the Ministry of Education and Culture administration and the Knesset Education Committee reveals a fundamental change in the philosophy of education in Israel. The decentralization trend that developed since 1985, which diverts the focus of power from the center (the Ministry of Education and Culture) to the periphery (schools and communities) will undoubtedly receive greater emphasis.

The reform plan known by the name of its sponsor, Shimshon Shoshani, Director-General of the Ministry of Education and Culture, is essentially a summary of ideas published in 1983 by John Goodlad, an American professor of education.[15] The plan rests on several assumptions:[16]

1. The gap between cumulative knowledge in various fields of psychology and the reality in the schools, as expressed in subject matter and teaching methods, is widening. Consequently, parents and students are dissatisfied with the performance of the schools. Parents demand more and more of their schools and wish to influence the quality of education services provided.
2. Unlike in the past, much learning is taking place outside school and is unrelated to the subject matter taught in school. As a result, teachers, who are exposed to criticism from all sides, feel frustrated and unneeded, and this feeling causes good teachers to leave the profession.
3. Budget cuts give teachers a sense of impotence when they try to implement changes and perform the tasks for which they were hired. These budget cuts make it difficult to narrow gaps between socioeconomically advantaged and disadvantaged students.
4. Since Israel was founded, its education system has fallen into patterns of rigidity that frustrate efforts to effect meaningful change.

Consequently, the Shoshani plan prescribes a holistic reform that would embrace all parts of the system and be completed in no more than eight years. Its major objectives are excellence, which means having high expectations of teachers and pupils and providing the tools to achieve these expectations, and adherence to the efficiency principle.

The comprehensive system reform that Shoshani wishes to implement would be carried out at several levels simultaneously:

The structural level: There would be four school divisions instead of the three that exist today. Children would start school at the age of 4, the age of cognitive maturity. Students would be allowed to graduate high school at 16. Top students would be able to complete post-secondary education at 19. This structure is more efficient, since it saves the system two years of high school as compared with the present structure.

The content and process level: There would be two types of curricula: compulsory curricula set forth at a country-wide level, and optional curricula designed by the school. The content and breadth of the curriculum would take into account the stages of pupils' cognitive development, permit diversity in teaching and learning methods in keeping with pupils' needs, and include foreign-language instruction and science and technology courses beginning in early childhood.

School autonomy would transfer the focus of decision-making and education from the center to the periphery. Principals and faculty members would design courses, formulate schools' education policies in conjunction with community representatives, and act to implement and evaluate the policies chosen. Teachers and administrators would be accountable for the results of their work. Schools would be orientated toward scholastic achievement. Pupils would be allowed to learn at their own pace; criteria would be set for measuring the success of teachers and rewarding teachers who excel. To develop "school pride," schools would be instructed to specialize in specific values (Jewish studies, Labor Movement values) or subjects (e.g., music or science). Parents would have the option of choosing their children's school, thus encouraging competition between schools and ensuring the survival of the most effective.

Because the revolutionary Shoshani plan threatens to shatter the equilibrium among social interest groups, it has aroused very strong opposition as well as reserved support. The most vociferous opponents have called for abolishing social integration and backtracking on the academic and social achievements of integration. This argument is heard chiefly from the Teachers' Union;[17] the Secondary Schoolteachers' Union has neither opposed nor supported the plan.[18] The social lobby in the Knesset considers the Shoshani plan an assault on everything that has been accomplished for the disadvantaged thus far, i.e., post-primary and higher education and access to social mobility. Academicians are divided. Some are enthusiastic about the plan, which coincides with their socio educational world-view;[19] others oppose it because of concern for the fate of integration if the enrollment-district system is breached.[20] Interestingly, even supporters of the plan, such as the then Education Minister Aloni, have taken exception to the breach of enrollment districts, fearing that this may scuttle the integration policy that meets the needs of the disadvantaged. This, however, did not keep Aloni from supporting the other components of the plan.[21] The controversy surrounding the Shoshani plan centers on the following points:

The age aspect: Having children start school at age 4 would increase the danger that children would lose all interest in creativity, games, art, and music. Parents of children who do not acquire literacy skills at age 4 would hire private tutors, to the irreversible detriment of the disadvantaged. The epicenter of the growing experience would move in the direction of achievement.

The age of 11 is too early to choose a post-primary curriculum; it would primarily reflect the parents' scholastic leanings, not necessarily those of the child.

Advancing high-school graduation to age 16 would increase unemployment and crime among teenagers who do not wish to attend college and who would have two years to wait before induction.[22]

The choice aspect: Might there not be the danger that parents would choose schools on the basis of their image, rather than their child's aptitudes and needs? Might the selection be made in reality by schools, and not by parents? What would happen to students who are rejected? Would a setting that suits their needs be found? Might different levels of schools, ranked by children's socioeconomic status, come into being?

Advocates of the Shoshani plan believe that controlled parental choice will ensure the maintenance of integration in post-primary schooling. Is it really possible to supervise the schools and prevent their selecting pupils based on ethnic or socioeconomic background? Furthermore, parents who choose from a list of several schools would not be making a true choice, because the demand for certain schools would exceed the number of places available. Thus many parents (especially the disadvantaged) would have to settle for the schools in lower demand (chiefly the scholastically poorer schools).

Education research has shown that schools which manage to retain the best pupils contribute indirectly to improving the level of weaker students, because the high achievers set their classmates an example which serves to pull the weaker ones up. Students who leave their communities in order to attend prestigious out-of-town schools also progress, while their former classmates who do not leave do not advance.[23] Consequently, one remains concerned that parental choice might empty some schools of their better pupils.

These observations bring several questions to the fore. Will the criticism of Shoshani's reform plan cause the plan to be abandoned, in which case we may expect a continuation of the status quo and social equilibrium policy that the education system has evinced for the past 20 years? Alternatively, are we about to witness an unprecedented revolutionary breakthrough in education? Will the Director-General of the Ministry of Education and Culture be able to marshall political and social backing for his plan?

Although the Shoshani plan has not yet been accepted as binding Government policy, a review of the present state of Israeli education shows that much of the plan has already been adopted by several local authorities, the best known of them being Tel Aviv, Ramat Hasharon, and Givatayim.

The Research Perspective

Israel's future education policy, proposed today by policy-makers, has come up for debate as part of the public agenda. Some favor this policy as a remedy for the ills of the Israeli education system. Others support it as a way to disengage from the status quo that has prevailed in the education system for the past 25 years. The opponents, on the other hand, stress the menace that the plan poses for educational integration.

The main disagreement in Israeli public opinion, as elsewhere in the world, revolves around parental choice and the establishment of super-regional schools. Research literature shows that the controversy exists in other countries as well, including the United States and Great Britain,[24] for the following reasons:

1. As with all issues that have an ideological element, parental choice is based on values. Parental choice is a fundamentally democratic act, but it can have undemocratic consequences, such as social segregation.[25]

2. This policy is being promoted for many diverse motives, both by various groups within a country and among countries. A study in the United States suggests several rationales for and against parental choice. Some regard it chiefly as an exercise in democracy; others believe it can reverse the decline in scholastic achievement.[26] Some regard parental choice as a way to empower teachers professionally,[27] since parents would choose the schools with the best teachers. Others see it as a way to improve racial integration,[28] and still others favor it as a means of rejuvenating education systems and shattering the massive administrative apparatus that the bureaucracy has built up.[29]

Parental choice in Great Britain, introduced in 1982 and reinforced by the 1988 education act, was meant to solve the problem of the economic inefficiency of small schools. The British administration found that parental choice would create large schools and lead to the closure of small schools.[30] Certain members of Parliament, however, favored this policy as a way of reducing the power of the Labor Party in local education authorities.[31]

Parental choice in the Netherlands, on the other hand, is part of the liberal ideology expressed in Section 23 of the relevant legislation,[32] and has nothing to do with school efficiency.

Parental choice in France was introduced in 1959 by legislation named for then-Prime Minister Michel Debré. The primary motivation for the law was economic, since its framers saw it as a way of coping with the great demand for education and the attendant increase in public expenditure for this item. The policy-makers hoped that the law would ease the burden on the public coffers and increase the burden on the parents.[33] The "Debré law" allows parents to choose between a regular public school (supported entirely by the state) and a private school that enters into a special contract with the state, in which the school receives some public funding in exchange for partial state supervision of teacher quality and certain parts of the curriculum. The data show that many citizens have selected the second option and sent their children to supported private schools.[34]

3. How strongly can a parental-choice policy help improve school quality and social integration? The research findings are not unequivocal. Bolstering our arguments is the statement by

American researcher Richard Elmore that we lack sufficient knowledge about the impact of various choice programs on the education system as a whole. Elmore agrees that the findings are not unequivocal. Furthermore, even the existing structure of education offers choice, since affluent parents may purchase supplementary education services directly or move to neighborhoods in which schools are considered "good."[35]

Most of the research findings on the efficacy of policies of parental choice of schools are based on case studies; few are culled from comprehensive surveys. Most of the studies are theoretical, with few probability studies. Several findings nevertheless exist that can give an indication of the type of future education policy to which we should aspire. A survey of 243 studies conducted in the United States of the efficiency and effectiveness of an education policy based on parental choice allows the following conclusions: schools that were exposed to parental choice had higher achievements and lower dropout rates, both parents and pupils felt greater commitment to the school, parents were more involved, and the schools were more receptive to public criticism.

One may wonder whether these findings, which suggest that parental choice is effective, may be caused by the composition of the student body and the vast resources invested in these schools. The research suggests that we can answer the first part of the question in the affirmative. Parental choice has led to differentiation between schools, not only in achievement but also socially. As for the second part of the question, Sosmiak and Ethington claim that no differences in inputs exist between closed-enrollment and open-enrollment schools.[36] If this argument is accepted, it is legitimate to say that the main contribution of parental choice to school effectiveness has to do with the students' socioeconomic status. If this is so, would a policy of parental choice in education be detrimental to the weaker social classes?

The research findings on these questions are not unequivocal. Several studies, such as the project in East Harlem, indicate that parental choice has a strongly favorable effect on the scholastic achievements of disadvantaged pupils.[37] Other studies lead to opposite findings.[38] Researchers agree, however, that parental choice may possibly encourage social segregation, even if the local community is not enthusiastic about integration and gives school administrations sole discretion in the selection of pupils. Studies in Britain and the Netherlands corroborate this position.[39] Thus, an education policy that encourages parental choice is not immune to segregation; it may offer the privileged significant advantages and thereby disrupt the social equilibrium, unless it meets the following criteria: controlled choice; establishment of information centers that apprise all parents, including minorities, of the available educational options; a role for parents in setting the curriculum; and a variety of curricula that meet the needs of weak pupils as well.[40]

Several American states have introduced controlled choice. A project carried out in Massachusetts has attracted special attention,[41] although there have been less successful efforts elsewhere.[42] All of the controlled-choice programs are similar. The community decides on a list of schools from which parents may choose. Each is made into a "magnet school" and is required to offer a unique and attractive curriculum, options for advancement and success, and proposals for advancing weaker students. Each school is autonomous, with a public council that works alongside the administration, selects the faculty, and gives it backing. The council even helps the school "sell" itself. Schools that operate according to the controlled-choice model permit parental choice to a point, forcing the parents to list first, second, and third preferences in their choice of school. They also inform parents that the final decision on placement of their children must conform to a policy that seeks to prevent racial and socioeconomic segregation.

An analysis of the efforts made in various U.S. localities has found positive results for controlled choice in terms of scholastic achievement, parental satisfaction with the school, and equality.[43] The success of controlled choice in several U.S. states raises the question of whether this paradigm can be duplicated in Israel. I shall consider this question below.

Education Policy in Israel: Where To?

A glance at the 1953 State Education Law makes it clear that the legislators were trying to balance conflicting educational goals: equality and the possibility of elitism (with an emphasis on achievement); parental choice among different types of education and the parental right to determine one-quarter of the curriculum on the one hand, and compulsory education with non-discretionary enrollment districts on the other. The essential question is: will this system of checks and balances continue to exist, and to what extent is this system desirable? The maintenance of an education policy based on checks and balances means the perpetuation of the status quo and the ossification of the education system. Overhauling the education system, in contrast, means amending the law and taking risks (possibly coupled with opportunities). It is not clear how willing Israeli society is to take risks when the prospects are ambiguous.

An analysis of Israeli education policy in the past 20 years shows that efforts to reform the system have sought, in the main, to solve the system's dysfunctions by tackling the socioeconomic problems of the country at large. Because the product of education is measured in the long term and, by and large, in terms of scholastic achievement, it is difficult to judge whether the education system reforms effected thus far have solved the problems in the fashion intended. Since 1965, programs meant to modify the education system have been based either on other countries' efforts that had been somewhat successful at solving problems similar to those of Israeli education (e.g., the Shoshani plan), or on evidence of the probability (based on partial information) that the proposed change may solve academic and/or social crises, e.g., the integration policy.

In contrast, an analysis of the content of the proposed changes in the education system in the past 20 years has shown that the basis for the changes proposed by education policy-makers, either at the macro level (the structural reform) or at the micro level (curriculum changes), has been primarily ideological/political. The ideological basis for the integration policy is a belief in equal opportunity as a preferred value. The ideological basis of Shoshani's education policy, in contrast, is connected with the economic philosophy of "market mechanisms," which may be construed as belief in economic efficiency as a preferred value or liberal faith as a preferred value. Because values are part of every education policy, preference of any particular policy is a value judgment. Curriculum policy may be analyzed according to the same criteria. A centralized, uniform curriculum may be interpreted as a value expression of national socialization, whereas a decentralized, pluralistic curriculum may indicate preference of the value of freedom.

An analysis of the sources also shows that Israeli education policy-makers have invoked one of two strategies when dealing with crises in the education system. The first is incremental change and avoidance of shocks to the social status quo. An example is the formal-equality policy of the 1950s and the differential resource allocation of the early 1960s. When these policies failed to improve the scholastic and social results of education, policy-makers decided to contend with the socio-educational crisis using shock treatment: the reform of the late 1960s. The framers of the reform hoped in this fashion to integrate Israel's social classes and improve the scholastic achievements of the disadvantaged. These two objectives were pretentious and led to unrealistic expectations.

This book has shown that the reform has been implemented only partially and has not been treated kindly by the research findings.[44] The testimony of a former chief scientist at the Ministry of Education and Culture indicates that proclamations about the centrality of integration as a goal of the education system do not stand the test of reality.[45] The schools direct weak and mediocre students to non-prestigious tracks, and the transition from junior- to senior-high schools is coupled with a high dropout rate.

A former Director-General of the Ministry of Education and Culture, Eliezer Shmueli,[46] revealed that full implementation of the reform was thwarted by actions taken by five groups: the kibbutz movement, religious organizations, the Teachers' Union, the Finance Ministry, and parental interest groups. Even in localities where the reform was carried out, it was not implemented in full and teachers found various ways to circumvent it by means of tracking or special classes.[47] The findings of Resh *et al.* indicate that junior-high school teachers are less optimistic about the prospects of successful social integration than their colleagues in primary and high schools.[48] In other words, the shock-treatment strategy became nothing but another incremental change, along the lines of those of the 1950s and 1960s.

There is no doubt that the reform policy of the late 1960s could have provided the momentum for a revolution in the Israeli education system had it included pre-school and primary school as well as the junior-high school. This would have required the consent of the major interest groups, endorsement by the Teachers' Union, the requisite human and physical resources for full implementation, and implementation throughout the education system simultaneously after a specified trial period.

Since the early 1980s, education policy-makers have followed in the wake of events in the schools instead of initiating or guiding education policy. The reason has to do with their inability to make decisions in an environment of conflicting pressures from social interest groups, each representing a different outlook and values. Continued implementation of the reform policy in all local authority jurisdictions is not realistic. To acknowledge that the reform has failed would be too bold a step for the policy-makers to take, since the public might interpret it as a failure for which a political price should be paid.

Criticism of integration in the Knesset plenum and the Knesset Education Committee made it difficult for the Education Ministry administration to carry on with its routine work. The education policy-makers were shocked to find that the intervention programs (group teaching, integrated classes), in which large sums of money had been invested, did not produce the expected results. Even if the immediate effect of these programs had been positive, teachers reverted to the old methods as soon as the ministry's facilitators left.[49] The national achievement tests sounded alarm bells in policy-making and public circles alike; they showed that the education system was not functioning. A country founded on the values of the melting pot and socialism could not favor privatization of the education system. Under these circumstances, the education policy-makers preferred to establish public committees – a school autonomy committee, a committee to study the integration policy (known as the Justice Aloni committee), the Kashti committee – to work out the problems and keep public pressure at bay. Forming the committees also made it possible to avoid all initiative at the local and/or school levels and treat realities with tacit consent. It was in this spirit that the Ministry of Education and Culture administration responded so feebly to the emergence of "gray education" and special-curriculum schools. Changes made by the Tel Aviv education system met with displeasure on the part of the previous Ministry of Education and Culture administration. Local authorities have been seizing the initiative in education and making changes without central government permission (the most prominent examples being Ofaqim and Tel Aviv).[50]

Under these circumstances, faced with loss of control over local educational initiatives, the Ministry of Education and Culture administration has decided to modify its centralization policy and shift the focus of power from the center to the periphery, i.e., to the schools. As detailed in earlier chapters, the Teachers' Union took exception to this idea because it feared losing control over its own locals. The Ministry of Education inspectors regarded school decentralization and autonomy as the first step toward the dilution of their functions and power. In fact, the primary schools (those that took part in the project) were given autonomy only in pedagogical affairs;[51] whereas school autonomy is also, and primarily, supposed to entail decision-making in matters of finance, hiring, and firing. Autonomy at the post-primary level included administrative matters as well.

The question facing education policy-makers remains how to ensure excellence and equality at the same time. Excellence and efficiency are essential if the system is to meet its need for high-level, skilled personnel. The system needs equality as a fig leaf that it can offer to a society divided by wide educational gaps; this is also a statement of loyalty to the ideology of the founders of the State. The six committees that were either formed or extended by then Education Minister Shulamit Aloni (although chosen by her predecessor) are proof that the system is groping for solutions to its problems and is seeking ways to resolve the value conflicts of various sectors of society. The plan propounded by the incumbent director-general, Dr Shoshani, is another attempt to resolve the two crises.

The present administration of the Ministry of Education and Culture is attempting to liberate the system from the status quo, even at the price of carrying out a plan about which research findings in the United States and Great Britain have not been particularly complimentary. One may question the advisability of adopting a plan that is so controversial abroad as the future policy of Israel. Will it harm the country's delicate social fabric? Because it has not been endorsed as policy or put into practice, only time will tell whether this is indeed the solution to the woes of the Israeli education system. Clearly, continuation of the present policy – a policy of the status quo, of rigidity, of "followership" instead of leadership – may cause the system to retreat rather than progress in today's rapidly changing world. Current realities require change and political backing for change. The social equilibrium that was created with the implementation of the social integration policy has already moved far from the center ground. Because the previous educational policy did not prove itself, a systemic change may ensure improved performance and meet the system's needs on both the social and the scholastic planes.

Social psychology research shows that true integration occurs when the two sides that come into social contact are similar in status.[52] This means that the success of social integration depends on improving the scholastic achievements, self-image, and social status of the disadvantaged. Forced integration has not attained these social and scholastic goals to any significant degree.[53] Teachers' salaries have risen slightly, but it is not clear whether their social status has improved. The pedagogic effort invested in the integrated junior-high schools has not produced the desired results. If this is so, how can we ensure excellence alongside equality, reduce teacher burnout, and make sure that pedagogic programs in which effort has been invested will bear fruit? This is the question to be studied in future research.

Education System Reform

A proposal for reform, made by Shoshani, is based on the following assumptions:

1. A high-quality education system requires pedagogic personnel who believe in quality and aspire to achieve it. To this end, the pedagogic personnel must be on a high professional level. The professional literature argues that it is possible to acquire professional skill by means of higher education in specific subjects (mathematics, literature, etc.) as well as through clinical pedagogic training.[54] The research also attributes great importance to in-service training both within the school framework and outside it. To ensure the professionalism of teaching personnel, teachers and schools should be given autonomy in designing courses and initiating new teaching projects. The autonomous school will be accountable for its activity and teachers will be responsible for the results of their work.
2. Professional personnel should be remunerated as warranted by their level. A transfer of financial autonomy to schools would enable them to compensate teachers who take initiatives and display excellence.
3. Publicizing school activities and achievements will increase efficiency, boost public confidence in the schools, and increase demand for their services.
4. Schools that wish to improve integration and scholastic achievement simultaneously must specialize in some respect, offer programs to advance both weak and strong pupils, and invest their resources in teaching and learning, not just on administration.[55]
5. Research shows that commitment and involvement in school

life are the results of choice of school. A school that offers attractive programs for weak students should receive commensurate financial compensation. A school that achieves superior results on the cognitive and other agreed-upon levels should receive additional bonuses from the State. The added revenues will allow the school administration to provide scholarships for outstanding students, thus permitting students of low and high socioeconomic level homes to learn side by side. Similarly, school revenue will enable the administration to increase teaching hours for weak pupils, thus improving their achievements.[56]

6. An Israeli education researcher, Rachel Elboim-Dror, argues[57] that the ability of an organization to withstand pressure groups is greater the more united and functional the organization is. A school with greater unity is therefore more stable against pressure. Hence,[58] the autonomous school will be more stable against pressures which conflict with its educational policy, because the teachers in it will be united.

7. School autonomy enables schools to set independent policy makes it easier for them to adjust to environmental changes and thereby increases their ability to stand.

In view of these basic assumptions, education system reform seems to be urgently needed – not only to extricate the system from its current stagnation but also, and primarily, to improve the system's economic and social functionality in an era of rapid environmental change.

To permit schools to carry out the necessary changes, the education system should be decentralized and the focus of power moved from the center to the periphery, i.e., to communities and schools.

The school administration should be supported by a public council comprised of community representatives, which would help the administration set education policy, determine priorities in keeping with community needs, and marshall the resources needed to implement the policy chosen. Schools should reflect the social composition of their communities.

Each school should develop its educational creed and specialization. In view of the high cost of developing specific-discipline specialization, most development of this type should focus on values rather than scholastic disciplines.

Parents should choose among schools in their area of residence (enrollment districts can be enlarged). Super-regional parental choice may indeed create social segregation that the education system will be unable to prevent. One should note that super-regional choice separates youngsters from their surroundings and friends in the community, creating estrangement and destroying their feeling of belonging. Regional parental choice would force schools to become more efficient, diversify their curricula, and show accountability *vis-à-vis* their customers.

The autonomous school of the future should design its own curriculum, review it, and modify it as needed; develop varied teaching methods commensurate with students' needs; and monitor student achievements. The autonomous school can also reward teachers who excel.

The central government would have several roles to play in this structure:

- It would set forth a minimum required curriculum for country-wide use, which would ensure national cohesiveness in Hebrew language, mathematics, foreign languages, and Jewish history.
- It would exercise control by administering achievement tests and monitoring the enforcement of education laws.
- It would serve as a headquarters for guidance and in-service training. Schools would be entitled to acquire guidance and in-service course material from alternative sources as well, provided that they meet the educational standards.
- It would finance schools on a per-capita basis, along with supplementary benefits for schools with a high percentage of disadvantaged pupils. The Education Ministry would also reward schools that excel.

Teachers would be state employees as they are today, but school administrators would be responsible for hiring and firing, on the basis of rules of professional ethics that the Teachers' Union would accept.

As professionals, teachers at all levels of education should hold degrees or teaching certificates. They should be required to participate in general and school-level in-service activities and should be accountable for the results of their work.

The education system should be restructured using a four-level paradigm:

Early childhood ages 4–7.

There is no doubt that readiness for school begins before age 5. Studies have shown that efforts on behalf of children from disadvantaged families, if made at the early-childhood stage, pay off in the long term and prevent the subsequent classification of these children as disadvantaged.[59]

Primary school: ages 8–11.

Junior high school: ages 12–14.

Senior high school: ages 15–18.

Especially outstanding students should be allowed to graduate high school at a younger age and join the army at age 20 with a bachelor's degree.

The present format of technological education should be over-hauled. An analysis of the sources presented in earlier chapters of this study showed that a broad general and scientific education is absolutely essential in an era of rapid technological change, even for those who seek technological, as opposed to theoretical, education.

Technological education in its present form is expensive and inefficient. Workshop-style vocational training should only be offered at the post-secondary stage. Investment of financial and pedagogic resources in students who presently enroll in the non-matriculation tracks of technological education (*masmam* and *masmar*) will improve their achievements and ensure them a better future – as the successful experience of the Meir Shefiyya and Kadoorie youth villages has shown.[60]

Will this plan vitiate the power of the interest groups that impede change today, and will it improve the performance of the education system? Only time will tell.

Notes

Preface and Acknowledgments

1   Ozga, J. (1987), "Studying Educational Policy Through the Lives of Policy-Makers: An Attempt to Close the Macro-Micro gap," in: Walker, S. and Barton, L. (eds), *Changing Policies Changing Teachers*, Milton Keynes, Open University Press.

2   Edwards, G. and Sharkansky, I. (1978), *The Policy Predicament*, San-Francisco, Freidman & Company.

3   Walker, A. (1981), "Social Policy, Social Administration and the Social Construction of Welfare," *Sociology*, 15: 255–71.

4   Mitchell, D. (1988), "Educational Politics and Policy: The State Level," in: Boyan, N. J. (ed.), *Handbook of Research in Educational Administration*, New York, Longman, ch. 22.

5   Mitchell, D. and Encarnation, D. J. (1984), "Alternative State Policy Mechanisms for Controlling School Performance," *Educational Researcher*, 13: 4–11.

Chapter 1   Linking Politics to Education

1   Kogan, M. (1975), *Educational Policy-Making*, London, Allen & Unwin.

2   Kogan, M. (1979), "Different Frameworks for Education Policy-Making and Analysis," *Education Analysis*, 1–2: 5–14.

3   Lodge, P. and Blackstone, T. (1982), *Educational Policy and Educational Inequality*, Oxford, Robertson.

4   Easton, D. (1965), *A Framework for Political Analysis*, Englewood Cliffs, New Jersey.

5   Dror, Y. (1974), *Public Policy-Making Reexamined*, New York, Leonard Hill Books.

6   Thomas, M. R. (1983), *Politics and Education: Cases from Eleven Nations*, London, Pergamon, ch. 1.

7   Popper, K. (1972), *Objective Knowledge*, Oxford, Calendar Press.

8   Scheffler, I. (1967a), *The Anatomy of Inquiry*, New York, Knopf.

9   Simon, H. A. (1957), *Administrative Behavior*, New York, Macmillan.

10 Burch, M. and Word, B. (1986), *Public Policy in Britain*, Oxford, Basil Blackwell.

11 Mahler, G. (1982) (ed.), *Readings on the Israeli Political System, Structures and Processes*, Washington, University Press of America.

12 Elboim-Dror, R. (1982), "Some Features of Educational Legislation in the Knesset," in: Ben-Baruch, E. and Neumann, Y. (eds), *Educational Administration and Policy-Making*, Ben-Gurion University Press, pp. 55–71.

13 Blondel, J. (1978), *Political Parties: A Genuine Case for Discontent?* London, Wildwood House.

14 Hall, S. and Jacques, M. (eds) (1983), *The Politics of Thatcherism*, London, Lawrence & Wishart.

15 Peters, G. (1984), *The Politics of Bureaucracy*, London, Longman, ch. 6. See also: Etzioni-Halevy, E. (1983), *Bureaucracy and Democracy*, London, Routledge & Kegan Paul.

16 Thomas, M. R. (1983), *Politics and Education*.

17 Dale, R. (1989), *The State and Education Policy*, Milton Keynes, Open University Press.

18 Thody, A. (1992), *Moving to Management: School Governors in the 1990's*, London, David Fulton Publishers.

19 Berger, S. (1981), *Organizing Interest Groups in Western Europe: Pluralism, Corporatism and the Transformation of Politics*, Cambridge, Cambridge University Press.

20 Thomas, M. R. (1983), *Politics and Education*.

21 Wildavsky, A. (1987a), *Frames of References Come for Cultures: A Predictive Theory*, Berkeley, Berkeley University Research Center.

22 Lane, J. E. (1993), *The Public Sector*, London, Sage, pp. 74–75.

23 Thompson, J. D. (1967), *Organization in Action*, New York, McGraw-Hill.

24 Elboim-Dror, R. (1970), "Some Characteristics of the Education Policy Formation System," *Policy Sciences*, 1: 231–53.

25 March, J. G. and Simon, A. H. (1958), *Organizations*, New York, Wiley.

26 Lindbloom, C. E. (1959), "The Science of Muddling Through," *Public Administration Review*, 9: 79–88.

27 Wildavsky, A. (1988), *The New Politics of the Budgetary Process*, Boston, Little and Brown.

28 Wanat, J. (1974), "Bases of Budgetary Incrementalism," *American Political Science Review*, 68: 1221–29.

29 Breton, A. (1974), *An Economic Theory of Representative Government*, London, Macmillan.

30 Downs, A. (1957), *An Economic Theory of Democracy*, New York, Harper & Row.

31 Dunsire, A. (1987), "Testing Theories: The Contribution of Bureaumetrics," in: Lane, J. E. (ed.), *Bureaucracy and Public Choice*, London, Sage.

32 Gaziel, H. (1972), *Policy-Making in French Education*, unpublished dissertation, Hebrew University of Jerusalem, School of Education.

33 Odden and Dougherty, V. (1982), *State Programs of School Improvement: A 50-State Survey*. Denver, CO: Education Commission of the States.

34 Cobb, R. W. and Elder, C. D. (1972), *Participation in American Politics: The Dynamics of Agenda Building*. Baltimore, Johns Hopkins University Press.

35 Aloni Calls for Advancement of Arab Education. *Al Hamishmar* (Daily Newspaper) of 20 January, 1993.

36 Wirt, F., Mitchell, D. and Marshall, C. (1988), "Culture and Educational Policy: Analyzing Values in State Policy Systems," *Educational Evaluation and Policy Analysis*, 10: 271–84.

37 Clark, D. and De Astuto, T. (1986), "The Significance of Permanence of Changes in Federal Educational Policy," *Educational Researcher*, 15: 4–13.

38 Wirt, F. (1982), "Policy Output: Institutionalization in Prisons and Schools," in: Jacob, H., Gray, V. and Vines, K. (eds), *Politics in the American States*, Boston, Little Brown, pp. 287–328.

39 Husen, T. (1980), "Strategies for Educational Equality," in: *Readings of Equal Education*, New York, Erwin Flaxman, ch. 1.

Chapter 2 Shaping Education Policy

1 Coombs, Ph. (1968), *The World Crisis of Education*, Paris, UNESCO.

2 Behrman, J. R., Hrubec, Z., Taubman, P. and Wales, T. (1985), *Socio-Economic Success: A Study of the Effects of Genetic Endowments, Family Environment and Schooling*, Amsterdam, North Holland Publishing Company.

3 Cohn, E. (1980), *The Economics of Education*, Oxford, Pergamon Press.

4 Eicher, J. C. and Orivel, F. (1980), *The Allocation of Resources to Education Throughout the World*, Paris, UNESCO.

5 Elboim-Dror, R. (1970), "Some Characteristics of the Policy Formation System in Education," *Policy Sciences*, 1: 231–53.

6 Cuban, L. (1990), "Reforming Again, Again and Again," *Educational Researcher*, 19: 3–13.

7 Carnoy, M. and Levin, H. (1985), *Schooling and Work in the Democratic State*, Stanford, Stanford University Press.

8 Woodhall, M. (1985), "Economics of Education," *International Encyclopedia of Education*, 3: 1546–53.

9 Levin, H. (1983), *Cost-Effectiveness: A Primer*, London, Sage.

10 Hanushek, E. A. (1981), "Throwing Money at Schools," *Journal of Policy Analysis and Management*, 1: 19–41.

11 Madaus, G. F., *et al.* (1980), *School Effectiveness: A Reassessment of the Evidence*, New York, McGraw-Hill.

12 Giroux, H. (1992), "Educational Leadership and the Crisis of the Democratic Government," *Educational Researcher*, 21: 4–12.

13 Guthrie, J., *et al.* (1983), "U.S. School Finance Policy, 1955–1980," *Educational Evaluation and Policy Analysis*, 5: 207–30.

14 Department of Education and Science (ed.) (1986), *Report by the HMI on the Effects of Local Authority Expenditure Policies on Education Provision in England*, London, DES.

15 Davis, D., *et al.* (1982), *Mi nehene mi-mashabei ha-hinukh: halukat tesumot beyn 1973– 1981* [Who Benefits from Education Resources? Allocation of Inputs between 1973 and 1981], Jerusalem, Ministry of Education and Culture.

16 Organization for Economic Cooperation and Development (1971), *Educational Policies for the 1970's, General Report of the OECD Conference on Policies for Educational Growth*, Paris.

17 Claydon, L. F. (1969), *Rousseau on Education*, London, Ollier.

18 Bourdieux, P. and Passeron, J. C. (1990), *Reproduction in Education, Society and Culture*, London, Sage.

19 Husen, T. (1980), "Strategies for Educational Equality," in: *Readings of Equal Education*, Erwin Flaxman, ch. 1.

20 Coleman, J. (1968), "The Concept of Equal Opportunity," *Harvard Educational Review*, 38: 7–22.

21 Husen, T. (1979), *The School in Question: A Comparative Study of the School and Its Future in Western Societies*, Oxford, Oxford University Press.

22 Kleinberg, F. (1967), "Hirhurim al ha-shivioniut be-hinukh," [Reflections on Equality in Education], *Megamot* [Trends], 13: 257–88.

23 Coleman, J. S. (1967), *Equality of Educational Opportunity*, Washington, D.C., U.S. Department of Health, Education and Welfare, Office of Education, 1967. See also: Leibowitz, A. 1977. "Parental Inputs and Children Achievements," *Journal of Human Resources*, 12: 242–50.

24 Central Advisory Council for Education (Plowden Report) (ed.) (1967), *Children and Their Primary Schools*, London, HMSO.

25 Carroll, S. J. (1979), *The Search for Equity in Social Finance: Summary and Conclusions*, Santa Monica, California.

26 Jencks, Ch. (1972), *Inequality: A Reassessment of the Effect of the Family and Schooling in America*, New York, Basic Books. .

27 Lesterc, Th. (1975), *Generating Inequality Mechanism of Distribution in the U.S. Economy*, New York, Basic Books.

28 Bell, D. (1973), *Coming of Post Industrial Society: A Venture in Social Forecasting*, New York, Basic Books.

29 Gardner, J. (1961), *Excellence: Can It Be Equal and Excellent Too?*, New York, Harper and Brothers Publishers.

30 Coons, J. E. (1988), "Can Education Be Equal and Excellent?" in: Guthrie, J. (ed.), *School Finance Policies and Practices*, Cambridge, Mass., Ballinger.

31 Harper, E. L., *et al.* (1969), "Implementation and Use of P.P.B. in Sixteen Federal Agencies," *P.A.R.*, 29: 623–632.
32 Chubb, J. and Moe, T. (1990), *Politics, Markets and American Schools,* Washington, D.C., Brookings Institution.
33 Shapira, R. and Haymann, F. (1991), "Solving Educational Dilemmas by Parental Choice: The Case of Israel," *International Journal of Educational Research,* 15: 277–91.
34 Nathan, J. (ed.) (1989), *Public Schools by Choice,* St. Paul, The Institute of Teaching and Learning Publications.
35 Coons, J. E. and Sugarman, S. (1978), *Education by Choice,* Berkeley, Calf., University of California Press.
36 Levin, H. (1987), "Education as Public and Private Good," *Journal of Policy Analysis and Management,* 6: 628–31.
37 Coleman, J. (1990), "Preface: Choice, Community and Future Schools," in: Clune, W. H. and Witte, J. F. (eds), *Choice and Control in American Education,* vol. 1, New York The Falmer Press, pp. 9–22.
38 Cooper, B. (1992), *What Future for School Choice,* New York, Fordham University School of Education.
39 Weiler, D. (1974), *A Public School Voucher Demonstration: The First Year at Alum Rock,* Santa Monica, Rand Corporation.
40 Cuban, L. (1990), *Educational Researcher,* 19: 3–13.
41 Parsons, T. (1970), *Structure and Process in Modern Society,* New York, The Free Press.
42 Lenski, G. (1966), *Power and Privilege: A Theory of Social Stratification,* New York, McGraw-Hill.
43 Paulston, R. G. (1976), *Conflicting Theories of Social and Educational Change: Typological Review,* Pittsburgh, University of Pittsburgh, Center for International Studies.
44 Elboim-Dror, R. (1975), "Some Aspects of the Educational Policy Formation System," in: Ianni, F. (ed.), *Conflict and Change in Education,* Glenview, Scott Foresman.
45 Homans, G. C. (1950), *The Human Group,* New York, Harcourt, Brace and World.
46 Bunce, V. (1976), "Elite Succession, Petrification and Policy Innovation," *Comparative Political Studies,* 9: 3–33.
47 State of Israel, *The Knesset, State Education Law, 5713–1953.*
48 Condor, Y. (1984), *Kalkalat Yisrael* [The Economy of Israel], Jerusalem, Schocken.
49 Lissak, M. (1982), "Konfliktim ideologi'im ve-hevrati'im be-Yisrael" [Ideological and Social Conflicts in Israel], *Seqira hodshit* [Monthly Review], 9: 4–14.
50 Adler, C. (1989), "Israeli Education Addressing Dilemmas Caused by Pluralism: A Sociological Perspective," in: Krausz, E. (ed.), *Education in a Comparative Context,* New Brunswick, Transaction, ch. 3.
51 Eisenstadt, S. N. (1989), *The Transformation of Israeli Society,* Jerusalem, Magnes Press, ch. 9 (Hebrew),

52 Elboim-Dror, R. (1989), "Conflict and Consensus in Educational Policy Making in Israel," in: Krausz, E. (ed.), *Education in a Comparative Context*, New Brunswick, Transaction, ch. 4.

Chapter 3 History of Education Policy in Israel

1 The Yishuv era was the one which preceded the establishment of the State of Israel, and it can be divided into two basic time frames: that before the British mandate in Palestine in 1917, and thereafter. See, Elboim-Dror, R. (1986), *Ha-hinukh ha-ivri be-Eretz Yisrael (Hebrew Education in Eretz Israel)*, Jerusalem, Yad Ben-Zvi, vol. 1.

2 Elboim-Dror, R. (1985), "Determining Education Policy in Israel," in Ackerman, V., Carmon, A. (ed.), *Hinukh be-hevrah mithavah: ha-hevrah ha-yisraelit (Education in a Society which is Being Formed: the Israeli Society)*, Tel Aviv, HaKibbutz HaMeuhad, vol. I.

3 The Hovevei Zion movement was a movement of educated Jewish young people in Russia at the beginning of the twentieth century, who reached the conclusion, as a result of pogroms against Jews, that the independent existence of the Jewish people was only possible in Eretz Israel. Among the most prominent of its leaders were Lilienblum and Pinsker. See, Ettinger, S. (1969), *Toledot am Yisrael ba'et ha-hadadashah (The History of the Jewish People in the Modern Era)*, Tel Aviv, Dvir, pp. 180–5.

4 Luria, Z. (1921), *Ha-hinukh be-Eretz Yisrael (Education in Eretz Israel)*, Education Department in Eretz Israel, p. 49.

5 *Sefer ha-hinukh veha-tarbut (1951) (Education and Culture Volume (1951))*, Ministry of Education and Culture, p. 4.

6 Bowman, H. E. (1942), *Middle East Window*. London, Longman.

7 Shelhav, Y. (1972), *Ha-temurot be-ma'arekhet ha-hinukh ha-yehudit be-Eretz Yisrael 1932–1939 [The Changes in the Jewish Education System in Eretz Israel 1932–1939]*, Thesis for the M.A. degree in Judaic studies, Ramat Gan, Bar-Ilan University.

8 Bentwich, J. (1960), *Ha-hinukh bi-Medinat Yisrael [Education in the State of Israel]*, Tel Aviv, Tzatzik, p. 32.

9 *Ibid.*, p. 33.

10 Carmon, M. (1955), "Histadrut ha-morim u-ba'ayat ha-hinukh ba-Yishuv," ("The Teachers Union and the Problem of Education in the Yishuv"), in Kimche, D., Reklis, L., Avigal, M. (eds) *Sefer ha-yovel shel histadrut hamorim 5663–5713 [Jubilee Volume of the Teachers Union 1903–1953]*, Tel Aviv, Histadrut Hamorim.

11 *Hed ha-hinukh*, Weekly of the Teachers Union (1932), Year 10, Issue 9–10, pp. 187–8.

12 Bein, A. (1942), *Toledot ha-hityashvut ha-tzionit [History of the Zionist Settlement]*, Massada, Jerusalem.

13 Elboim-Dror, R. (1985), "Determining Education Policy in Israel,", p. 37.

14   Bentwich, J. (1960), *Ha-hinukh bi-Medinat Yisrael*, p. 49.
15   Luria, Z. (1921), *Ha-hinukh be-Eretz Yisrael*, p. 8.
16   Rinot, M. (1978), *"Ha-pulmos al itzuv ma'arekhet ha-hinukh ha-ivri be-Eretz Yisrael"* ["The Polemic about the Formulation of the Hebrew Education System in Eretz Israel"], *Ha-tzionut (Zionism)*, vol. 5, pp. 114–78.
17   Lamm, Z. (1973), *"Metahim ideologi'im, ma'avakim al matrot ha-hinukh"* ["Ideological Tensions, Struggles about the Aims of Education"], *Ha-hinukh be-Yisrael* [*Education in Israel*], Jerusalem, Ministry of Education and Culture, pp. 69–84.
18   Ahad Ha'am (1933), *"Tehiyat ha-ru'ah"* ["Revival of the Spirit"]. *Ha-shiloah*, vol. 10, Issue 5–6. See also his work, *Al parashat derakhim* [At the Crossroads], part II, pp. 139–42.
19   *Sefer ha-hinukh veha-tarbut* (1951), p. 6.
20   Avigal, M. (1971), *Hazon ve-hinukh* [*Vision and Education*]. Tel Aviv, Tarbut Ve-hinukh pub.
21   Arnon, A. (1953), *"Al bet ha-sefer ha-kelali"* ["On the General School"], in Kimche, D., and Reklis, L. (eds), *Sefer ha-yovel shel histadrut hamorim 5663–5713*.
22   Ben-Yehudah, B. (1962), *Le-toledot ha-hinukh be-Eretz Yisrael* [*Toward a History of Education in Eretz Israel*], Jerusalem, Keren Kayemet Le-Yisrael.
23   Reshef, S. (1980), *Zerem ha-ovdim ba-hinukh* [The Labor System in Education], Tel Aviv, Tel Aviv University. See also, Dror, Y. (1994), *"Ha-hinukh ha-hevrati-erki be-zerem ha-ovdim bi-tekufat ha-mandat ha-Briti"* ["Social-Moral Education in the Labor System in the British Mandate Era"], a special issue of *Dor le-dor*, which deals with the history of Hebrew education.
24   Azaryahou, Y. (1939), *"Ha-hinukh ha-ivri be-Eretz Yisrael"* ["Hebrew education in Eretz Israel"], in Kimche, D. (ed.), *Sefer ha-yovel shel histadrut hamorim 5663–5713* [*Jubilee Volume of the Teachers Union 1903–1953*], Tel Aviv, Histadrut Hamorim.
25   Ussishkin, M. (1939), *"Mikhtav hozer"* ["Circular"], in Kimche, D. (ed.), *Sefer ha-yovel shel histadrut hamorim 5663–5713* [*Jubilee Volume of the Teachers Union 1903–1953*], Tel Aviv, Histadrut Hamorim.
26   Rinot, M. (1976), *"Histadrut ha-morim, ha-tenuah ha-tzionit veha-ma'avak al he-hegmoniyah be-Eretz Yisrael"* ["The Teachers Union, the Zionist Movement and the Struggle for the Hegemony in Eretz Israel], in *Tziyonut* [*Zionism*], vol. 4, pp. 114–45.
27   Bentwich, J. (1960), *Ha-hinukh bi-Medinat Yisrael*, p. 28.
28   Rubinstein, A. (1974), *Hithavut ha-shilton ha-mekomi be-Eretz Yisrael* [The Formation of Local Government in Eretz Israel], the Sixth National Conference on Local Government, Jerusalem.
29   Rinot, M. (1976), *"Histadrut ha-morim . . . "*, vol. 4, pp. 114–45.
30   Elboim-Dror (1985), "Determining Education Policy in Israel, p. 40.
31   Bentwich, J. (1960), *Ha-hinukh bi-Medinat Yisrael*, pp. 54–56.

32 Matras, J. (1965), *Social Change in Israel*, Chicago, Adline Publications, pp. 44–46.

33 Stanner, R. (1963), *Dinei hinukh [Laws of Education]*, Jerusalem, Ministry of Education and Culture.

34 Bentwich, J. (1960), *Ha-hinukh bi-Medinat Yisrael*, p. 63.

35 Grinwald, L. (1975), *Hishtatfut bein ha-shilton ha-merkazi levein ha-shilton ha-mekomi be-hinukh [Cooperation between the Central Government and the Local Authority in Education]*. Thesis for M.A. degree in education, Ramat Gan, Bar-Ilan University.

36 Israel, Ministry of Education and Culture (1950), *Din ve-heshbon shel va'adat ha-hakirah le-inyanei hinukh be-mahanot ha-olim [Report of the Investigative Committee on Educational Matters in the New Immigrant Camps]*. Jerusalem.

37 Kleinberger, A. P. (1973), *"Hakikah, politikah ve-hakhvanah bi-tehum ha-hinukh"* ["Legislation, Politics and Guidance in the Educational Realm"], in Ormian, H. (ed.), *Ha-hinukh be-Yisrael*., pp. 51–68.

38 Kleinberger, A. F. (1969), *Society, Schools and Progress in Israel*, London, Pergamon, p. 121.

39 Bentwich, J. (1960), *Ha-hinukh bi-Medinat Yisrael*, p. 70.

40 Lamm, Z. (1978), *"Metahim ideologi'im be-hinush"* ("Ideological Tensions in Education"), in *Emdah*, 6, pp. 32–37.

41 Stanner, D. (1963), *Dinei hinukh*, ch. 1.

42 Kleinberger, A. F. (1973), *"Hakikah, politikah ve-hakhvanah bi-tehum ha-hinukh"*, p. 60.

43 Elboim-Dror, R. (1985), "Determining Education Policy in Israel", p. 57.

44 Sikrun, M. (1957), *Ha-aliyah le-Yisrael ba-shanim 1949–1955 [Immigration to Israel in the Years 1949–1955]*, Jerusalem, Falk Center for Social-economic Research.

45 Frankenstein, K. (12952), *"Ha-gishah ha-psikhologit le-ba'ayat ha-hevdelim he-etni'im"* ["The Psychological Approach to the Problem of Ethnic Differences"], in *Megamot*, 3, pp. 158–70.

46 Smilansky, M. (ed.) (1960), *Child and Youth Welfare in Israel*, Jerusalem, Szold Institute.

47 Volk, Y. (1956), *"Le-inyan hakhasharat morim le-veit-sefer kefari"* ["On Training Teachers for the Village School"], *Ha-hinukh*, vol. 28, pp. 24–28.

48 *Al batei ha-sefer be-mahanot ha-olim [On the Schools in the New Immigrant Camps]* (1950). See document in State Archives, 1720/Gimmel 15/5/060/Mem Ayin.

49 Hanoch, G. (1960), *Income Differentials in Israel*. Jerusalem, Falk Institute for Social-Economic Research in Israel.

50 Klinov-Malul, R. (1966), *Rivhiut ha-hashka'ah be-hinukh be-Yisrael*, Jerusalem, Falk Institute.

51 Jerusalem, Ministry of Labor and Welfare, the Personnel Planning Authority (1965), *Ko'ah adam be-Yisrael [Personnel in Israel]*, *Annual*

Report, p. 50.

52   Jerusalem, Ministry of Labor and Welfare, the Personnel Planning Authority (1966), *Annual Report*, p. 136.

53   Israel, Central Bureau of Statistics (1966), *Statistical Abstracts of Israel*, 17, p. 612.

54   Jerusalem, Ministry of Labor and Welfare, the Personnel Planning Authority (1962), *Survey of University Graduates*, Hebrew University, p. 29.

55   Dror, Y. (1978), *The Israeli Political System*. New York, Harper and Row.

56   Elboim-Dror, R. (1980), "Educational and Cultural Policy-making as Reflected in Education," *Studies in Education*, 27, pp. 1–49.

57   Gaziel, H. (1991), *Yisum mediniut be-hinukh, iyunim be-minhal uve-irgun ha-hinukh* [*Implementation of Policy in Education, Studies in the Administration and Organization of Education*], 17, pp. 5–22.

58   Elboim-Dror, R. (1985), "Determining Education Policy in Israel, p. 75.

59   Tomer, Y. (1993), *Hatza'ah shel haver ha-knesset Shitreet le-yom hinukh arokh be-arei ha-pitu'ah uvi-shekhunot ha-metzukah"* [*"Proposal by Member of Knesset Shitreet for an Extended School Day in the Development Towns and in the Distressed Neighborhoods"*], *Yedioth Aharonoth*, July 22, 1993.

60   The Minister of Education and Culture, Prof. Amnon Rubinstein, appointed a public committee in March 1995 to examine the implementation of an extended school day in the educational system in Israel. The committee has nine members, two from academia, two from the Ministry of Education, two from the teachers unions, two from the local authorities, and one representative of the parents.

61   Yisraeli, A. (1987), "Mivneh misrad ha-hinukh" ["The Structure of the Ministry of Education"], in *Be-hinukh uve-tarbut*, Issue 4, pp. 6–8.

62   Yonnai, Y. (1988), *Mi mefahed mi-pedagogim: pedagogiya u-minhal be-misras ha-hinukh (Who is Afraid of Pedagogues: Pedagogy and Administration in the Ministry of Education)*, Tel Aviv, Yahdav, ch. 5.

63   Interview with Miriam Schmida, office head of the Minister of Education, the late Zalman Aranne, April 1994.

64   Klein, Z. (1995), "Va'adah be-rashut Prof. Adler tivhan ma'avar le-yom limudin arokh" ["A Committee Headed by Prof. Adler will Examine the Transition to an Extended School Day"], in *Globes*, March 13, 1995.

65   Fishbein, Y. (1987), "Shmueli: misrad ha-hinukh soveil mei-redidut umi-hoser manhigut" ["Shmueli: the Ministry of Education Suffers from Superficiality and from a Lack of Leadership"], in *Davar*, March 18, 1987.

66   Yonnai, Y. (1988), *Mi mefahed mi-pedagogim*, p. 82.

67   Sela, A. (1987), *Ha-hinukh ha-dati: zeramim, megamot u-ma'avakim* [*Religious Education: Systems, Streams and Struggles*], Thesis for the M.A. degree in education, Jerusalem, Hebrew University.

68 Kleinberger, A. F. (1969), *Society, Schools and Progress in Israel*, p. 124.

69 Yonnai, Y. (1988), *Mi mefahed mi-pedagogim*, ch. 2.

70 When Minister Hammer took over the Ministry of Education and Culture, he brought with him staffers who eventually forced various senior officials to leave their positions. Two religious district heads were appointed (South and Tel Aviv), as well as five senior officials in the staff.

71 This politicization reappeared when Minister Aloni of Meretz took over the Ministry of Education. She, too, switched the staff. See, Hendel Y. (1992). "Al tzaid ha-makhsheifot shel ha-makhsheifah Aloni" ["Concerning the Witchhunt of the Witch Aloni"], *Hadashot*, October 25, 1992.

72 Stanner, R. (1963), *Dinei hinukh*, ch. 1.

73 Kubarsky, H. (1965), "Mif'al ha-hinukh be-misgeret ha-ahrayut shel ha-shilton ha-merkazi veha-shilton ha-mekomi" ["The Education Enterprise within the Framework of the Responsibility of the Central Government and the Local Authority"], in *Temurot be-minhal*, 2, pp. 10–20.

74 Ayalon, P. (1977), "Ha-yehasim bein ha-shilton ha-merkazi le-vein ha-shilton ha-mekomi" ["The Relationship between the Central Government and the Local Authorities"], *Devar ha-shilton ha-mekomui*, Tel Aviv, Hamerkaz Leshilton Mekomi.

75 Gaziel, H. (1980), "Taktziv ha-hinukh ke-sugya be-yehasim bein ha-shilton ha-merkazi le-vein ha-shilton ha-mekomi" ["The Education Budget as a Factor in the Relationship between the Central Government and the Local Authorities"], *Iyunim be-hinukh*, 27, pp. 43–64.

76 Israel, the Local Authority (1984), *Din ve'heshbon ha-va'adah le-inyanei ha-shilton ha-mekomi (Dokh va'adat Zanbar)* [*Report of the Committee on Local Authorities – the Zanbar Report*], Jerusalem.

77 Schmida M., Scherzer, M. (1991), "Bein shivyon li-metzuyanut bi-shenot ha'shemonim be-ma'arekhet ha-hinukh be-Yisrael" ["Between Equality to Excellence in the 1980s in the Education System in Israel"], *Iyunim be-minhal ve'irgun ha-hinukh* [*Studies in Administration and Organization of Education*], 17, pp. 5–23.

78 The most striking examples are Yavneh and the revolution in education which Meir Shitreet, the head of the local authority at the time, accomplished, and the investment in education in the town of Eldar in Carmiel.

79 Peleg, Z. (1993), *Ahrayut ve-otonomia shel reshut mekomit* (Responsibility and Autonomy of a Local Authority), Jerusalem, Szold Institute.

80 Azaryahou, Y. (1954), *Ha-hinukh ha-ivri be-Eretz Yisrael (Hebrew Education in Eretz Israel)*, Tel Aviv, Massada.

81 *He ha-hinukh* (1968), vol. 42, Issue 33, p. 4.

82 Shelhav, Y. (1972), *Ha-temurot be-ma'arekhet . . . .*

83 Penn, A. (1942), "Li-r'ot mibifnim" ["To See from the Inside"], *Hed hahinukh*, vol. 6, Issue 1, pp. 5–7.

84 Dagan, S. (1984), *Esrim ve-hameish shanim le-irgun ha-morim [Twenty Five Years of the "Irgun" – Teachers Union]*, Tel Aviv, Ma'alot.

85 Gaziel, H. and Taub, D. (1992), "Teachers Unions and Educational Reform: a Comparative Perspective: the cases of France and Israel", *Educational Policy*, 6., pp. 72–86.

86 Israel, Ministry of Education and Culture (1974), *Director-General's Circular*.

87 Rafman, A. (1989), "Ba'alei ha-me'ah veha-de'ah" ["Those with the Money and the Say"], *Yedioth Aharonoth*, September 11, 1989.

88 Goldring, A. (1990), "Ba'ayat yahasei ha-gomlin she-bein horim le-vein ma'arekhet ha-hinukh" ["The Problem of the Reciprocal Relationship between Parents and the Education System"], *Havat da'at: psikhologiyah ve-yei'utz be-hinukh [Opinion: Psychology and Guidance in Education]*, 23, pp. 146–58.

89 Levi, V. (1989), "Lo be-veit sifreinu: horim dorshim et piturehah shel menahelet bet-sefer ilanit be-Tel-Aviv" ["Not in Our School: Parents Demand the Dismissal of the Principal of Ilanit School in Tel Aviv"], *Al hamishmar*, September 1, 1989.

90 Dovrat, N. "Al ha-hatum: va'ad ha-horim" ["Signed: the Parents Committee"], *Ma'ariv*, June 22, 1990.

91. Hakham, A. (1990), "Le-fi hahlatat va'ad ha-horim" ["By Decision of the Parents' Committee"], *Arim: Mekomon*, July 20, 1990.

92. Elboim-Dror, R. (1985), "Determining Education Policy in Israel," p. 89.

93. "Ha-lobi ha-hevrati ba-knesset tove'a meiha-universita'ot ba-aretz le-hahil aflaya metakenet bekhol ha-mosadot le-haskalah gevohah" ["The Social Lobby in the Knesset demands of the Universities the Application of Corrective Discrimination in all the Institutes of Higher Education"], *Ha-tzofeh*, May 9, 1995.

Chapter 4   Education Policy Landmarks

1 Horowitz, D., and Lissak, M. (1977), *Meyishuv le-medina* [From settlement to state], Tel Aviv, Am Oved.

2 Smooha, S., and Peres, Y. (1974), "Pa'ar 'adati be-Yisrael" [Ethnic Gap in Israel], *Megamot* 5: 20–43.

3 Zucker, D. (1985), "Beyn shivioniut, elitism, ve-hesegiut" [Between Egalitarianism, Elitism, and Achievementism], in Ackerman, V., *et al.* (eds), *Hinukh be-hevra mit'hava, ha-ma'arekhet ha-Yisraelit* [Education in a Society in Formation, the Israeli System], Hakibbutz Hameuhad and the Van Leer Jerusalem Institute, vol. 1, 187–214.

4 Lamm, Z. (1973), "Metahim ve-ideologiot: ma'avaqim 'al matrot ha-hinukh" [Tensions and Ideologies: Struggles over the Goals of

Education], in Ormian, H. (ed.), *Ha-hinukh be-Yisrael* [Education in Israel], Jerusalem, Ministry of Education and Culture, 69–84.

5 Dinur, B. (1953), budget speech of the Ministry of Education and Culture in the Knesset, 1953–1954, *Divrey ha-knesset* [Knesset Proceedings], 1719–25.

6 Elboim-Dror, R. (1985), "Qeviat mediniut ha-hinukh be-Yisrael" [Making Education Policy in Israel], in Ackerman, V., *et al.* (eds), *Hinukh be-hevra mit'hava, ha-ma'arekhet ha-Yisraelit* [Education in a Society in Formation, the Israeli System], Hakibbutz Hameuhad and the Van Leer Jerusalem Institute, 65.

7 Adler, C. (1974), "Social Stratification and Education in Israel," *Comparative Educational Review*, 18: 10–24.

8 Aranne, Z. (1959), speech in the Knesset plenum on the education budget for fiscal year 1959/60, *Divrey ha-knesset* [Knesset Proceedings], 1607–22.

9 Eban, A. (1962), Budget speech of the Minister of Education and Culture in the Knesset, 1960/61, *Divrey ha-knesset* [Knesset Proceedings], 1397–1403.

10 Zucker, D. (1985), "Beyn shivioniut, elitism, ve-hesegiut," pp. 202–3.

11 Shemida, M. (1987), *Beyn shivion li-metsuyanut* [Between Equality and Excellence], Ramat Gan, Bar-Ilan University, p. 173.

12 Smilansky, M. (1973), "Hitmodedut ma'arekhet ha-hinukh 'im be'ayoteyhem shel yeladim te'uney tipuah" [How the Education System Copes with the Problems of Disadvantaged Children], in Omrian, H. (ed.), *Ha-hinukh be-Yisrael* [Education in Israel], Jerusalem, Ministry of Education and Culture.

13 Adler, C. (1969), "Le-be'ayat ha-neshira mi-beyt ha-sefer ha-tikhon ha-'iyuni" [On the Problem of Dropping Out from Academic High Schools], in *Kivunim rabim, kavana ahat: divrey 'iyun u-mehqar* [Many Directions, One Intent: Study and Research Proceedings], Jerusalem, School of Education, the Hebrew University of Jerusalem.

14 Kleinberger, A. (1969), *Society, Schools and Progress in Israel*, London, Pergamon Press.

15 Smooha, S., and Peres, Y. (1974), "Pa'ar 'adati be-Yisrael" [Ethnic Gap in Israel], *Megamot* 5: 19.

16 *Din ve-heshbon shel ha-va'ada ha-parlamentarit li-vehinat mivne ma'arekhet ha-hinukh ha-yesodi ve-ha-'al yesodi be-Yisrael* [Report of the Parliamentary Committee for Examination of the Structure of the Primary and Post-Primary Education System in Israel] (1970), the Knesset, 122–3.

17 Amir, S. (1976), *Pa'ar be-hakhnasot dor rishon ba-arets* [Disparity in Incomes of the First Generation in Israel], Jerusalem, Falk Institute for Economic Research in Israel.

18 Minkovich, A., *et al.* (1977), *Ha'arakhat ha-hesegim ha-hinukhi'im be-veyt ha-sefer ha-yesodi be-Yisrael* [Evalution of Education Achievements in Primary School in Israel], Jerusalem, School of Education, the Hebrew University of Jerusalem.

19   Eban, A. (1961), Budget speech of the Minister of Education and Culture in the Knesset, 1961/62, *Divrey ha-knesset* [Knesset Proceedings], 1397–403.

20   Glasman, N. S. (1969), *Developments Toward a Secondary Education Act: The Case of Israel*, unpublished doctoral thesis, the University of California at Berkeley.

21   Elboim-Dror, R. (1985), "Qevi'at mediniut ha-hinukh be-Yisrael" [Making Education Policy in Israel], *op. cit.*, pp. 35–116.

22   The Knesset passed the reform law on Tamuz 16, 5729 (July 2, 1969). See *Sefer Huqim* [Book of Laws] (1960), no. 563, dated Tamuz 25.

23   "Masqanot ha-va'ada li-vediqat mivne ha-hinukh ha-yesodi ve-ha-reforma ba-hinukh" [Conclusions of the Committee for Examination of the Structure of Primary Schooling and the Education Reform] (1981), *Divrey ha-knesset* [Knesset Proceedings], 354–56.

24   "Seqer sar ha-hinukh ve-ha-tarbut 'al pe'ulot misrado" [Review of the Minister of Education and Culture on the Operations of His Ministry], *Divrey ha-knesset* [Knesset Proceedings], 2717–19.

25   Perah, Y. (1983), "Hatsa'a le-seder ha-yom: hafsaqat haqamatan shel hativot beynayim hadashot" [Motion for the Agenda: Moratorium on the Construction of New Junior-High Schools], *Divrey ha-knesset* [Knesset Proceedings], 629–30.

26   "Masqanot va'adat ha-hinukh be-nose haqamatan shel hativot beynayim hadashot" [Conclusions of the Education Committee on the Construction of New Junior-High Schools] (1984), *Divrey ha-knesset* [Knesset Proceedings], 2626–7.

27   Motion by MK Sartani: "Ha'im ha-reforma hisiga et ya'adeha?" [Has the Reform Attained its Objectives?] (1987) *Divrey ha-knesset* [Knesset Proceedings], 3635.

28   "Masqanot va'adat ha-hinukh be-nose beyt ha-sefer ha-yesodi" [Conclusions of the Education Committee on the Subject of Primary Schools] (1987), *Divrey ha-knesset* [Knesset Proceedings], 2421.

29   "Teguvoteyhem shel haver ha-knesset Yehuda Perah (Likud) ve-haver ha-knesset Hagai Meirom ('Avoda) le-divrey sar ha-hinukh ve-ha-tarbut 'al pe'ulot misrado" [Responses of MK Yehuda Perah (Likud) and MK Hagai Meirom (Labor) to Remarks by the Minister of Education and Culture on Operations of His Ministry] (1990), *Divrey ha-knesset* [Knesset Proceedings], 2429–35.

30   Chen, M., Levi, A., and Adler, C. (1978), *Halikh ve-totsa'a be-ma'ase ha-hinukh: ke-ha'arakhat terumatan shel hativot ha-beynayim le-ma'arekhet ha-hinukh* [Process and Result in the Act of Education: Toward Evaluation of the Contribution on Junior-High Schools to the Education System] study on junior-high schools, Tel Aviv University, School of Education, and the Hebrew University of Jerusalem, the Institute for the Study of Fostering in Education.

31   Reported in Shemida M. (1987), *Beyn shivion li-metsuyanut* [Between Equality and Excellence], Ramat Gan, Bar-Ilan University, 193–4.

32 "Masqanot va'adat ha-hinukh be-nose misrad ha-hinukh ve-ha-integratsia" [Conclusions of the Education Committee on the Subject of the Ministry of Education and Integration] (1988), *Divrey ha-knesset* [Knesset Proceedings], 3267–8.

33 Goldstein, S. (1980), "Judicial Intervention in Educational Decision Making: An Israeli-American Comparison," in Goldstein, S. (ed.), *Law and Equality in Education*, Jerusalem, The Van Leer Jerusalem Foundation.

34 Kleinberger, A. P. (1973), "Haqiqa politit ve-hakhvana bi-tehum ha-hinukh" [Political Legislation and Guidance in the Field of Education], in Ormian, H. (ed.), *Ha-hinukh be-Yisrael* [Education in Israel], Jerusalem, Ministry of Education and Culture, 51–68.

35 Shemida, M. and Shertser, M. (1991), "Beyn shivayon li-metsuyanut bi-shenot ha-shemonim be-ma'arekhet ha-hinukh be-Yisrael" [Between Equality and Excellence in the 1980s in the Education System in Israel], *'Iyunim be-minhal u-ve-irgun ha-hinukh* [Studies in Education Administration and Organization], 17: 23–38.

36 Shemida, M., *Beyn shivion li-metsuyanut*, p. 31.

37 "Mankal misrad ha-hinukh higia' li-Netanya leshakhne'a otam bi-zekhut ha-reforma ba-hinukh" [The Director-General of the Ministry of Education Reached Netanya to Convince Them of the Merits of the Education Reform], *Hadshot Netanyah* [Netanya News], 45, January 24, 1992.

38 Gaziel, H., and Taub, D. (1992), "Teachers Unions and Education Reform, A Comparative Perspective: The Cases of France and Israel," *Educational Policy*, 6: 72–87.

39 Adiel, S. (1973), "Ha-ma'avaqim 'al ha-temurot be-mivne ma'arekhet beyt ha-sefer" [Struggles for Changes in the Structure of the School System], in Ormian, H. (ed.), *Ha-hinukh be-Yisrael* [Education in Israel], Jerusalem, Ministry of Education and Culture, pp. 144–9.

40 Amir, B., and Blass, N. (1985), "Hitpat'huta shel mediniut misrad ha-hinukh ve-ha-tarbut bi-tehum ha-integratsia ha-hevratit be-ma'arekhet ha-hinukh be-Yisrael" [Development of Ministry of Education and Culture Policy in the Field of Social Integration in the Education System in Israel], in Amir, Y., Sharan, S., and Ben-Ari, R. (eds), *Integratsia ba-hinukh* [Integration in Education], Tel Aviv, Am Oved, 31–54.

41 Klein, Z., and Eshel, Y. (1980), *Integrating Jerusalem Schools*, New York, Academic Press.

42 Inbar, D. (1989), "A Back Door Process of School Privatization: The Case of Israel," in: Boyd, W. and Cibulka, G. (eds), *Private Schools and Public Policy: International Perspectives*, Basingstoke, Falmer Press.

Chapter 5   The Past Decade: Conflicting Aims

1 "Seqirat sar ha-hinukh ve-ha-tarbut 'al pe'ulot misrado" [Review of

the Minister of Education and Culture on the Operations of His Ministry] (1985/86), *Divrey ha-knesset* [Knesset Proceedings], 3573.

2 "Seqirat sar ha-hinukh ve-ha-tarbut 'al pe'ulot misrado" [Review of the Minister of Education and Culture on the Operations of His Ministry] (1982/83), *Divrey ha-knesset* [Knesset Proceedings], 3135–55.

3 Klinov, Ruth, "Public Resource Allocation for Education," in Kop, Y. (ed.), *Resource Allocation for the Social Services*, Jerusalem, the Center for Social Policy Studies in Israel, 1987. Contrary to the economists' attitude, educational sociologists Yogev and Eylon found that the law has a perceptible impact on perseverance rates in this context, especially up to the completion of studies in twelfth grade, but had no effect on rates of initial high-school enrollment. Perseverance is stronger among boys than girls, and stronger in academic than in vocational tracks. The law had a favorable effect on inter-ethnic equality by dissuading students of Asian-African origin from dropping out of the highest grades. See Yogev, A. and Eylon, H. (1986), *Hoq hinukh tikhon hinam ve-shivyon hizdamnuyot be-hinukh: hebetim hevrati'im be-tsad shiqulim kalkali'im* [The Free Secondary Education Law and Equal Opportunity in Education: Social Aspects Alongside Economic Considerations], Tel Aviv University, School of Education, the Unit for Sociology of Education and Community.

4 Response by MK Shoshana Arbeli-Almozlino (Labor) to the Compulsory Education Bill (Amendment no. 11), presented to the Knesset by the Deputy Minister of Education and Culture, Miriam Ta'asa-Glaser (Likud), *Divrey ha-knesset* [Knesset Proceedings], 1982/83, 3085.

5 Response by MK Michael Bar-Zohar (Labor) to a speech by the Minister of Education and Culture on the Ministry's gray education policy: *Divrey ha-knesset* [Knesset Proceedings], 1988/89, 3269.

6 Minister of Education and Culture, *Mediniuteynu be-yahas la-hinukh ha-afor* [Our Policy on Gray Education], *Divrey ha-knesset* [Knesset Proceedings], 1988/89, 3265.

7 Bar Simantov, R. and Langerman, S. (1988), *Tokhnit limudim nosefet be-mimun horim be-vatey sefer yesodi'im* [Parent-Funded Supplementary Curriculum in Primary Schools], Jerusalem, The Henrietta Szold Institute.

8 Rotem, M. (1990), *Ma'arekhet shi'urey ha-'ezer ha-perati'im, le-or mediniut hinukh mishtane* [The Private Lessons System in View of Changing Education Policy], thesis for the degree of Master in Social Science, Bar-Ilan University.

9 Rotem, M., *ibid.*, ch. 5.

10 James, E. (1988), "The Public-Private Division of Responsibility for Education: An International Comparison," in: James, Th. and Levin, H. (eds), *Comparing Public and Private Schools*, Stanford, Stanford University, Series on Education and Public Policy, pp. 95–128.

11 Peled, E. (1976), *Ha-hinukh bi-shenot ha-shemonim* [Education in the

1980s], Jerusalem, Ministry of Education and Culture.

12 Israel Ministry of Education and Culture (1973), *Hozer mankal meyuhad* [Special Circular of the Director-General], No. 4.

13 *Ibid.*, paragraph 17.

14 Danilov, Y. (1986), "Ha-'atsmaut ha-pedagogit shel ha-mosad ha-hinukhi" [The Pedagogical Independence of the Education Institution], in *Nos'ey hinukh merkazi'im be-ma'arekhet ha-hinukh* [Major Education Themes in the Education System], Jerusalem, Ministry of Education and Culture, Pedagogical Secretariat.

15 Goldberger, D. (1991), *Beyt ha-sefer ha-qehilati* [The Community School], Qaley Mahshava Publication Company.

16 Israel Ministry of Education and Culture (1984), *Otonomia be-hinukh: mashma'ut ve-yisum* [Autonomy in Education: Meaning and Practice], Jerusalem.

17 "Aloni ma'avira 'od samkhuyot le-vatey ha-sefer" [Aloni Transfers Further Powers to Schools], *Hadashot*, September 18, 1992.

18 The report on the committees' existence was presented by Ami Walinski, director of the Ministry of Education Planning and Budgeting Division, at a meeting of the Knesset Education Committee on March 21, 1993.

19 "Masqenot va'adat ha-hinukh shel ha-kneset be-nose beyt ha-sefer ha-yesodi" [Conclusions of the Knesset Education Committee on Primary Schools] (1987/88), *Divrey ha-knesset* [Knesset Proceedings].

20 Shapira, R., Goldring, A., Flor, H., and Shavit, R. (1991), *Otonomia beyt sifrit be-merhavey rishum meshutafim: behirat horim mevuqeret be-Yisrael* [School Autonomy in Shared Enrollment Districts: Controlled Parental Choice in Israel], Tel Aviv University School of Education, Unit for Sociology of Education and Community. See also Shapira, R. (1988), *Yihudiut hinukhit-hevratit: batey sefer yihudi'im – reqa', hitpat'hut u-ve'ayot* [Socio-educational Singularity: Special-Curriculum Schools – Background, Development, and Problems], Tel Aviv University School of Education, Unit for Sociology of Education and Community.

21 Israel Ministry of Education and Culture (1991), *Doh ha-va'ada ha-tsiburit li-vediqat ma'amadan shel misgerot ha-hinukh ha-'al ayzoriot* [Report of the Public Committee for Examination of the Status of Open-Enrollment Schools], Jerusalem.

22 A 1976 regulation by Minister of Education Aharon Yadlin entitled local authorities to determine the size and nature of enrollment districts and the number of schools within each. This regulation was meant to help local authorities integrate socially polarized neighborhoods. The regulation could force children from different neighborhoods to attend one school even if the neighborhoods were not geographically close to each other. In equal measure, however, this regulation might help a local authority set up several schools in a given area and permit "parental choice" in this fashion, even if this

circumvented integration. There is no gainsaying the fact that the mayor is an elected official who values his voters' opinions in this matter, as in any other, very highly. If his constituency dislikes the integration policy, the mayor may invoke this regulation to carry out the electors' wishes.

23 On December 31, 1989, Minister of Education Navon appointed a public committee to examine the status of super-regional schools on the primary and junior-high levels. The formation of this committee reflected a desire to keep the schools integrated while permitting and promoting special emphases of various kinds in schools and among communities of parents and teachers, while thwarting processes and rules that would cause integration to fray. When Zevulun Hammer took over as Minister of Education and Culture, he asked the committee to continue with its work. The committee report was officially presented to Hammer on February 5, 1992. It contained a review of the committee's work, discussions, and findings, and recommendations for policy and future implementation modalities. Hammer accepted the recommendations and confirmed that his ministry and the local authorities would operate under several of them. Existing super-regional schools, he said, would be endorsed on condition that they maintained social integration; greater efforts would be made to open regionally based special-curriculum schools; resources would be allocated for development of the special characteristics of all schools in a given locality or district; and pupils would be allowed to choose the school of their liking, as long as the local authority provided supervision. This supervision was meant to prevent the evolution of socially homogeneous schools. See Israel Ministry of Education and Culture, *Hozer mankal meyuhad/15* [Special Circular of the Director-General, No. 15], March 5, 1992.

24 For the committee report, see Israel Ministry of Education and Culture (1991), *Doh ha-va'ada ha-tsiburit li-vediqat ma'amadan shel misgerot ha-hinukh ha-'al ayzoriot* [Report of the Public Committee for Examination of the Status of Open-Enrollment Schools (the Kashti Committee report)], Jerusalem. For responses to the report, see Bar-Lev, M. (ed.), *Hatsofe: musaf le-'inyeney hinukh ve-hora'a* [Hatsofe (daily newspaper): Supplement on Education and Teaching], March 25, 1992, p. 5.

25 Gaziel, H. and Romm, Z. (1988), "From Centralization to Decentralization: The Case of Israel as a Unique Pattern of Control," *European Journal of Education*, 23: 345–55.

26 For the response of the Director-General, Zevulun Orlev, see *Hatsofe*, March 25, 1992, p. 5.

27 The minister's response to the Kashti Committee report is described in Fishbein, Y., "Bekhirim mat'hu biqoret 'al mediniut misrad ha-hinukh le-'asor ha-qarov" [Senior Officials Criticized Ministry of Education Policy for the Coming Decade"], *Davar* (daily newspaper), February 4, 1992.

28 Shapira, R. and Haymann, F. (1991), "Solving Educational Dilemmas by Parental Choice: The Case of Israel," *International Journal of Educational Research*, 15: 277–91.

29 Gur, M., "Raq ha-horim yekholim" [Only the Parents Can], *Ha'aretz* (daily newspaper), August 6, 1992.

30 Kiel, Y. (1977), *Ha-hemed – shorashav, toledotav u-ve'ayotav* [State-Religious Education – Its Roots, History, and Problems], Jerusalem, Ministry of Education and Culture.

31 Schwartzwald, Y. (1990), *Ha-hinukh ha-mamlakhti dati: metsiut u-mehqar* [State–Religious Education: Reality and Research], Ramat Gan, Bar-Ilan University Press, p. 23.

32 Ron, A. (1973), "'Al ha-tefisa ha-kolelanit ba-hinukh ha-dati" [On the Comprehensive Philosophy in Religious Education], *Bi-sede hemed* (journal for State–Religious Education), 16: 195–206.

33 Shremer, O. (1985), "Ha-hinukh ha-mamlakhti dati: beyn mehuyavut yesod le-amot mida operativiot" [State–Religious Education: Between Basic Commitment and Practical Criteria], in Ackerman, V., *et al.* (eds), *Hinukh be-hevra mit'hava – ha-ma'arekhet ha-Yisraelit* [Education in a Society in Formation – The Israeli System], Hakibbutz Hameuhad and the Van Leer Jerusalem Institute, pp. 349–77.

34 Izak, P. (1989), *"No'am" ke-veyt sefer u-khe-ma'arekhet hinukhit ve-ha-hashlakhot legabey ha-hinukh ha-mamlakhti dati* [No'am as a School and as an Educational System and the Implications for State–Religious Education], thesis for the degree of Master of Arts in Social Sciences, School of Education, Bar-Ilan University.

35 Response of the Minister of Education and Culture at the time, Yitzhak Navon, to a motion for the agenda by MK Rabbi Haim Druckman on the status of State–Religious education, *Divrey ha-knesset* [Knesset Proceedings], 1986/87, 1433.

36 Egozi, M., *Hashpa'at ha-herkev ha-hevrati shel ha-kita 'al ha-hesegim ha-limudi'im mi-shekhavot hevratiot shonot* [The Impact of the Social Composition of the Class on Scholastic Achievements of Different Social Strata], Jerusalem, Ministry of Education and Culture.

37 Schwartzwald, Y. (1990), *Ha-hinukh ha-mamlakhti dati*, ch. 6.

38 Stahl, A. (1976), *Mizug tarbuti be-yisrael* [Cultural Integration in Israel], Tel Aviv, Am Oved.

39 Greenbaum, N. (1992), "Ha'hinukh ha-mamlakhti dati ve-ha-reforma: be'ayot be-tikhnun u-mipui batey ha-sefer" [State–Religious Education and the Reform: Problems in Planning and Mapping the Schools], *Bi-sede hemed* (journal for State–Religious Education), 6: 78–84.

40 Schwartzwald, Y. (1985), "Ha-reforma ba-hinukh ha-dati: hazon u-metsiut" [The Reform in Religious Education: Vision and Reality], *Megamot* 29, 173.

41 Israel Ministry of Education and Culture (1979), *Doh ha-va'ada ha-tsiburit li-vediqat ha-reforma be-ma'arekhet ha-hinukh be-Yisrael* [Report

of the Public Committee for Examination of the Education-System Reform in Israel], Jerusalem.

42   Chen, M., Levy, A., and Adler, C. (1978), *Halikh ve-totsa'a be-ma'ase ha-hinukh: terumata shel hativat ha-beynayim le-ma'arekhet ha-hinukh* [Process and Product in Educational Endeavor: The Contribution of the Junior-High Echelon to the Education System], Jerusalem, Ministry of Education and Culture.

43   Israel Ministry of Education and Culture, Religious Education Administration (1993), *Qavim manhim li-mediniut ha-hinukh ha-mamlakhti dati* [Guidelines for State–Religious Education Policy], Jerusalem.

44   Coleman, G. (1985), "Integratsia ve-shivyon hizdamnuyot be-Yisrael" [Integration and Equal Opportunity in Israel], in Ackerman, V., *et al.* (eds), *Hinukh be-hevra mit'hava – ha-ma'arekhet ha-Yisraelit* [Education in a Society in Formation – The Israeli System], Hakibbutz Hameuhad and the Van Leer Jerusalem Institute, 875–84.

45   Chen, M. and Kfir, D. (1981), "Ketsad qidma hativat ha-beynayim et talmideha" [How the Junior-High Echelon Advanced Its Students], *'Iyunim be-hinukh*, 32: 59–82.

46   "Ma'avaq ba-hahlata leqatsets ba-hinukh ha-mamlakhti dati" [Struggle Against the Decision to Slash (Budgets of) State–Religious Education], *Hatsofe* (daily newspaper), February 19, 1993. "The Minister of Education and Culture decided on a new decree to cut 15,000 teaching hours from many classes that do not have 40 pupils," quoted from *Igeret le-morey ve-horey ha-talmidim be-hemed* [Letter to Teachers and Parents of Students in State–Religious Education] (1993), Jerusalem, the Center for Religious Education.

47   "Manhig shas taqaf be-harifut et ma'arekhet ha-hinukh shel ha-mafdal" [Shas Leader in Sharp Attack on NRP Education System], *Ha'aretz* (daily newspaper), October 4, 1992.

48   A special program called Shelef organizes twelfth-grade students from advantaged State–Religious high schools for service in corresponding schools in development towns. The advantaged students spend their last year of high-school studies as rank-and-file students in development-town schools, in order to help their peers meet the demands of matriculation. The program is sponsored by the Center for Religious Education.

49   Elkayam, S. (principal of the Religious comprehensive school in Ofaqim), "Beyt ha-sefer ha-maqif tsarikh lir'ot ba-yeshiva degem le-hiqui" [The Comprehensive School Should Regard the Yeshiva as a Model for Emulation], *Hatsofe* (daily newspaper), April 29, 1992.

50   Zucker, D. (1985), "Ha-hinukh ha-miqtso'i – ma'arekhet be-lahatsim tsolvim" [Vocational Education – A Battle of Conflicting Pressures], in Ackerman, V., *et al.* (eds), *Hinukh be-hevra mit'hava – ha-ma'arekhet ha-Yisraelit* [Education in a Society in Formation – The Israeli System], Hakibbutz Hameuhad and the Van Leer Jerusalem Institute, 449.

51   Ackerman, V., *et al.* (eds), *Hinukh be-hevra mit'hava*, p. 220.

52 Aranne, Z., *Hevley hinukh* [Education Pains], Jerusalem, 220.
53 Karmi, S. (1989), "Hitpat'hut ha-hinukh ha-tekhnologi ha-miqtso'i be-r'i hitpat'hut ha-hinukh ha-tikhoni – temurot, be'ayot ve-hebetim nivharim" [Development of Technological-Vocational Education in View of Development of Secondary Education – Selected Changes, Problems, and Aspects], *'Iyunim be-minhal u-ve-irgun ha-hinukh*, 15: 119–42.
54 The course programs ("tracks") of vocational education are described below:

- Secondary-vocational (Hebrew abbreviation: *masmat*), a four-year course leading to a vocational matriculation certificate that entitles the holder to vocational certification and eligibility for further study.
- Regular-vocational (Hebrew abbreviation: *masmar*), a three- or four-year secondary course permitting a one-year extension for the degree of *tekhna'i* (technician) or a two-year extension for the degree of *handesa'i* (practical or civil engineer).
- Practical-vocational (Hebrew abbreviation: *masmam*), meant for the less qualified. This course of study can be completed at the end of tenth grade and entitles graduates to government vocational certification. It can also be completed after twelve years' study, in which case a a high-school diploma is given.
- "Guidance" classes – established in 1968 for pupils who finished primary school but could not gain admission to any other post-primary setting. Duration: one year (ninth grade).

All of these course programs are supervised by the Ministry of Education and Culture. Additional vocational-education frameworks are not Ministry-supervised; they include industrial schools, adult vocational-training schools, and the technological syllabus of the agricultural-education system. See Peled, E., *Ha-hinukh bi-shenot ha-shemonim* [Education in the 1980s], Jerusalem, Ministry of Education and Culture.
55 Israel Ministry of Education and Culture (1990), *Hozer ha-mankal 39/8* [Circular of the Director-General, 39/8].
56 Israel Ministry of Education and Culture (1975), *Ma'arekhet ha-hinukh ha-tekhnologi: ha-nativ ha-tekhnologi be-vatey ha-sefer ha-'al yesodi'im bi-shenot ha-limudim tashlad-tashla* [The Technological Education System: The Technological Path in Post-Primary Schools in the 1973/74 and 1974/75 School Years], Jerusalem.
57 The matriculation-examination reform, introduced in 1979, was meant to allow more students, especially those of Asian-African origin, to earn matriculation certificates. Two changes made in this reform stand out: a transition to electives based on students' areas of interest, and the right to be tested on a lower level in each subject,

provided that the matriculation candidate be tested on a minimum overall level of 20 points. See Y. Levi (1990), *Temurot ve-shinui'im bi-vehinot ha-bagrut be-Yisrael* [Changes and Modifications in Israeli Matriculation Examinations], Jerusalem, Ministry of Education and Culture.

58 *Seqirat sar ha-hinukh ve-ha-tarbut mar Yitzhak Navon 'al pe'ulot misrado* [Review by the Minister of Education and Culture, Mr Yitzhak Navon, of the Operations of His Ministry] (1990), *Divrey ha-knesset* [Knesset Proceedings], 1989/90, 421.

59 *Divrey ha-knesset* [Knesset Proceedings], 1989/90, 2422.

60 Since the 1992/93 school year, the Technion has given preference in admission to vocational high-school graduates in the matriculation track. Based on an interview with the Deputy Director-General of the ORT school system, Zvi Peleg, on April 4, 1992.

61 *Ha-hinukh ha-tekhnologi be-Yisrael liqrat shenot ha-alpayim, doh ha-va'ada ha-tsiburit le-'idkun matarot ha-hinukh ha-tekhnologi* [Technological Education in Israel Toward the Year 2000, Report of the Public Committee for Updating the Goals of Technological Education] (1985), Jerusalem, Ministry of Education and Culture.

62 Zucker, D. (1985), "Ha-hinukh ha-miqtso'i," p. 459.

63 Nitsan, A. (1970), *Beyt ha-sefer ha-miqtso'i, tokhnit ha-limudim ve-tsorkhey ha-mesheq be-'anfey mis'har, banqa'ut u-minhal* [The Vocational School, Curriculum and Needs of the Economy in Commerce, Banking, and Administration], Jerusalem, Henrietta Szold Institute. See also Kahana, R. and Star, L. (1973), *Kama dilemot be-ma'arekhet ha-hinukh ha-miqtso'i ha-tekhnologi be-Yisrael* [Several Dilemmas in the Vocational-Technological Education System in Israel], The Hebrew University of Jerusalem, School of Education and Institute for Research of Labor and Social Affairs.

64 Klinov, R. (1991), *Haqtsa'at mashabim tsiburi'im le-ma'arekhet ha-hinukh: seder adifuyot* [Public Resource Allocation for the Education System: Priorities], Jerusalem, The Center for Social Policy Studies in Israel.

65 Tilak, J. B. G. (1988), "Economics of Vocationalization: A Review of the Evidence," *Canadian and International Education*, 17: 45–62.

66 Psacharapoulos, G. (1987), "To Vocationalize or Not To Vocationalize: That is the Curriculum Question," *International Review of Education*, 33: 187–211.

67 Neuman, S. and Ziderman, A. (1991), "Vocational Schooling, Occupational Matching, and Labor Market Earnings in Israel." *The Journal of Human Resources*, 26: 256–81.

68 Ziderman, A. (1989b), "Alternative Training Modes for Youth in Israel: Results from Longitudinal Data," *Comparative Education Review*, 33: 243–55.

69 This is, alleged by the Religious Education Administration in the Ministry of Education and Culture. The Administration is also striving to close down religious vocational schools. See Fishbein, Y,

"Minhal ha-hinukh ha-dati hora lisgor kitot tekhnologiot le-tovat kitot yeshivatiot" [Religious Education Administration Orders Closure of Technological Classes in Favor of Yeshiva Classes], *Davar* (daily newspaper), February 10, 1992.

70 Shavit, Y., "Ba-maqom ha-revi'i: beney 'edot ha-mizrah" [In Fourth Place: The Oriental Ethnics], *Yedioth Ahronoth* (daily newspaper), October 28, 1992. In a letter to the Director-General of ORT, Mr. Goralnik, on September 30, 1992, Matti Dagan, director of the Religious Education Administration, wrote: "My arguments against technological education stem not from criticism of its quality and curricula but from its very existence in post-primary schooling, in view of the dynamics that it creates *vis-à-vis* a population group of normal potential."

71 Israel Ministry of Education and Culture (1992), *Doh ha-va'ada ha-'elyona le-hinukh mada'i-tekhnologi (doh va'adat Harari)* [Report of the Supreme Committee for Scientific-Technological Education (the Harari Committee), Jerusalem.

72 Sarsour, S. (1985), "Li-sh'elat hinukho shel mi'ut zar bi-medinato" [On the Education of an Alien Minority in Its (own) State], in Ackerman, V., *et al.* (eds), *Hinukh be-hevra mit 'hava – ha-ma'arekhet ha-Yisraelit* [Education in a Society in Formation – The Israeli System], Hakibbutz Hameuhad and the Van Leer Jerusalem Institute, 475–525.

73 Ackerman, V., *et al.* (eds), *Hinukh be-hevra mit 'hava*, p. 494.

74 Israel Ministry of Education and Culture, *Doh tsevet ha-hinukh ha-'aravi le-tikhnun ha-hinukh li-shenot ha-80* [Report of the Arab Education Team for Planning of Education for the 1980s], Jerusalem, Ministry of Education and Culture Archives.

75 Shmueli, E. (1977), "Mesimot ha-misrad li-shenat tashlah" [Ministry Tasks for 1977/78], in *Va'adat tikhnun ha-hinukh li-shenot ha-80* [Committee for Planning of Education for the 1980s], Jerusalem, Ministry of Education and Culture, Pedagogical Secretariat.

76 Peled, E. (1977), statement on Director-General's position on Arab education, forwarded to the Arab education team, in *Va'adat tikhnun ha-hinukh li-shenot ha-80* [Committee for Planning of Education for the 1980s], Jerusalem, Ministry of Education and Culture Archives.

77 Bashi, J., Kahan, S., and Davis, D. (1981), *Ha-hesegim ha-limudi'im shel beyt ha-sefer ha-yesodi ha-'Aravi be-Yisrael* [Scholastic Achievements of the Arab School in Israel], Jerusalem, School of Education, the Hebrew University of Jerusalem.

78 Mar'i, S. K. (1978), *Arab Education in Israel*, New York, Syracuse University Press.

79 Zoabi, O. (1971), "'Arvi'ey Yisrael bi-dilemat ha-ne'emanut ha-kefula" [Israeli Arabs in the Dilemma of Dual Allegiance], *Ma'alot*, 5: 27–32.

80 Koplevitz, O. (1973), "Ha-hinukh be-migzar ha-'Aravi: 'uvdot u-ve'ayot" [Education in the Arab Sector: Facts and Problems], in Ormian, H. (ed.), *Ha-hinukh be-Yisrael* [Education in Israel], Jerusalem, Ministry of Education and Culture, 323–6.

81 Sarsour, S. (1985), "Li-sh'elat hinukho shel mi'ut zar bi-medinato."
82 Adler, C. (1986), "Israeli education addressing dilemmas caused by pluralism," in: Rotherdan, D. and Simon, J. (eds), *Education and Integration of Ethnic Minorities*, London: Pinter.
83 Report of the Arab Education Team for Planning of Education for the 1980s.
84 Israel Ministry of Education and Culture (1985), *Doh ha-va'ada li-vediqat ha-hinukh ha-'Aravi* [Report of the Committee for Examination of Arab Education], Jerusalem.
85 Israel, Office of the State Comptroller (1992), *Doh mevaqer ha-medina mispar 43* [Report of the State Comptroller, no. 43], Jerusalem, 314-39.
86 Eliezer Shmueli, Minister of Education between 1978 and 1987, wrote: "The attempts to decentralize the powers of the Arab Education Division have met with opposition by the Arabs, of all people, who claimed that the administrative differentiation gives them special status. Today, however, the Arabs are proclaiming their wish to integrate into the government administrative system. Shmueli, E., "Nifradim u-vilti shavim" [Separate but Not Equal], *Ha'aretz* (daily newspaper), September 16, 1992.
87 Israel Ministry of Education and Culture, Arab Education and Culture Division, *Ha-hinukh ha-'Aravi liqrat tashmaz: seqirat menahel ha-agaf* [Arab Education for 1986/87: Review of the Division Director], internal document, August 25, 1986.
88 Israel Ministry of Education and Culture (1992), "Tokhnit ha-homesh le-qidum ha-hinukh be-migzar ha-'Aravi" [Five-Year Plan for the Advancement of Education in the Arab Sector], *Hozer mankal meyuhad dalet/92* [Special Bulletin of the Director-General d/92].
89 "Aloni qoret leqadem ha-hinukh ha-'aravi limno'a islamizatsia" [Aloni Calls for Advancement of Arab Education to Prevent Islamization], *Al Hamishmar* (daily newspaper), January 20, 1993.
90 Consider remarks by Juma'a al-Qesasi, chairman of the Rahat Local Council, at a workshop on the fate of Arab education, held at the rural Arab locality of Basmat Taboun: "[We] ought to boycott the government education institutions and set up independent Arab schools to educate a new generation that will achieve victory and liberation from the aliens' yoke." Quoted by A. Mansour, "Apatia hinukhit" [Educational Apathy], *Al Hamishmar* (daily newspaper), January 31, 1992.

Chapter 6 Budget and Curriculum

1 Fournier, J. (1970), *Politiques d'enseignement* [Educational Policies], Paris, PUF.
2 Rosevitz, Shimon (1993), *Megamot be-taqtsivei ha-hinukh bi-shenot ha-shemonim* [Trends in Education Budgets in the 1980s], Jerusalem, ISES, the Institute for the Study of Educational Systems.

3 Klinov, Ruth (1988), "Haqtsa'at mashabim tsiburi'im le-hinukh" [Allocation of Public Resources for Education], in Kop, Y. (ed.), *Haqtsa'at mashabim le-sherutim hevrati'im* [Resource Allocation for the Social Services], Jerusalem, the Center for Social Policy Studies in Israel.

4 Israel Ministry of Education and Culture (1992), *Ma'arekhet ha-hinukh bi-re'i ha-misparim, 5752*, [The Education System in Numbers, 1991/92], Jerusalem, Ministry of Education and Culture, Senior Division for Economics and Budgets, ch. 5.

5 Klinov. R. (1988), "Haqtsa'at mashabim tsiburi'im le-hinukh."

6 Sharkansky, I. (1987), *The Political Economy of Israel*, New Jersey, Transaction Books.

7 Besok, M. (1992), "Ha-hotsa'a ha-le'umit le-hinukh 'altah be-90 ve-91 be-7 ahuz le-shana" [National Expenditure on Education Rose in 1990 and 1991 by 7 Percent per Annum], *Davar*, December 15, 1992.

8 Klinov, R. (1988), "Haqtsa'at mashabim tsiburi'im le-hinukh", p. 66.

9 Israel Ministry of Education and Culture (1992), *Facts and Figures about Education and Culture in Israel*, Jerusalem, pp. 16–17.

10 Tsadok, M. (1990), "Kivunim efshari'im be-tiqtsuv ma'arekhet ha-hinukh" [Possible Directions in Budgeting the Education System], in *Tikhnun mediniut ha-hinukh* [Education Policy Planning], Jerusalem, Ministry of Education, pp. 19–47.

11 State of Israel, State Comptroller's Office (1992), *Duah mevaqer ha-medina, 42* [State Comptroller's Report No. 42].

12 Israel Ministry of Education and Culture, *Ma'arekhet ha-hinukh bi-re'i ha-misparim, 5752*, [The Education System in Numbers, 1991/92], *ibid.*, p. 22. See the 1991 edition of the same publication, pp. 29–32.

13 Israel Ministry of Education and Culture (1992), *Facts and Figures about Education and Culture in Israel*, Jerusalem, Division for Economics and Budgets, p. 36.

14 Israel Ministry of Education and Culture (1992), *Ma'arekhet ha-hinukh bi-re'i ha-misparim, 5752*, ch. 7.

15 Hecht, A. (1987), "Hoq ha-shilton ha-meqomi be-Yisrael" [The Local Authority Law in Israel], in Elazar D. *et al.* (eds), *Ha-shilton ha-meqomi be-Yisrael* [Local Authorities in Israel], Jerusalem, Jerusalem Center for Public Affairs, pp. 177–243.

16 State of Israel, Central Bureau of Statistics and Ministry of the Interior, *Ha-rashuyot ha-meqomiot be-Yisrael* [Local Authorities in Israel], Jerusalem, 1980–1990 data.

17 Gaziel, H. (1982), "Urban Policy Outputs," *Urban Education* 17, pp. 139–55.

18 State of Israel, Central Bureau of Statistics (1989–1991), *Supplement to Monthly Bulletin of Statistics*, vols 39, 40, 41, nos 11, 12, and 13.

19 "Shulamit Aloni hitsiga reformot marhiqot lekhet" [Shulamit Aloni Proposed Far-Reaching Reforms], *Yedioth Ahronoth*, February 25, 1993.

20 Klinov, R. (1988), "Haqtsa'at mashabim tsiburi'im le-hinukh", p. 62.

21 Bar Siman Tov, R. and Langerman, S. (1988), *Tokhnit limudim nosefet be-mimun horim be-vatey sefer yesodi'im* [Parent-Financed Supplementary Curriculum in Primary Schools], Jerusalem, Henrietta Szold Institute.

22 Sharan, S. and Sharan, Y. (1975), *Hora'a beqevutsot qetanot* [Teaching in Small Groups], Tel Aviv, Schocken.

23 Rotem, M. (1990), *Ma'arekhet shi'urey ha-'ezer ha-prati'im, le'or mediniut hinukh mishtane* [Private Tutoring in View of Changing Education Policy], thesis submitted for the degree of Master of Arts in the Social Sciences, Ramat Gan, Bar-Ilan University.

24 Yogev, A. and Ayalon, H. (1987), "Hoq hinukh tikhon hinam ve-shivyon ha-hizdamnuyot be-hinukh: hebetim hevrati'im be-tsad hebetim kalkali'im" [The Free Secondary Education Law and Equal Opportunity in Education: Social Aspects alongside Economic Aspects], *Riv'on le-kalkalah* [Economic Quarterly], 131, pp. 873–83.

25 Carlson argues that schools developed the selection mechanism in order to deny access to undesirable population groups. See: Carlson, R., "Hagbalot ha-seviva ve-hashpa'atan 'al irgunim – beyt ha-sefer ha-tsiburi u-lequhotav" [Environmental Constraints and Their Impact on Organizations – the Public School and its Clientele] in: Elboim-Dror, R. (ed.), *Minhal ve-hinukh* [Administration and Education], Academon, Jerusalem, 1977, pp. 89–102.

26 Interview with Dr Amram Melitz, Southern District Director, Ministry of Education and Culture, December 30, 1992.

27 Friedman, Y. *et al.* (eds) (1988), *Efeqtiviut, tarbut ve-aqlim shel batey sefer* [Effectiveness, Culture, and Climate in Schools], Jerusalem, Henrietta Szold Institute.

28 Davis, D. *et al.* (1982), *Mi nehene mi-mashabey ha-hinukh* [Who Benefits from Education Resources], Jerusalem, Ministry of Education and Culture, Educational Welfare and Urban Renewal Department.

29 Israel Ministry of Education and Culture (1992), *Ma'arekhet ha-hinukh bi-re'i ha-misparim, 5753*, ch. 4.

30 The system is based on the father's origins, father's education, and housing density. See Algrabli, M. (1975), "Medadim le-ifyun hevrati shel beyt ha-sefer ve-shita le-haqtsa'at taqtsiv tipuah beyn batey ha-sefer" [Social Indicators of Schools and a Method for Allocating Welfare Budgets among Schools], *Megamot* [Trends], 21: 215–19. According to Algrabli's criteria, a pupil is defined as disadvantaged if he/she belongs to a subgroup (based on the father's origins, father's level of education, and number of children in the family) of whom 40 percent or less passed the survey test (at the end of eighth grade) with a minimum score of 70 percent. Schools are defined as disadvantaged and eligible for assistance, to various degrees, based on the number of disadvantaged pupils enrolled and by another continuous indicator weighted according to the degree of disadvantage. This index, which is called "pupil disadvantage scoring," awards disadvantage points

for each pupil in inverse proportion to his/her subgroup's chances of passing the survey test. The index has attracted a great deal of criticism, the main focus of which is that it is based on social criteria and has a high degree of error in identifying low-achievers, i.e., successful pupils are misdiagnosed as disadvantaged and vice versa. If so, which policy is preferable? What kind of criterion should be used to determine the target population for the allocation of resources: a socio-ethnic criterion or an instrumental criterion based on scholastic performance? Whereas both criteria relate to the pupil as the focus of change, Yogev proposes treating the school as the focus of change. In other words, resource allocation should be biased in favor of disadvantaged schools, while there should be intervention that will lead to change in scholastic acitivity. That is to say, emphasis should be placed on productive learning rather than accelerated learning. The purpose is to avoid a waste of resources, benefit disadvantaged schools, and help the disadvantaged schools achieve better results. See also: Yogev, A. (1989), "Mediniut ha-hinukh be-Yisrael kelapey qidumam shel talmidim mi-qevutsot hevratiot halashot" [Education Policy in Israel for the Advancement of Pupils from Disadvantaged Social Groups], in Pur, D. (ed.), *Tikhnun mediniut ha-hinukh* [Education Policy Planning], position papers submitted to the Pedagogical Secretariat of the Ministry of Edcuation and Culture, Jerusalem, pp. 177–200.

31   Klinov, R. (1991), *Haqtsa'at mashabim tsiburi'im le-ma'arekhet ha-hinukh: sidrey 'adifuyot* [Allocation of Public Resources for the Education System: Priorities], Jerusalem, the Center for Social Policy Studies in Israel.

32   Friedman, Y. (1988), "'Al efeqtiviyut ve-aqontabiliyut be-irgun" [On Effectiveness and Accountability in Organizations], *'Iyunim be-minhal u-ve-irgun ha-hinukh* [Studies in Education Administration and Organization], 16, pp. 81–105.

33   Tsadok, M. (1990), "Kivunim efshari'im be-tiqtsuv ma'arekhet ha-hinukh."

34   Benavot, A. (1983), "The Rise and Decline of Vocational Education," *Sociology of Education*, 56, pp. 63–76.

35   Klinov, R. (1988), "Haqtsa'at mashabim tsiburi'im le-hinukh", p. 9.

36   Tsarfati, A. (1989), *Tefisat "tokhnit ha-limudim" be-'eyney qov'ey mediniyut ha-hinukh ha-ahra'it le-haf'alat mediniyut ha-hinukh ve-tsorkhaney ha-mismakh "tokhnit limudim"* [The Perception of the Curriculum by Education Policymakers Responsible for Setting Education Policy, and Consumers of the Curriculum Document], thesis for the degree of Master of Arts in the Humanities, Tel Aviv, Tel Aviv University School of Education.

37   Yonai, Y. (1990), *Ma'arekhet ha-hinukh shel medinat Yisrael* [The Education System of the State of Israel], Jerusalem, Ministry of Education and Culture.

38   Silberstein, M. (1984), "Maqom ha-moreh be-tikhnun ha-limudim be-Yisrael" [The Teacher's Role in Planning Curricula in Israel], *'Iyunim be-hinukh* [Studies in Education], 40, pp. 131–51.

39   Israel Ministry of Education and Culture, *Hozrey ha-menahel ha-kelali mem bet/10, mem zayin/10* [Circulars of the Director-General, 42/10, 47/10].

40   Ben Peretz, M. and Seidman, A., "Shloshah dorot shel pituah tokhniot limudim be-Yisrael" [Three Generations of Curriculum Development in Israel], *'Iyunim be-hinukh* [Studies in Education], 43/44, pp. 317–27.

41   Eden, S. and Levi, A. (eds) (1978), *Halakhah le-ma'aseh be-tikhnun limudim* [Theory and Practice in Curriculum Planning], Jerusalem, Ministry of Education and Culture, Curriculum Division.

42   Oliver, D. (1976), *Education and Community: A Radical Critique of Innovative Schooling*, Berkeley, McCutchan.

43   Eden, S. (1971), "Tokhniyot ha-limudim ha-hadashot: 'eqronot ve-tahalikhim" [The New Curricula: Principles and Procedures], in Eden, S. (ed.), *'Al tokhniyot ha-limudim ha-hadashot* [On the New Curricula], Tel Aviv, Ma'alot.

44   Eden, S., Moses, S., and Amiad, R., (1986), *Interaqtsia beyn ha-merkaz le-veyn ha-periferia be-tikhnun limudim* [Center-Periphery Interaction in Curriculum Planning], Jerusalem, Ministry of Education and Culture, Curriculum Division.

45   Israel Ministry of Education and Culture (1976), *Netunim statisti'im 'al ma'arekhet ha-behinot, totsa'ot behinot ha-bagrut u-vehinot ha-gemer ha-'iyuniyot be-vatey ha-sefer ha-'al yesodi'im, 5752, 5753* [Statistical Data on the Examination System and on the Results of Academic Matriculation Examinations and Final Examinations in Secondary Schools, 5732, 5733], Jerusalem, Examinations Department.

46   Eden, S. and Levi, A. (eds) (1978), *Halakhah u-ma'aseh betikhnun limudim*.

47   Tyler, R. W. (1949), *Basic Principles of Curriculum and Instruction*, Chicago, University of Chicago Press.

48   Bloom, B. C. (1956), *Taxonomy of Educational Objectives: Handbook I: Cognitive Domain*, New York, Davis McKay.

49   Ben Peretz, M. and Seidman A., "Shloshah dorot shel pituah . . . ," p. 323.

50   Interview with Mr. Shlomo Ben Eliyahu, former director of Curriculum Division, Ministry of Education and Culture.

51   Israel, Ministry of Education and Culture (1969), *Horaot le-vatey-sefer 'al yesodi'im* [Instructions for Primary Schools], Jerusalem, chs. 3 and 4.

52   Israel, Municipality of Tel Aviv-Jaffa (1971), *Duah ha-va'adah ha-tsiburit li-vediqat ha-be'ayah shel shi'urim prati'im le'talmidei batei-sefer tikhoni'im* [Report of the Public Committee Investigating the Problem of Private Tutoring for High-School Students], Tel Aviv.

53 Israel, Ministry of Education and Culture (1970), *Pirtey-kol ha-kenes ha-artsi shel menahaley batey-ha-sefer ha-tikhoni'im miyom 11.3.1970* [Minutes of the National Convention of High-School Principals on March 11, 1970].

54 Israel, Ministry of Education and Culture (1973), *Duah ha-va'adah ha-tsiburit le-vitsu'a ha-shinuyim bi-vehinat ha-bagrut* [Report of the Public Committee for Implementing Changes in the Matriculation Examination], Jerusalem.

55 On the cultural bias of the psychometric exam, see Shimon Shetreet's article on the Education Minister's intention to abolish the psychometric exam: "Temikha be-hatsa'at Aloni levatel et ha-behinot ha-psikhometriot" [Support for Aloni's Proposal to Abolish the Psychometric Exams], *Al-Hamishmar*, September 23, 1992. See also the debate between Professor Friedman of the School of Administration's Law School and Dr Blair of the National Center for Testing and Evaluation, *Ha'aretz*, November 17, 1992; article entitled: "Ha-behinah ve-ha-pa'ar ha-hevrati" [Examinations and the Social Gap].

56 Based on internal data we received from the Student Admission Department at Bar-Ilan University.

57 Israel, Ministry of Education and Culture (1979), *Mimtsa'ey duah ha-va'adah le-ma'amad ha-moreh u-le-miktso'a ha-hora'ah* (va-'adat Etzioni) [The Findings of the Committee on the Status of Teachers and the Teaching Profession (Etzioni Committee)], Circular of the Director-General, Special 1/79.

58 Israel, Ministry of Education and Culture, Pedagogical Secretariat, *Ha-otonomia ba-mosad ha-hinukhi u-markiveha* [Autonomy and Its Components in Educational Institutions], internal document.

59 Reshef, S. (1985), *Otonomia be-hinukh: reka', sikuyim ve-'ekronot le-vitsu'a* [Autonomy in Education: Background, Chances and Principles for Implementation], Tel Aviv, Tel Aviv University School of Education.

60 Lewy, A. (1985), *School-Based Curriculum: An Adversary View*, Tel Aviv, Tel Aviv University.

61 Silberstein, M. (1985), "Hakhsharat ha-morim le-tikhnun limudim u-le-fituham" [Training Teachers to Plan and Develop Curricula], in Silberstein M. (ed.), *Hakhsharat ha-morim le-tikhnun limudim u-le-fituham* [Training Teachers to Plan and Develop Curricula], Jerusalem, Curriculum Planning Institute.

62 Dory, A. (1982), *Shnei pirushim le-otonomia shel ha-moreh: ha-'adafot ha-morim le-teva'* [Two Explanations of Teachers' Autonomy: Teachers' Preference for the Sciences (or Giving Preference to Science Teachers)], Jerusalem, Ministry of Education and Culture, Curriculum Division.

63 Israel, Ministry of Education and Culture (1982), *Circular of the Director-General*, 42/10, Paragraph 344.

64 Tserlin, M. (ed.) (1987), *Tikhnun limudim: mabat la-'atid* [Curriculum Planning: Looking to the Future], Ministry of Education and Culture, Curriculum Division, pp. 38–54.

65 Silberstein, M. (1985), *Curriculum Development in Israel in the Eighties: A Dialogue between Teachers and Professional Developers*, International Seminar on SBCD, Tel Aviv University, School of Education.

66 Shermer, A. (1983), "Beyn tokhnit limudim le-hora'atah ba-kitah" [The Curriculum and Its Application in Class], in: Nisan, M. and Last, A. (eds), *Beyn hinukh le-psikhologia* [Education and Psychology], Jerusalem, Hebrew University.

67 Sabar, N. (1987), "School-Based Curriculum Development: The Pendulum Swings," in: Sabar, N., *et al.* (eds), *Partnership & Autonomy*, Sheffield, University of Sheffield Press.

68 Israel, Ministry of Education and Culture (1979), *Sugiyot bi-vehinot ha-bagrut ve-te'udot ha-bagrut* [Aspects of Matriculation Examinations and Matriculation Certificates], Shild Committee, Jerusalem.

69 Israel, Ministry of Education and Culture (1986), *Hatsa'ah le-shinuy bi-vehinot ha-bagrut* [A Proposal for Changing the Matriculation Examinations], Jerusalem, Committee for Post-Primary Education.

70 Israel, Ministry of Education and Culture (1992), *Behinot ha-bagrut* [Matriculation Examinations], Jerusalem, Circular of the Post-Primary Education Committee.

71 Skilbeck, M. (1985), *School-Based Curriculum Development and Central Curriculum Policies: A Paradox in Three Acts*, International Seminar on SBCD, Tel Aviv University School of Education.

72 Lawton, D. (1980), *The Politics of School Curriculum*, London, Routledge and Kegan Paul.

Chapter 7 Education Policy in Israel: Toward the Millennium

1 Feld, Y. (1987), "Ha-reshut ha-meqomit – ha-mivneh ha-mishpati" [The Local Authority – the Juridical Structure] in: Elazar, D. and Kalcheim, H. (eds), *Ha-shilton ha-meqomi be-Yisrael* [Local Government in Israel], Jerusalem, Published by the Jerusalem Center for Public Affairs, ch. 5.

2 Onay, D. (1988), *Keytsad oleh noseh be-hinukh le-diyun tsiburi* [How Does an Educational Issue Become the Topic of Public Debate?], Thesis for the degree of Master of Arts in the Humanities, Tel Aviv, Tel Aviv University School of Education.

3 Interview with Mr. Dagan, head of the Religious Education Administration, February 25, 1993.

4 Levi, A. (1992), "'Ivut be-haktsa'at taktsivey ha-revaha ha-tikhonit yotser qipuah shel ukhlusiat ha'oni" [Unfair Distribution of High-School Welfare Allocations Discriminates against the Poor], *Davar*, December 7, 1992.

5 Fischbein, Y. (1993), "Kefar Sava ma'aminah be-integratsia" [Kefar Sava Believes in Integration], *Davar*, January 1, 1993.

6   Bashi, Y. (1992), "Lamah nehutsim mivhaney hamashov" [Why Are the Achievement Tests Necessary?], *Ha'aretz*, June 19, 1992.

7   Israel Ministry of Education and Culture (1993), *Ma'arekhet ha-hinukh bi-re'i ha-misparim*, [The Education System in Numbers], Jerusalem, Senior Division for Economics and Budgets, ch. 2.

8   Kazal-Thresher, D. (1993), "Educational Expenditures and School Achievement," *Educational Researcher*, 22: 30–32.

9   Fischbein, Y. (1992), "Meqif klali ORT Hatsor ba-maqom ha-rishon be-vagrut be-viologia" [ORT Hatsor Comprehensive Comes in First in the Biology Matriculation Examinations], *Davar*, February 11, 1992.

10 Mendler, N. (1993), "Bi-Sederot, Ofaqim, u-Netivot gadal pi shalosh shi'ur ha-matslihim bi-vehinot ha-bagrut" [A Threefold Rise in Matriculation Success Rate in Sederot, Ofaqim, and Netivot], *Ha'aretz* January 20, 1993.

11 Burg. A. (1993), "Ha-integratsia hi mas sefatayim ve-lo soger pe'arim" [Integration: Lip Service and Not a Gap-Closer], *Hed-Ha-Qrayot*, January 29, 1993.

12 Tsadoq, M. (1988) "Kivunim efshari'im be-tiqtsuv ma'arekhet ha-hinukh" [Possible Orientations in Budgeting for the Education System], in: *Tikhnun mediniyut ha-hinukh* [Planning Education Policy], Jerusalem, Ministry of Education and Culture, Pedagogical Secretariat, pp. 19–47.

13 "Ha-hinukh ha-mamlakhti ha-dati lo yipaga' mi-shinuy shitat ha-teqen" [State–Religious Education Will Not Be Affected by a Change in the Staffing Method], *Ha-Tsofeh*, June 3, 1993.

14 Boyer, E. L. (1982), *High School: A Report on Secondary Education in America*, New York, Harper & Row.

15 Goodlad, J. (1983), *A Place Called School: Prospects for the Future*, New York, McGraw-Hill.

16 Shoshani, S. (1993), *Efshar gam aheret – Tel Aviv-Yafo ma'aminah be-hinukh* [There Is Another Way – Tel Aviv-Jaffa Believes in Education], Tel Aviv Municipality, Education Department.

17 Asa, Y. (1993), "Tiltul ha-hinukh o hisul ha-integratsia" [Roaming Education or Abolition of Integration], *Hed ha-hinukh*, 87, p. 10.

18 Friedman, S. (1992), "Misrad ha-hinukh ve-ha-morim: qodem nilmad et ha-homer" [The Ministry of Education and the Teachers: Let's First Do Our Homework], *Ma'ariv*, October 15, 1992.

19 Shapira R. (1992), "Tefisah hinukhit – batey-sefer otonomi'im" [Educational Perspective – Autonomous Schools], *Davar*, August 18, 1992.

20 Kashti, Y. (1992), "Petihat ezorey rishum tifga' ba-integratsia" [Opening Enrollment Districts Will Harm Integration], *Ha'aretz*, December 22, 1992.

21 Aloni, S. (1992), "Hitnagdut le-tokhnit Shoshani" [Opposition to the Shoshani Plan], *Ha'aretz*, November 12, 1992.

22 Antler, R. (1922), "Kitah aleph begil 4, siyum tikhon begil 16, teguvot

shel doktor Goldberg yo'etz bakhir lesar ha-hinukh ve-ha-tarbut le-
'tokhnit Shoshani'" [Starting Grade One at Age 4, Graduating High
School at Age 16, the Reactions of Dr. Goldberg, Senior Adviser to the
Minister of Education and Culture, to the "Shoshani Plan"], *Yedioth
Ahronoth*, October 15, 1992.

23 Smilenski, S., Shaftiya L. (1977), "Hakesher beyn integratsia u-
mishtanim kitati'im aherim le-veyn hesegim bekitot aleph u-vet"
[The Connection between Integration and Other Classroom Variables
and Achievements in Grades 1 and 2], *Megamot 50* [Trends], 23, pp.
79–87.

24 Raywid, A. M. (1991), "Is There a Case for Choice?, *Educational
Leadership*, 10(48): 14–15.

25 Heckman, P. E. (1991), "Evidence, Values and the Revitalization of
Schools," *Educational Leadership*, 48: 14–15.

26 Chubb, J. E. and Moe, T. M. (1990), *Politics, Markets and America's
Schools*, Washington, D.C., Brookings Institution.

27 Deering, P. and Kraft, R. (1989), "School Choice: What Choice for
Teachers?" *Teaching*, 1: 22–31.

28 Metz, M. H. (1986), *Different by Design: The Context and Character of
Three Magnet Schools*, New York, Routledge and Kegan Paul.

29 Finn, E. E. (1990), "Why Do We Need Choice? in: Boyd, E. & Walberg,
H. L. (eds), *Choice in Education: Potential and Problems*, Berkeley, CA:
McCutchan.

30 Walford, G. (1992), "Educational Choice and Equity in Great Britain,"
Educational Policy, 6: 123–38.

31 Halpin, D. *et al.* (1991), "Local Education Authorities and the Grant-
Maintained Schools Policy," *Educational Management and Administration*, 19: 233–42.

32 Ministry of Education and Science (MOW) (1988), *Newsletter on
Freedom of Education in the Netherlands*, Dociform 22, E. Zoetermeer.

33 Tanguy, L. (1972), "L'état et l'école," [State and School], *Revue française
de sociologie* [French Sociology Review], 13: 325–75.

34 Fowler, F. L. (1992), "School Choice Policy in France: Success and
Limitations," *Educational Policy*, 6: 429–43.

35 Elmore, R. F. (1991), "No Easy Answers to the Complex Question of
Choice," *Educational Leadership*, 48: 17–18.

36 Sosmiak, L. A. and Ethington, C. A. (1992), "When Public School
Choice Is Not Academic: Findings from the National Education
Longitudinal Study of 1988," *Educational Evaluation and Policy Analysis*,
14:. 35–52.

37 Brand, R. (1991), "On Public Schools of Choice: A Conversation with
Seymour Fliegel," *Educational Leadership*, 48: 20–25.

38 Moore, D. & Davenport, S. (1989), "High School Choice and Students
at Risk," *Equity and Choice*, 5: 5–10.

39 Louis, K. S., *et al.* (1990), *Review of Educational Policies in the Netherlands*,
Paris, OECD.

40 Adler, M., *et al.* (1989), *Parental Choice and Educational Policy*, Edinburgh, Edinburgh University Press.

41 Willie, Ch. (1991), "Controlled Choice Avoids the Pitfalls of Choice Plans," *Educational Leadership*, 48: 62–64.

42 Elmore, R. E. (1990), *Working Models of Choice in Public Schools*, Washington, D.C., Education Center for Policy Research in Education.

43 Alves, M. J. and Willie, C. V. (1987), "Controlled Choice Assignments: A New and More Effective Approach to School Desegregation," *The Urban Review*, 19: 67–88.

44 "The interethnic and interclass encounter in junior-high schools does not lead to any real change in the pupils' scholastic achievements or to marked or significant social and emotional fluctuations. . . . The gaps between groups with respect to scholastic achievement or placement in high school did not narrow." Chen, M., *et al.* (1977), "Efsharut ha-mifgash ha-beyn-'adati be-hativot ha-beynayim, mimusho ve-tots'otav" [Possibilities, Reality, and Results of the Interethnic Encounter in Junior High School], *Megamot* [Trends], 23, pp. 101–23.

45 This comment by Yosef Bashi, former chief scientist at the Ministry of Education and Culture, was part of a speech he delivered at a conference on schools in the twenty-first century. See: Mendler, N. (1992), "Misrad ha-hinukh hitsig tokhnit beli musag aykh yeraeh beyt-hasefer bi-shnot ha-alpayim" [The Ministry of Education Has Submitted a Plan without Any Idea of What Schools Will Be Like in the Twenty-First Century], *Ha'aretz*, February 4, 1992.

46 Shmueli, A. (1987), *Ha-reformah be-hinukh u-mitnagdehah* [The Education Reform and Its Opponents], lecture to the Jerusalem Forum.

47 Said by Avraham Yogev in reaction to the Ministry of Education and Culture's plan for the next decade. See: Mendler, N. (1992), "Misrad ha-hinukh hetsig tokhnit beli musag aykh yeraeh beyt-hasefer bi-shnot ha-alpayim" [The Ministry of Education Has Submitted a Plan without Any Idea of What Schools Will Be Like in the Twenty-First Century], *Ha'aretz*, February 4, 1992.

48 Resh, N., *et al.* (1977), "'Emdot morim klapey integratsia beyn 'adatit u-matarot ha-hinukh be-hativat ha-beynayim" [Teacher's Attitudes to Interethnic Integration and Educational Objectives in Junior High School], *Megamot* [Trends], 23, pp. 221–9.

49 In an interview, Dr Hannah Shahar, senior researcher at the Institute for Integration of Bar-Ilan University, disclosed that a great deal of effort was expended on in-service courses and on training teachers to teach in heterogenous classes, and that the teachers applied what they were taught. However, when training ceased and the teachers had to fend for themselves, they tended to revert to their former methods of teaching. As a result, the administration of the Institute decided to rethink its entire approach and adopt the concept of system-wide intervention. The focus of change was not only the teacher, but

the entire school. It is still too early to assess the results of this change.

50 "Ha-mahapekhah ha-hinukhit shel 'iriyat Tel-Aviv" [The Educational Revolution of the Municipality of Tel Aviv], *Yedioth Ahronoth*, October 15, 1992.

51 The information is based on interviews with a sample of twelve principals of autonomous schools in the Jerusalem and Tel Aviv districts. The interviews were conducted by students in the "Autonomy in Education" course offered as part of the master's degree inthe School of Education of the Hebrew University of Jerusalem.

52 Amir, Y. (1977), "Ha-mifgash ha-etni ve-hashlakhotav 'al 'emdot ve-yahasim beyn-'adati'im" [The Ethnic Encounter and Its Repercussions on Interethnic Attitudes and Relationships], *Megamot* [Trends], 23, p. 65.

53 Chen, M. and Adi, A. (1992), *Ha-mivneh ha-politi shel ha-qehilah, ha-reformah shel beyt-ha-sefer ve-ha-hesegim ha-limudi'im* [The Political Structure of the Community, the School Reform, and Scholastic Achievements], paper presented at an international seminar run by the Special Assistance Research Institute, Jerusalem, Hebrew University, School of Education.

54 The Perfect School: 9 Reforms to Revolutionize American Education, *U.S. News and World Report*, January 11, 1993.

55 Cooper, B. (1993), *School-Site Cost Allocations: Testing a Micro-Financial Model in 23 Districts in Ten States*, Albuquerque, N.M., paper prepared for the American Association of Finance Evaluation.

56 Walberg's findings were cited in *U.S. News and World Report*, January 11, 1993, p. 56.

57 Elboim-Dror, R. (1987), "Mispar hashqafot 'al tashtit ha-politika shel ha-hinukh," [Several Aspects of the Political Infrastructure of Education], in: Elboim-Dror, R. (ed.), *Minhal u-mediniyut: te'oriyah ve-yisumim be-hinukh*, [Administration and Policy: Theory and Practice in Education], Jerusalem, Magnes Press, pp. 135–61.

58 Dimmock, C. (1993), *School-Based Management and School Effectiveness*, London, Routledge.

59 S. Shaftiya, L. (1973), *Meni'at kishalon ha-limudi ha-mitstaber etsel yeladim te'uney-tipuah be-emtsa'ut hora'at ha-qeriah ba-gan* [Preventing Cumulative Scholastic Failure among Disadvantaged Pupils by Teaching Preschoolers to Read], Jerusalem, Henrietta Szold Institute.

60 From an interview with Mr Nisim Cohen who is conducting these experiments in the Meir Shafiya Youth Village and, currently, at the Kadoorie School.

Ministers of Education, 1949–1993

1949–1950   Mr Zalman Shazar
1950–1951   Mr Aaron Remez
1951–1955   Prof. Bez-Zion Dinur
1955–1960   Mr Zalman Aran
1960–1963   Mr Abba Eban
1963–1969   Mr Zalman Aran
1969–1974   Mr Igal Alon
1974–1977   Mr Aaron Yadlin
1977–1984   Mr Zevulun Hammer
1984–1990   Mr Itzhak Navon
1990–1992   Mr Zevulun Hammer
1992–1993   Mrs Shulamit Aloni

Short Bibliography of Books in English about the Educational System in Israel

Adar Z. (1977). *Education in Israel and in the United States.* Jerusalem, Hebrew University Publications.

Ben Baruch, E. and Neumann, Y. (1982) (eds). *Educational Administration and Policy Making: The Case of Israel.*

Iram Y. (1994). *Education in Israel: A source book.* Garland Publishing Company.

Iram Y. (1993). Recurring Reforms and changes in Israeli educational system: An analytic approach. *International Journal of Educational Development,* vol. 3, pp. 217–26.

Israel, Ministry of Education and Culture (1992). Facts and Figures about Education and Culture in Israel.

Kleinberger, F. A. (1969). *Society, Schools and Progress in Israel.* Pergamon Press.

Index